AUTO/BIOGRAPHY & PEDAGOGY

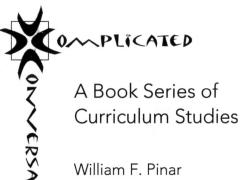

omplicated

A Book Series of Curriculum Studies

William F. Pinar
General Editor

Vol. 42

The Complicated Conversation series
is part of the Peter Lang Education list.
Every volume is peer reviewed and meets
the highest quality standards for content and production.

PETER LANG
New York • Washington, D.C./Baltimore • Bern
Frankfurt • Berlin • Brussels • Vienna • Oxford

Freema Elbaz-Luwisch

AUTO/BIOGRAPHY & PEDAGOGY

Memory & Presence in Teaching

PETER LANG
New York • Washington, D.C./Baltimore • Bern
Frankfurt • Berlin • Brussels • Vienna • Oxford

Library of Congress Cataloging-in-Publication Data

Elbaz, Freema.
Auto/biography and pedagogy: memory and presence in teaching /
Freema Elbaz-Luwisch.
pages cm. — (Complicated conversation:
a book series of curriculum studies; vol. 42)
Includes bibliographical references.
1. Education—Biographical methods. 2. Discourse analysis, Narrative.
3. Critical pedagogy. I. Title. II. Title: Autobiography and pedagogy.
LB1029.B55E53   370.72—dc23   2013018780
ISBN 978-1-4331-1642-1 (hardcover)
ISBN 978-1-4331-1641-4 (paperback)
ISBN 978-1-4539-1155-6 (e-book)
ISSN 1534-2816

Bibliographic information published by **Die Deutsche Nationalbibliothek**.
Die Deutsche Nationalbibliothek lists this publication in the "Deutsche
Nationalbibliografie"; detailed bibliographic data is available
on the Internet at http://dnb.d-nb.de/.

The paper in this book meets the guidelines for permanence and durability
of the Committee on Production Guidelines for Book Longevity
of the Council of Library Resources.

© 2014 Peter Lang Publishing, Inc., New York
29 Broadway, 18th floor, New York, NY 10006
www.peterlang.com

Printed in the United States of America

For Danni and Shelley

TABLE OF CONTENTS

LIST OF ILLUSTRATIONS

Following Chapter 2

Following Chapter 7

FOREWORD

Devorah Kalekin-Fishman

Elbaz-Luwisch describes the form of her chapter on memory as 'resembl[ing] a meandering stream that curves back on itself at times but still arrives, eventually, at a wider and deeper place'. To me, this oxymoron is in fact a description of the 'form' of the entire book. Beginning with a chapter on memory, the book goes on to chronicle different kinds of memories and different kinds of accounts. There are several returns to clarify some of the narratives. But when the author sees fit to stop the meandering, she leaves her readers in a place that is indeed far broader and deeper. Reading *Autobiography and Pedagogy* on a trip to Jerusalem, I discovered that 'the journey that constitutes the book' split neatly into the 'there and back'. When the bus returned to what was for me home base, I realized too that the textual mosaic assembled in it does not disappear with the final page. The stories that Elbaz-Luwisch bears with her as 'the underside of a cheerful Canadian childhood', and to which she curves back several times in the course of the book, disclose increasingly more subtle details. Somewhat ironically, too, the descriptions of intimate struggles with writing, with conflict, with teaching, outline a concern with the world that mercilessly invades private experience but may ultimately be shaped by the accumulation of clandestine triumphs and failures.

Writing frankly about her experiences and about the layered experiences of her parents and their extended families, Elbaz-Luwisch shows how stories shape trajectories from generation to generation. No wonder it turned out to be highly appropriate to be reading about this stream on a bus winding up the hills to Jerusalem. I was on my way to participate in a family fête. Without faltering, the welcoming relatives towed me back into a planet that I had made every effort to escape. The customs that governed the celebration of the wedding—the ceremony and the festivities—have not been part of my repertoire for dealing with daily life for many years. But of course, like compost, as in the author's life, they are merely lying fallow and can easily be stirred up. Savoring the stories that I read it was brought home to me with something of a start that memories that I thought had been left behind, were embodied in my postures, echoing in my tone of voice and bearing unimpeachable witness to desires that only seemed to be quelled.

A large part of this book is taken up with stories that 'had to be told,' and that turns out to be a major strength. The easily accessible conversational style combines with highly serious investigations of the nature of memory, of storying and conflict, and of the varied connections of their configuration with how people teach. Elbaz-Luwisch's decision to intersperse summaries of theory and quotes from narratives with comments describing how she finds herself talking and writing evokes awarenesses of traces that make people the persons they are, on the one hand, and wonder about how these traces fit into the world that is contrived by memories, on the other. The stories told in the book call attention to memories that have had a decisive impact on shaping the private lives as well as the more or less public work of the pedagogue-tellers. They make it easy to identify with the challenges and the dilemmas that confront teachers at whatever phase of students' careers they are involved in, and above all the dilemmas of those who have responsibility for teacher education.

In relation to the tradition of narrative inquiry which Elbaz-Luwisch has done much to further since the 1980s, the chapters of this book highlight the idea that learning is made possible only when there is mutual awareness of the selves called upon to act in the classroom. Over and over again, during the last several decades, researchers have found that students of all ages seek a truly human(e) relationship with people who are positioned as their teachers. To their minds, such warmth is a necessary, if not sufficient, condition for enabling learning. This underlines the fact that narratives of self are not solely a channel to therapy, or mere self-indulgence, but rather constituents of action. It is the narrated self that is the 'presence' in the classroom and that self which builds, or avoids building, relationships with students. With Elbaz-Luwisch, who shares her feelings and her experiences frankly, the warmth is not described, it is illustrated.

Elbaz-Luwisch quotes stories of and by different students and colleagues. Her own story is about her experiences in teacher education, and about how those experiences are buttressed by her unavoidable legacy, the gnawing telling and re-telling of her parents' stories. Their stories of impoverished childhood, of threats in adulthood, of family members lost in the Holocaust guide her and her children to repeated, but still not exhaustive, searches for evidence of the definitive key to the code of a tale that endures. Though visited and revisited, these stories have no finality, and remain with the reader echoing and re-echoing in one's own search for understanding.

The stories with no endings are encountered in contextualized dialogues; they form, therefore, invitations and promises, as the author says, of re-imagining and re-storying in further contexts, and even an invitation to re-readings. Whether or not we are privy to the re-tellings, readers are part of the dialogue. The book ends with reminders of the importance to memory and to pedagogy of 'presence,' 'embodiment,' of 'imagination,' and of 'dialogue. The concluding remarks do not put paid to the book. Instead, they involve the reader anew in the situated problematic of storying. As a volume about narrative, *Auto-biography and Pedagogy* ends in medias res and implicates the reader in the webs of questions that have arisen. The printed matter comes to an end, but the story and the search for cues continues, in response to the challenging dialogue that the book initiates.

Not only does the dialogue go on, but it raises issues that are barely hinted at in the text. While this is a highly personal book, there are signals throughout of possibilities for a broader social theorization. Locating the material in a 'post-modern' frame is, to my mind, too facile. There are several indications of what social approach is suggested albeit, perhaps luckily, not yet worked out. Above all, the confluence of teaching and warmth, of openness and learning, is congruent with the ideal of the democratic classroom, thus raising a series of new questions. Among other salient themes, Elbaz-Luwisch points out that space and place are central to all the stories that teacher educators and mentors tell. Whether childhood is recalled with joy or sadness, the where of it and its flavor is indelibly etched in memory. Still, the complex networks of people and things that constitute those memories are not called up in detail in this volume. Views and objects are referred to, if at all, only summarily. What is the nature of the interaction with the immediate environment that is embedded in memory and embodied in unconscious but persistent behaviors? None of the story-tellers that Elbaz-Luwisch cites seems to find it necessary to describe in detail the 'things' with which they have to deal in their homes. None seems to have spent any time in describing the physicalities of the classrooms in which teaching and mentoring is per-

formed. All the teachers and teacher-educators who tell their stories seem to take for granted a situated room, shapes of walls, distributions of desks,
places for a black- or a white-board, means of communication and of recording events. Thus, while the stories quoted are told by people from a variety of cultural backgrounds, with its attempt to describe the prevalence of difference, the book actually manages to underscore similarities. Depending on your place on the globe, I guess, you can learn exactly what defines the - uni- versalities of human perception at least in a given site from what is 'left out'. Here we learn the particularities of what it means to be living in Israel — for teachers and students alike.

In line with current streams of theory in sociology, this book actually hints, then, at the applicability of actor-network theory, the theory based on recognition of the fact that relations with objects are integral to the experience of the social. The embodied self with its world of memory sees, hears, smells, feels, tastes the objects with which it necessarily has contact. It also must consider the kinds of actions that objects intimately involved in our lives elicit. This oblique contribution to a comprehension of the social indicates further directions for exploring memory in dialogues.

So much is said, and so much is left unsaid. The broadening stream twists and turns, and deepens.

Haifa, 13 March, 2013

ACKNOWLEDGMENTS

Several chapters of this book are based on published articles or book chapters; I am grateful to the publishers for permission to draw on the following materials:

1. Chapter 4 is a revised and expanded version of Elbaz-Luwisch, F., (2009). Life stories in time and place: Narratives of Israeli teachers. In S. Gill (Ed.), *Exploring selfhood: Finding ourselves, finding our stories in life narratives.* Brighton, UK: Centre for Research in Human Development, Guerrand-Hermes Foundation.

2. Chapter 6 is a revised and expanded version of: Elbaz-Luwisch, F. (2010) Writing and professional learning: The uses of autobiography in graduate studies in education. *Teachers and Teaching, Theory and Practice 16*(3), 307–327, published by Taylor and Francis, http://www.tandfonline.com/doi/abs/10.1080/13540601003634404.

3. Chapter 8 is based on: Elbaz-Luwisch, F. (2009). The uses of conflict in the pedagogy of teacher education. *Perspectives in Education 27*(2), 169–176, and also draws on material written by me for Chapter 2 of Li, X., Conle, C., Elbaz-Luwisch, F. (2009) *Shifting polarized positions: A narrative approach in teacher education.* New York: Peter Lang.

4. Chapter 5 (not previously published) is based in part on material collected in the framework of the *Memory and Pedagogy* project, funded by the Israel Science Foundation, Grant No. 1038/04, 2004-2007.

For permission to include photographs of their work, I am most grateful to Kalliopi Lemos, for the images of "Wooden Boat with Seven People," from her installation *Navigating in the Dark Part III* at St. Pancras Church, London, November 2012; and to Rebecca Soudant for images from her exhibit *ReCover* shown at Union Gallery, Queen's University, Kingston, in summer 2005.

I am most grateful to Lily Orland-Barak and Debbie Golden for reading and commenting on the article which was the starting point of this book; to my daughter Shira for her patience and attention to detail in formatting the text; and to my amazing family for their love and support.

INTRODUCTION

The world—whatever we might think when terrified by its vastness and our own impotence, or embittered by its indifference to individual suffering, of people, animals, and perhaps even plants...whatever we might think of this measureless theater to which we've got reserved tickets, but tickets whose lifespan is laughably short, bounded as it is by two arbitrary dates; whatever else we might think of this world— it is astonishing.

Wisława Szymborska, 1996

Where to begin? This question only begins to bother me after I've written a matter-of-fact opening which I decide fails to invites the reader into the dark wood represented by this book. I envisage a short, evocative paragraph that somehow sketches the precise spot where a path can be discerned leading into the undergrowth...but how to write that?

Many life story interviews begin precisely this way, with the teller, the research participant, hesitating and wondering where to begin. In part this hesitation is the doing of the researcher: asking a stranger to tell about her life is not an everyday conversational opener. But generally, the teller also brings her own doubts to the situation, and one seems to hear the voice of an inner critic who fears the teller doesn't have much that is worth talking about, or, perhaps, that there is too much to tell and no way to impose order on the telling. Sometimes the hesitation indicates that the teller wants to be accommodating, to tell the researcher what she needs to know. At other times, rather than probing for the researcher's direction, the teller manages her hesitation by putting it aside and jumping right in: one of the women educators who told their stories as part of a women's circle (see Chapter 5) began her life story by talking about the meeting she'd had with a group of teachers the day before. Another member of the same group (not included here) launched into a rambling account of everything that had happened to her after leaving our last meeting: a war, a trip to India and the death of her mother, all events that could be expected to give rise to far-ranging reflections on one's life. Both of these were strategies, unexpected but highly effective ones as it turned out, for finding one's way into the story of lives in education.

It seems the hesitation (whether acknowledged or ignored) in telling one's life story—and beginning a book that is in large measure personal is not very different—is there because having a life to tell about is not trivial. Rather, it's a mystery: at moments it can seem an accomplishment, but one which can easily dissolve into a random series of events that merely overtook us. The possibility of telling it anew each time is precious: to make sense of what we did not understand while it was happening, perhaps to get it right the next time round, and if not, at least to be able to start over, to have the freedom to choose, right now, in this moment, how to begin is an inestimable gift.

This book represents an ongoing inquiry carried out in a non-linear fashion over the past 15 or more years, within the frame of an approach to education that is both narrative and auto/biographical. As elaborated by Clandinin & Connelly (2000), narrative inquiry calls for careful attention to experience (Dewey, 1938) as a starting point for inquiry; thus the study of education means paying close attention to educational experience and the ways it is storied by individuals and groups. The term "auto/biography" is used to denote the focus on personal and individual stories and on "the intersection between individual experience and the social context" (Griffiths & Macleod, 2008, 123). The diverse views of narrative elaborated by Paul Ricoeur (1984) and Hannah Arendt (1958, 1993), and the links between education and imagination forged by Maxine Greene (1995, 2000) have also influenced the present inquiry. Finally, my perspective has been shaped by Mindell's (e.g., 1982, 2010) view of human experience as a multi-layered process guided by access to diverse levels and states of consciousness; he holds that this ongoing process is *the whole story*, and that, in the lives of individuals and groups, "everything is happening within the context of an overall story direction, a powerful story trying to create greater awareness" (Mindell, 2010, 150–151).

There are many possible entry points to the study of educational experience, and I can trace the beginning of this inquiry from more than one point of departure. From an academic perspective, the inquiry here is a continuation of previous work on narrative (Elbaz-Luwisch, 2005), on the uses of autobiographical writing in work with teachers (e.g., Elbaz-Luwisch, 2002, 2010a; Elbaz-Luwisch & Pritzker, 2002), and on the place of personal history in thinking about multiculturalism and multicultural education (Li, Conle & Elbaz-Luwisch, 2009).

From a personal perspective, the inquiry is grounded in my life story and life history: I grew up listening to family stories, and recognized a certain urgency in the telling which made them, in Ricoeur's (1984) words, "stories which demand to be told." I wanted to explore these stories and in particular to understand what made them compelling for me. I wanted to listen more carefully to myself telling my own story, to figure out how those stories which demanded to be told had had an influence on my life and on how I story it. And then, as the academic and personal perspectives came together, I wanted to know more about how and why other people hold on to and want to tell their individual stories, and how this impacts on our collective narratives. The tradition of autobiographic work in education, in curriculum and teaching, dates back to the notion of "currere" first formulated by Pinar in 1975 (see Pinar, 1994) and more recently described as a process in which

> ...one re-enters the lived present. Conscious of one's breathing, indeed, of one's embodied otherness, one asks, 'who is that?' Listening carefully to one's own inner voice in the historical and natural world, one asks, 'what is the meaning of the present?'...currere allows the student of education to "tap [into the] intense current within, that which courses through the inner person, that which electrifies or gives life to a person's energy source" (Pinar, 2004, 37).

Mindful of my breath, attentive to the lived present, I nonetheless chose to begin with memory. The first chapter of the book does the groundwork for the rest of the book by examining the complex issue of memory in philosophy and in education, interweaving a theoretical discussion with accounts of personal memories, both my own and those of other educational practitioners whose stories will feature later in the book, as well as accounts drawn from the literature. My relationship with philosophy is an ambivalent one: I chose to do a first degree in philosophy, partly because all the other choices I was considering then (psychology, political science, literature) seemed too narrow at a time when I wanted to remain connected to the wideness of the academic horizon just opening up to me. Reading philosophical treatments of educational issues, over the years, I still feel that they offer essential grounding and clarification of concepts and ways of understanding; but sometimes, they lead into what can seem like a labyrinth of jargon-heavy argument where I lose sight of experience. Smeyers and Verhesschen (2001), however, suggest that we can view narrative research as itself a form of philosophical analysis because of its aim to understand human practice, in education as in other practical domains. In this light, I tried to write Chapter 1 in a way that would offer both clarification and connection: to the ways that educators remember, to the uses of memory, to an understanding of how and why memory moves us forward as much as it draws us back.

Trusting that a story which demands to be told has not only shaped who I am but still has much to teach me about being a scholar and an educator, I decided to continue, in Chapter 2, with episodes from my family story, drawing particularly on memories of my mother and stories of her early life to explore the possibility of retrieving and telling a life through auto/biographical narrative. Here the ideas of embodiment (Johnson, 1987, 1989) and imagination (Greene, 1995) come into play. In writing about my mother, I am interested in understanding how her stories live on in concrete ways in my body in gesture, posture and movement, in how I live in the world, in how I stand as an academic and a teacher in the university classroom.

Teachers' stories show that they take up what has been called a "position of presence" in front of students (Estola & Elbaz-Luwisch, 2003), and the idea of teaching presence is becoming more prominent in the discussion of teaching in recent years. This notion underlines the importance of embodiment in understanding teaching as both lived experience and as narrative. In Chapter 3, picking up on the experience of embodiment as told in the stories of Chapter 2, I examine the diverse connections between the body and lived experience, particularly in relation to ideas around motherhood and mothering. I then question the pedagogical implications of these explorations for an understanding of teaching and for the notion of presence in teaching in particular.

Moving on from my personal story to the retrieval of memory in the stories of others, Chapter 4 examines the written autobiographies of a group of teachers, graduate students in education who participated in an advanced methods course on narrative inquiry in multicultural settings. The chapter highlights the themes that are prominent in the teachers' presentations of their stories, dealing with their stories of origins, of belonging and marginalization in society and in the teaching profession, and with the participants' ways of storying growth and development in teaching, and their sense of purpose and calling to the profession. The chapter concludes by highlighting and puzzling over the somewhat surprising similarities among the stories despite the diverse backgrounds of the participants, as well as the ways that these teachers manage to produce coherent stories that seem to integrate diverse voices rather than being fragmented by them.

Chapter 5 continues the theme of 'retrieval of memory' with respect to teacher educators, adding to the relatively limited research on the lives and stories of teachers who teach teachers. The chapter presents and discusses the stories of teacher educators from different backgrounds, working in the complex and multicultural setting of teacher education in Israel. I interpret these stories within their very specific context, yet it seems that this close view has something to contribute to an understanding of teacher education in a global context.

Imagination, as Maxine Greene argues, is vital for critical thinking about education and teaching. Chapter 6 discusses the use of personal writing and awareness methods to engage the imagination and facilitate teacher development through autobiographical writing. This chapter expands on my experience with the use of autobiographical writing by teachers in the context of graduate study (Elbaz-Luwisch, 2010a) and highlights the potential contribution of auto/biography to the professional learning of teachers.

Chapter 7 wrote itself unexpectedly, responding to Hannah Arendt's (1958) injunction to "take the imagination visiting." In this chapter I retell my own story from a different perspective, going back in time through fragments from my travel journals over the years. I chose to take Arendt's idea of visiting, and Lugones' (1987) notion of "world"-travelling quite literally here, not to reduce the complex theorizing involved in their work but rather because drawing on the scenes, colors and tastes of real-time embodied travel allows me to understand in new ways the journey of my own life and may offer a way for others to reimagine their own stories as well.

Another way of taking the imagination visiting is found in Chapter 8, where I return to my earlier work on the use of narrative and life story for multicultural education (for example, in Li, Conle & Elbaz-Luwisch, 2009). This chapter examines some possible benefits of engaging actively and consciously with conflict (as suggested by Mindell, 1995) in educational settings. I look back at my own efforts over the years to promote pedagogical encounters across borders of difference in the teacher education setting and draw on this experience to conceptualize and discuss ways of making possible a more nuanced and multi-voiced understanding of lives in education— an understanding which, in turn, would foster more productive meetings and experiences of border-crossing.

In the final chapter, I suggest ways that we might reimagine a critical language of teaching that is grounded in the multivocal lived experience of teaching. Chapter 9 highlights ways that auto/biographical inquiry provides opportunities for students and teachers from different cultural, religious and ethnic backgrounds to learn about one another's lives and experience through the sharing and examination of their personal and professional narratives. In this chapter I look back at how attention to memory, in the form of personal and collective narratives, allowed the themes of body, place and imagination to come forward in the varied stories that are told throughout the book. This makes it possible to theorize an understanding of presence in teaching and to suggest ways to foster such presence in the concrete world of schooling.

In the preface to *The View from Castle Rock* (Munro, 2007), Alice Munro reflects on the writing of a collection of short stories labeled "semi-fictional." The stories in the first part of that book are based in Munro's digging into the historical records of one side of her family, the Laidlaws, hailing from the south of Scotland. A good deal had been written about as well as by various family members. Munro gathered this material and "almost without my noticing what was happening, it began to shape itself, here and there, into something like stories. Some of the characters gave themselves to me in their own words, others rose out of their situations." At the same time she began writing another set of stories, more akin to memoir, in which Munro was in the center and wrote to understand her own life, yet fictional in that the other characters in the story seemed to take charge of their own lives, doing "things they had not done in reality. They joined the Salvation Army, they revealed that they had once lived in Chicago." For Munro, these stories seemed to pay "more attention to the truth of a life than fiction usually does." Finally, Munro decided that the two sets of stories had come close enough together to be included in the same volume.

Munro's book is labeled a work of fiction, yet I find her comments suggestive in regard to the writing of the present book. I too had been fascinated by family history for some time and, like Munro, began to feel a need to write about it; a certain amount of historical digging was called for, although there was little documentation to go on and in some cases I had to guess into the lives family members might have lived. In the accounts to which I will refer, of both family members and teachers, it is fair to say that often they "gave themselves to me in their own words" but also that they "rose out of their situations." Like Munro, I have put together different kinds of narratives: stories of personal and familial experience are juxtaposed with accounts of professional experience. Unlike Munro's book where the two sets of stories are kept separate, here they often appear together, intertwined and linked by the broader claim that personal and family experience, as embodied and emplaced, as shaped by historical time and cultural context, are formative of who one becomes as a teacher and educator.

As to how this formation comes about—how one becomes a teacher or a teacher educator, and indeed how one can usefully talk about this development in people's narratives of their lives— several different metaphors come to mind. One is the notion of a *parade* as suggested (in relation to the conceptualization of educational change) by Clandinin and Connelly (1998a). Not only change processes but also educators' lives in general often seem to be non-linear, not directed univocally towards a single goal but rather to ramble, meander, casually making their way, in a process that can be theorized as one of *improvisation* (Gur-Ze'ev, 2007).

Another metaphor is that of the *rhizome*, first noted by Jung (1989/1961) who suggested that life can be compared to "a plant that lives on its rhizome. Its true life is invisible, hidden in the rhizome...something that lives and endures underneath the eternal flux." As elaborated by Deleuze and Guattari (1987), this metaphor speaks of an open, non-hierarchical network that branches out in all directions, a root system that takes on diverse forms and has many points of entry; rhizomatic thinking is always multiple: many truths and many perspectives are possible. Drawing on this metaphor, some narrative researchers have theorized selfhood in terms of a "rhizomatic story" (Sermijn et al., 2008). Since rhizomatic thinking is always multiple, this metaphor emphasizes that many truths and many perspectives are possible, and life stories can be told and retold from different starting points to create new layers of significance for individuals and for their communities.

In this light, what Bakhtin says about any utterance in general certainly holds true for the story of a life: it is "never just a reflection or an expression of something already existing and outside it that is given and final. It always creates something that never existed before, something absolutely new and unrepeatable, and, moreover, it always has some relation to value—the true, the good, the beautiful" (Bakhtin, 1986, 119–120). The present book was written in this spirit.

CHAPTER 1

Mixing Memory and Desire Like Spring Rain

> A bit of reinvented truth. A child with a story full of holes, can only reinvent for herself a memory. Of this I am certain. Therefore the autobiography in all of this can only be reinvented. Memory is always reinvented in a story full of holes as if there is no story left. What to do then? Try to fill in the holes—and I would say even this hole—with an imagination fed on everything one can find, the left and the right and the middle of the hole. One attempts to create one's own imaginary truth.
>
> *Chantal Akerman* (in Pollock, 2008, 2010)

The words of French filmmaker Chantal Akerman seem to capture perfectly the complexities of the topic of memory, perpetually stretched between truth and invention, dealing in fragments yet always searching for the whole story. This chapter begins the inquiry into the complex relations of autobiography and pedagogy by examining the difficult but necessary issue of memory in education. I will try to fill in some of the holes in this issue through an interweaving of theoretical discussion with accounts of personal memories, mine and those of other educational practitioners whose autobiographical accounts will feature later in the book as well as accounts drawn from the literature. There has been much discussion of memory from diverse perspectives and almost as much discussion of autobiographical writing, a central form of 'memory work' in pedagogical settings, but much less direct consideration of memory in relation to pedagogy (see, however, Mitchell et al., 2011; R. Simon, 2005; Strong-Wilson, 2008). Thus, the central focus here is on bringing the discussion of memory to bear on questions of education, to understand how memory work can illuminate the pedagogical enactments of who we are and what we believe and aspire to in teaching.

Holding in mind classrooms, learners and teachers, and the diverse settings in which they interact, it is clear that memory plays, indeed must play a pivotal role in the conceptualization and understanding of teaching and learning processes from the point of view of the teachers. According to Warnock (1987, 6) memory can be defined as "that by the possession of which an animal learns from experience." In the tradition of teacher knowledge research from a narrative perspective (see Elbaz-Luwisch, 2007), which relies centrally on interviews and conversations with teachers to bring to light their experience and stories of teaching, an understanding of memory is crucial. In the foreword to a study of teacher memories (Ben-Peretz, 1995b), Connelly claims that "memory represents the assumptional basis for research on teacher knowledge" (1995, xvi). He noted that the retired teachers who participated in Ben-Peretz's study tended to recall negative experiences from their work yet still expressed satisfaction with their careers. Interpreting this paradoxical finding along Deweyan lines, Connelly suggested that a life in teaching should be viewed, and lived, as an educational pursuit, "as a narrative of inquiry, a life filled with tensions and problematic situations and with the growth that ensues from moving successfully from one inquiry to another." (1995, xv) The study of teaching is a study of experience, and of how through the construction and reconstruction of experience the knowledge of teaching is elaborated and an inquiry is taken forward. Experience is what we remember and can tell about, yet memory has yet to be given full attention in relation to teaching. In this chapter, I fill in some of the gaps by attending to memory in the context of autobiographical writing and stories of teachers' lives and experience.

Memory is held and brought forward by teachers in classroom performance, in discussion with colleagues, in solitary reflection and in writing about their work and lives. In each of these contexts, the body and the notion of embodiment play a significant role. And from the body we are led to a consideration of the concepts of presence and wide-awakeness without which it is not possible to speak about pedagogy unless we content ourselves with a pedagogy that is yet another "story full of holes," such as is found all too often in schools today. Imagination and truth, as foregrounded by Akerman above, are also central to any discussion of memory. And inevitably, writing, with all its attendant difficulties, comes to the fore as one medium for the retrieval of memory and a privileged if sometimes problematic vehicle for its safekeeping. These notions of body, presence, imagination and truth, and writing, will be examined more closely in later chapters; here they are only prefigured in relation to the discussion of memory. Given this intermingling of topics and concepts, the form of this chapter may resemble a meandering stream that curves back on itself at times but still arrives, eventually, at a wider and deeper place, a fuller understanding of memory in its connections to teaching and pedagogy and to the research on these topics.

Theories of memory

In the introduction to an edited volume on theories of memory, Rossington and Whitehead (2007) point out that there has been a "memory boom" starting in the last decade of the 20th century. They attribute this surge of attention to multiple sources, first among them, the postmodern view that historical memory has been commodified and rendered uncertain to such a degree that it can no longer be retrieved faithfully. In addition, they mention technological developments leading to new digital archives and the possibilities of virtual memory; concern with remembrance of the 20th century record of wars, genocide and other traumas; the debate around False Memory syndrome as well as developments in the fields of Holocaust studies, postcolonialism and poststructuralism. All of these concerns impact on education and on pedagogical commitments in different ways and to varying degrees, and they will echo in the discussion that follows.

Rossington and Whitehead also claim that "it would be mistaken to suggest that thinking about memory has undergone a chronological development over the centuries" (2007, 4). Rather, their compilation of seminal texts on memory in Western thought seems to show that while memory is not amenable to any simple definition, there are nevertheless a number of common ideas around memory that reappear and are rearticulated in different periods, often in combination rather than as separate and one-sided views.

One persisting idea about memory, famously elaborated in the Socratic dialogue *Meno* (Hamilton & Cairns, 1961) is that of recollection: the soul, being immortal, has learned before birth everything that is to be learned, and thus "it can recall the knowledge of virtue or anything else which (…) it once possessed" (364). The notion of recollection still has currency, for example in cultures that maintain a belief in reincarnation, such as the Druze living in Israel and other parts of the Middle East today as well as in some 'new-age' ideas. A less literal version of the idea of recollection is at work in the Jungian notion of the collective unconscious (Jung, 1991), the repository of archetypical images and contents to which all of us potentially have access.

From Plato, we have also inherited the still pervasive and, indeed, persuasive notion of memory as a copy of reality:

> Imagine, then, for the sake of argument, that our minds contain a block of wax (…)
> whenever we wish to remember something we see or hear or conceive in our own
> minds, we hold this wax under the perceptions or ideas and imprint them…whatever
> is so imprinted we remember and know so long as the image remains; whatever is
> rubbed out or has not succeeded in leaving an impression we have forgotten and do
> not know. (*Theaetetus* 191c-e, Hamilton and Cairns, 897)

A modern formulation of this idea, drawing on similar imagery, is Freud's notion of the "mystic writing pad" (Freud, 1991), the child's toy on which one writes with a pointed stick, causing an imprint to appear on a plastic covering sheet, to be erased when the sheet is lifted. The faint traces that remain on the soft layer underneath the plastic surface served Freud well as a representation of the contents of the unconscious, not easily brought to mind yet 'remembered' in some way. Although this toy still exists, somewhat anachronistically in the computer age (for sale on the internet under the name "magic sketch tablet"), the block of wax as a metaphorical representation of the working of memory no doubt seems archaic to a generation aware of the possibility of observing different areas of the brain lighting up on a computer screen in response to changing stimuli. However, the idea that memory can or should represent a faithful copy of experience does persist for example in legal contexts where witnesses are enjoined to tell the truth about what they observed. And whether memory is laid down over the course of our lived experience or is in some way thought to predate it, there is also a clear understanding that considerable effort may be required to retrieve memories. Walter Benjamin expresses the psychological force of this idea:

> Language has unmistakably made plain that memory is not an instrument for
> exploring the past, but rather a medium. It is the medium of that which is
> experienced, just as the earth is the medium in which ancient cities lie buried. He
> who seeks to approach his own buried past must conduct himself like a man digging.
> Above all, he must not be afraid to return again and again to the same matter; to
> scatter it as one scatters earth, to turn it over as one turns over soil (Benjamin, 1999,
> 576).

This understanding of the effort and persistence needed to call up some memories, particularly difficult ones, exists alongside the familiar experience of the "flashbulb memory" (Brown & Kulik, 1977)—a memory of a significant, often life-changing event that is retained in vivid (if not always accurate) detail. The strong imprint of early memories can be seen in the autobiographical writings of Israeli teachers, whose accounts are vivid and engaging, and in some ways more varied than the theories around early memory would suggest. For example, Lisa (see Chapter 5), an Israeli teacher born in the former Soviet Union, remembers: "When I was 5 we visited my father's relatives and vacationed in St. Petersburg (then called Leningrad); we toured every part of this amazing city through which the Neva River flows. I remember the white nights, the many beautiful water fountains and of course we visited the Palace of the Czar Peter decorated in gold."

Lisa's memories of the visit to St. Petersburg are clear and apparently significant for her story of herself, although she doesn't elaborate on how they are important; perhaps the elegant and glittering views she remembers are something she misses in her everyday life? Another teacher, Marie, holds with loving detail the memory of a repeated experience despite the fact that it was not particularly pleasant: "What I really didn't like was to go after school to father's store, a stationery store that was not far from the school— and to wait until 2 o'clock to go home with him."

Ella, who grew up in a small agricultural community (a "moshav"), begins her autobiography with what sounds like a flashbulb memory: "When I was 13, I parachuted from a plane for the first time." The adventure was a long-awaited birthday gift she had requested from her parents, but surprisingly she claims to remember little of the experience itself, only her own immense excitement before and after. Perhaps the early memory was dimmed by later experience: Ella learned to parachute on her own as soon as she was old enough, and this activity is now a regular part of her life. However, reflecting on her decision in the 9th grade to leave behind her friends and the familiar school setting in which she felt bored, and "jump" to the unfamiliar setting of a democratic school, Ella is convinced that her first parachute jump was the beginning of "my desire to choose for myself, to make decisions about my life and to accept the responsibility for those decisions."

The teachers' accounts underline the diversity and unpredictability of both what is retained in memory, and how we draw on memories in telling our stories. The notion that early experiences leave lasting and indelible imprints in memory is an idea that can be taken forward in different ways. On the one hand, we might see the bank of early memories as a rich storehouse of potential imagery to be used in active and creative ways, in cognition and in the development of personality; on the other hand, this idea may contribute to the belief that the character and abilities of young people are determined early in life and are not open to significant modification through education. Since most educators probably hold a view, even implicitly, of how memory works and how it influences learning and development, these divergent possibilities underline the importance of reflecting on our given conceptualizations and their pedagogical implications.

In discussing classical views of memory, Richards (2007, 20) points out that even in antiquity memory was seen as more than the passive reception of impressions but rather was viewed as an active and dialectical process involving both collection and recollection, storage and retrieval. Worry about the reliability of memory, its proximity to and possible contamination by emotion, by the imagination, or by writing, has also been a concern in research on teaching based on teachers' self-reports. This is a long-standing philosophical issue found in different periods, from Plato and Aristotle through to Hume. Freud's early work (1899) focused on the notion of the "screen memory": early memories that were used as a cover for memories of later events the person wished to repress, or the reverse—recollection of a later event covering for the memory of an early sexual experience. Eventually Freud came to the idea that supposed 'early' memories were probably reconstructed in later periods, and while they continued to be significant their veracity could not be relied upon (Davis, 1994). According to Rossington and Whitehead (2007), a change comes with Hegel whose "theory of memory enlists imagination to rescue images from the 'night-like mine or pit'" (73); this collaboration between memory and imagination inaugurates a sense of memory as *re*construction which remains influential— if not unproblematic—today, and is critical to a narrative understanding of the self.

The links between memory and emotion, also noticed in antiquity, have sparked considerable research interest in recent years. Reisberg and Hertel (2004), in the preface to a diverse collection of work on the interconnections between memory and emotion, note that researchers in this area take up diverse perspectives, including a range of psychological, biological and neurological approaches, looking into what is remembered from both everyday and extreme experiences. They also highlight the complexity of the interrelations and the 'mixed effects' of emotion on memory, noting that, in general, emotion has a positive effect on memory, increasing its vividness, accuracy, completeness and longevity. However, a focus on the central visual stimuli recorded in memory may impair memory for details at the periphery of the event, and emotion that is "assigned to an event after the fact may also spur memory reconstruction based on too little information" (Heuer & Reisberg, 2007, 55). Further, it has also been found that trauma, and its accompanying stress, may lead to events being recorded in a fragmented manner rather than integrated into a coherent narrative. As poet Sujata Bhatt tells it, "history is a broken narrative" (2000, 40–43). Thus, under difficult conditions merely having a story to tell may already be an accomplishment for the autobiographer.

Immigration is an experience that offers a particular challenge to the autobiographer: how to tell a coherent story that integrates then and now, here and there; how to reconcile the perspectives of one's country of origin with those of the new place, of the older generation born in one country with the younger generation growing up in another (Lieblich, 1993). One can detect the autobiographer at work reconstructing memory in a vignette of childhood written by Eliana, another Israeli teacher born in the former Soviet Union; she recalls "long trips to Odessa on the shore of the Black Sea...driving through the night my mother and brother slept but I didn't close an eye—I 'drove' with Father." Although we cannot know what does or does not conform to fact in this anecdote, it is clear that portraying herself as 'driving with father' is the writer's way of establishing something about herself and her relationship to her father that goes beyond mere representation.

As I wrote this section, returning to the text of Plato's dialogues (Hamilton & Cairns, 1961) that I've had since my second year at university, I remembered Professor Demos—Raphael Demos, a world expert in Plato, then recently retired from Harvard, who taught the first semester of the Introductory Philosophy course I took in my second year at McGill

University. The course was held in Moyse Hall, one of the largest lecture halls on campus, and we sat in pre-assigned seats so that our attendance could be monitored. I was alternately intrigued and puzzled by the encounter with Greek philosophy: it was exciting to read the dialogues but hard to imagine their significance for everyday life. Then one November day—it was 1963—I left the library and walked back to the Arts building through the glassed-in corridor where students gathered to smoke, talk and flirt. Feeling a bit uncomfortable there I walked quickly but noticed an unusual buzz in the air, waves of excited talk that suggested something out-of-the-ordinary had happened. Finally I met a friend who passed on the news: John Kennedy, president of the United States, had been shot.

It hardly needs saying that the effects of Kennedy's assassination were felt strongly around the world, not least across the border in Canada; the university announced that American students and teachers were released from class on the day of the State funeral, and our class in Introductory Philosophy was cancelled. The next time we met with Professor Demos he stood gravely in front of the three hundred or so students and told us we would not deal with our regular subject matter that day. A great tragedy had taken place, and it was his duty as a teacher and an elder to help his students, the young generation, make sense of this terrible event and come to some understanding about the presence of evil in the world. He spoke about Kennedy's youth and about how he had instilled in the young people of his country hope for a better future and a desire to contribute to it. He mentioned that the White House had become a home for the arts, for literature and philosophy, for ideas. He praised Jacqueline Kennedy's dignified behavior as she stood by her husband and, later, as she led her children to pay their respects to their father.

After the lecture three hundred students filed out of the hall in near silence, awed and moved by what we had heard. Following Demos's lecture, I went with anticipation to my other classes, especially the one in political science, where, as it happened, we were studying the American presidency. I was puzzled and disappointed that none of my other professors saw fit to make even an oblique reference to the assassination. A week or two later, a transcript of the talk was handed out, apparently prepared by a student who had managed to copy it down verbatim, and it has remained in my files. At first the presence of a written text seemed to reduce the experience we had shared to an item on the professor's vita, but I was glad to have it as a concrete reminder. Over the years the text gathered new and sometimes ironic meanings, in the light of revelations about Kennedy's personal life and the many tragic and difficult events that have marked the Kennedy family's continuing history. However, what still shines clearly for me is the memory of this teacher's willingness to stand before us, his young students, to try to offer us consolation, and to confront together the fact of evil in the world. Demos' lecture was an example of what Smith refers to as "teaching-as-truth-dwelling": an effort to be connected to students in the present, and to make the classroom "a place of truth seeking, truth discovering and truth sharing" (Smith, 2000, 19).

This account of my personal recollections around the Kennedy assassination brings together several of the points raised above about memory and adds something new. It is a clear example of a flashbulb memory, vivid and detailed as to time and place. I can't say to what extent it was a life-changing memory, but it remains relevant for my own understanding of myself as an educator, which I did not plan or expect to become at that time. And it also illustrates the nature of memory as social and cultural at the same time that it is individual. The notion of social and collective memory was pioneered by Halbwachs (1992), who first wrote about the topic in 1925; more recently it has been taken up by Haug (1987), Connerton (1989), Hirsch & Smith (2002) and others.

The ethics of memory

Generally, the discussion of memory and its retrieval or reconstruction through autobiographic writing suggests that exploring and bringing forward our memories is a salubrious practice, promoting personal growth and integration as well as professional development (e.g., Schaafsma, 1996). According to Pennebaker (1997), disclosing one's experience, whether orally or in writing, has been shown in a series of empirical studies to be helpful in itself, positively influencing various measures of physical health and emotional well-being; further, "people who benefited from writing began with poorly organized descriptions and progressed to coherent stories" (165). On another view, in writing one is required to focus on specific images and to recreate them in detail as well as to pull them together in narrative form, and, as MacCurdy (2007) suggests, "re-experiencing sensory details encoded during extreme life moments is at the core of trauma recovery" (36). Autobiographical writing in which the writer seeks to come to terms with difficult experiences of the past constitutes one form of 'caring for the self'; it might even be seen as a special case of the ethical obligation to care for others (Margalit, 2002), in particular those with whom we have close relationships (parent-child, teacher-student, intimate partners).

Margalit, however, raises a different issue about the 'goodness' of memory, concerning the *obligation* to remember. He recalls an episode reported in the Israeli press concerning a soldier killed by friendly fire. In an interview, the soldier's commanding officer did not remember the name of the fallen soldier; subsequent public response was swift to blame the officer for his lapse, suggesting that he had failed in his obligation to remember the soldier. Margalit analyzes this obligation to remember in terms of a distinction between morality and ethics, where morality has to do with what he terms 'thin' relations—those based on the mere attribute of being human, our relations to the stranger or to those who are far away—while ethics is grounded in 'thick' relations—those we have with parents, friends, lovers, fellow countrymen and countrywomen. Memory is crucial to our ethical relations with those close to us: Margalit suggests that memory is "the cement that holds thick relations together" (2002, 8).

Thus we have an ethical obligation to remember, but what exactly? To answer this, Margalit invokes the notion of caring, which is enmeshed with memory and is thus central to ethical relations. He concludes that we should remember whatever is needed to maintain our ethical relations with those who are close to us, to allow us to care for and about them in an ethical manner. In this context an interesting recent phenomenon is the practice taken up by some children and grandchildren of Holocaust survivors of tattooing the grandparent's number on their own arm (see Rudoren, 2012). On hearing of this my instinctive reaction was negative: the practice seemed at worst offensive to other survivors, at best merely provocative. But from a film made about this topic, it was apparent that while some of the survivors had also rejected the idea at first, they were very moved by the gesture which confirmed the closeness between them and their grandchildren. This phenomenon underlines the slippery nature of memory and suggests that perhaps, what exactly should be remembered, and how, will have to be worked out within the relationship according to the needs of each case.

When my son was in the 10th grade, and had just started at a new school, one day the dog ate his geography homework. He was enthusiastic about geography and had done the homework carefully, but Jenny, the boxer, got into his room and mangled the pages. It was too late to redo the homework, and Shai went to school the next morning with a heavy step, unsure about how he would tell this story, the ultimate trumped-up excuse turned truth, to his teacher. I thought about him all the way to work but then got busy with the tasks of the day. When I returned home, he was in his room, listening to music; I did not remember the homework until about an hour later. I rushed to his room, contrite that I had forgotten, to ask what had happened in geography class. Ah, he said—it seemed that he too had almost forgotten— "the teacher hugged me, and he told me to do it over and bring it in by the end of the week." Writing this now, almost 20 years later, I still feel a pang of conscience: although things had gone well, it seems ethically wrong of me to have been so preoccupied with other obligations that I forgot my son's distress. The episode brings home the sense of an obligation to remember virtually everything that concerns our children. For teachers, this obligation is attenuated: on the one hand, the teacher is not a priori required to know, much less remember, everything about her pupils; but on the other hand, she can never know in advance what information she *should* have about them in order to do her work ethically. Only when a situation becomes critical will it be apparent that the teacher should have known about the family's economic difficulties, the parents' impending divorce or the death of a beloved grandparent.

Another aspect of the ethical force of memory relates to the obligation to remember truthfully. It's not enough to simply remember: we ought to remember fully; we should get the facts straight, should remember things as they truly happened. It would be wrong to remember events in a self-serving way that casts us in a better light than we deserve and even worse to 'remember' the misdeeds of others if those did not in fact take place. This is the basis for the "memory wars" (Campbell, 2003) in relation to the controversies surrounding cases of recall in adult life (or false recall) of childhood sexual abuse.

The obligation to remember truthfully also comes up sharply in relation to remembrance of the Holocaust. Gotfryd (2000) tells about his Holocaust experiences with the vivid detail of the photographer he became after the war, yet the failure of memory is a recurrent motif in his stories: peers from his home town who were a few years ahead of him in school insisted they did not remember him (yet faithfully invited him to all their gatherings). Even a man whose life he saved in the evacuation of a camp was later unable to remember him or the events they had experienced together. Sometimes the lapses in memory had an explanation: one former schoolmate was from a poor family and confessed he had not wanted to remember the miseries of his own childhood; in other cases, the stories of absent memory remained a mystery. Yet it is around this mystery that Gotfryd's stories turn and hold the reader.

But it is not just failures of memory that make it impossible to represent adequately the events of the Holocaust. The sheer inadequacy of memory itself is emphasized repeatedly by Langer, who claims that the Holocaust is "a phenomenon alien to our usual patterns of speech or belief" (Langer, 1998, 3–4). He argues that chronological time is simply not appropriate to speak about the "duration" of Holocaust time, "a constantly re-experienced time (which) threatens the chronology of experienced time" (1995, 15). Since writing about experienced events normally invokes some form of temporal order, writing about the Holocaust inevitably does violence to "the uniquely imprisoned persistence of the Holocaust event in the memory of its witnesses" (Langer, 1995, 16). In the words of Yehiel Dinur, a writer and survivor of Auschwitz, taken from his testimony at the Eichmann trial in June 1961, moments before he passed out on the witness stand:

> Time there was not like it is here on earth. Every fraction of a minute there passed on a different scale of time. And the inhabitants of this planet had no names, they had no parents nor did they have children. There they did not dress in the way we dress here; they were not born there and they did not give birth; they breathed according to different laws of nature; they did not live—nor did they die—according to the laws of this world. (Dinur, 1961)

Watching the film of Dinur's testimony on Israeli television recently, I recalled seeing it on Canadian television in 1961. At the time I thought that Dinur was highly dramatic and when I saw him collapse I wondered at first if this might be an act; I was a teenager and had no basis for understanding the unbearable strain he must have been under, facing Eichmann in his glass box, speaking before an Israeli court. The fact that such a trial was even taking place must have seemed completely unreal to him: the former victims accusing the one who had engineered and administered their humiliation, bearing witness in the legitimate courtroom of a sovereign Jewish state. Thus any attempt to portray the events and sufferings of the Holocaust not only risks misrepresenting the truth of what happened but indeed *must* necessarily misrepresent it; and such (mis)representation potentially does harm both to survivors and to the memory of victims. Suleiman suggests that "memory is a 'shifting and many-layered thing,' never reaching the bedrock one longs for," and the only solution is to continue to write and rewrite (1993, 557). As Felman and Laub note about Holocaust testimony, it "seems to be composed of bits and pieces of a memory that has been overwhelmed by occurrences that have not settled into understanding or remembrance, acts that cannot be constructed as knowledge nor assimilated into full cognition, events in excess of our frames of reference."(1992, 5)

There seems to be an inevitable tension between the notion of witness testimony deriving its authority from the status of the narrator who experienced the events personally and the impossibility of establishing the authenticity of any given narrative. The now infamous case of the text entitled *Fragments* (Wilkomirski, 1996), the purported autobiography of a child survivor, Benjamin Wilkomirski, highlights this tension: the text was initially acclaimed as a powerful and unique autobiography told from a child's perspective; a few years later the veracity of the text and identity of its author were placed in question. It was established that the author did not experience the events he described in the book but, it seems, used a Holocaust story as a stand-in (a sort of "screen memory") for his own genuinely traumatic childhood experience of repeated abandonment, probably fully believing the story he 'retrieved' with the help of a therapist (Gross & Hoffman, 2004). And yet a noted scholar of Holocaust history, himself a survivor, Israel Gutman, held that the story is important, *even if untrue*, because the author experienced it deeply (Lappin, 1999).

Spence's notion of 'narrative truth' (1982) might be helpful in understanding this paradoxical situation: although it is right to object to a misrepresentation of the author's experience, one can see that the text in question might still bear a strong narrative truth value in that it offers a coherent account of previously disorganized and incomprehensible events, that it makes possible the expression of what was previously unsayable and does so in a persuasive manner. Writing on the 40th anniversary of the end of the Second World War, poet Mary Oliver (1986) begins from her own experience of living in close connection to nature: she would like to live in the world as someone who just walks in the woods, curious, interested in life, doing no harm, not defined by ethnic or religious identity, occupation or hobbies. But she has seen films taken in the concentration camps of Dachau, Auschwitz and Bergen Belsen; she has seen something which can be neither understood nor forgotten, the "iron claw" of Germany, which "slowly, for years, scrape(d) across Europe, while the rest of the world did nothing." Oliver juxtaposes to this a series of disparate images: a fawn wandering carefree in the woods near her home, a garden in which she imagines someone eating a peaceful lunch, sipping wine from a crystal glass— Mengele; and then, back in the woods, a doe, sensing danger, returns to look for and nuzzle her fawn (Oliver, 1986, "1945–1985, Poem for the Anniversary," 81–83). Poetry such as this provides significance and meaning not by establishing what happened in the past as a matter of historical record but in providing a 'story to live by' for the future, or at least the ingredients from which the reader may construct such a story.

This brings us back to a pedagogical context: we can assert that events that have been experienced deeply, and that can be conveyed to others in a way that allows them to identify with and understand the experience, can be pedagogically useful. They serve to flesh out Margalit's notion of an ethical community, one in which members have 'thick' relations with one another based on shared experience. Some of that shared experience may be vicarious experience (see Conle, Li & Tan, 2002), based in a narrative understanding of communal events. While schools and classrooms can be considered to be ethical communities in this sense, it is clear that very often they are structured and organized in ways that make it difficult if not impossible for them to function as such. Very large classes, for example, and the pressures of standardized testing, are conditions which make it more difficult to constitute an ethical community in the classroom. Classrooms are more likely to realize their potential as ethical communities if they can engage pupils with subject matter and learning processes that are meaningful both for them personally and for the communities to which they belong. Attending to historical memory in complex ways is critical to the realization of such potential; one such way is through a "dystopic" curriculum (Morris, 2001) that "opens up the possibility of learning anew how to live in the present with each other" (R. Simon, 2005, 4).

Memory and desire

The link between memory and desire made by T. S. Eliot (1922) in *The Waste Land* has stirred the imagination of many. In a philosophical discussion with the same title, Baier (1976) subsumes desire under the more general and less resonant category of intentions and finds several similarities between memory and intention, yet is forced to conclude her argument with the still unanswered question:

> Having pointed out the parallels between intending and remembering, I would like to be able to explain them, and to find some present directed mental state which would serve as the link. (…) How and through what mediator does one's past story affect one's intentions for the future? Through what present filter do intended acts, and their failures become fate? (Baier, 1976, 220)

A positive link between story and desire is made by Brooks (1984), who builds his discussion of how we read literary works around the term 'narrative desire' to indicate several layers of meaning: first, the plot of a novel is typically *about desire*; further, reading is itself *a form of desire* that carries us forward through the plot of a novel or story in a passionate search for the meaning that comes at the end of the tale. And finally, there is the *desire for narration* itself, the desire to tell, to be heard, recognized and listened to. Storytelling, according to poet Jane Hirshfield, "answers both our curiosity and our longing for shapely forms: our profound desire to know what happens, and our persistent hope that what happens will somehow make sense" (Hirshfield, 1998, 26). Such desire is not confined to writers of narrative fiction but is an everyday occurrence that motivates many of our small and large exchanges with others around us, not least the impulse to engage in autobiographic writing.

Lest we see this discussion as applying only to the reading of literature, the work of Paul Ricoeur (1984) on time and narrative (and on memory and forgetting, 2004) stakes out a much broader terrain. Ricoeur sees experience itself as bearing a prenarrative quality or "an inchoate narrativity"; he identifies stories that "demand to be told" (1984, 74). He further suggests the notion of "being entangled in stories": life is about being caught up in a web of stories. Ricoeur sketches that web as woven of stories being lived right now and stories past which are held in memory and which make up the 'background' or larger whole.

> The story "happens to" someone before anyone tells it. The entanglement seems like the "prehistory" of the told story, whose beginning has to be chosen by the narrator. This "prehistory" of the story is what binds it to a larger whole and gives it a "background". The background is made up of the "living imbrications" of every lived story with every other lived story. Told stories therefore have to "emerge" (…) from this background. (p. 75)

The notion of entanglement derives from quantum physics. As Mindell (2010) explains,

> Entanglement was first intuited…by Erwin Schrodinger, one of the parents of quantum theory. He predicted that particles could connect with one another nonlocally, which means at speeds apparently faster than the speed of light…he saw the possibility that two particles…that were originally connected will always be so, even if they travel to opposite sides of the world. (188–9)

Mindell's approach, known as "process-oriented psychology," is an eclectic one, focused on awareness, and grounded in the work of Jung but also in physics (in which he trained), Eastern philosophy and aboriginal worldviews. Mindell invokes the ideas of physics to help explain and work with psychological and social processes. He acknowledges that the phenomenon of entanglement is counter-intuitive and poses difficulties for a rational mind-set: no known signals are exchanged by the entangled particles, yet the phenomenon can be observed empirically. He asks, "How can one particle be connected with another without any signals going between them? How do you sometimes know something without any visible message or transfer of information" (Mindell, 2010, 191). Physics refers to this "space-defying connection" as *nonlocality*; it bears some similarity to Jung's (1981) notion of *synchronicity*, which refers to the occurrence of meaningful coincidences. For Mindell, both notions—entanglement and synchronicity—are grounded in what he terms the "processmind," defined as "the palpable, intelligent, organizing 'force field' present behind our personal and large group processes and, like other deep quantum patterns, behind processes of the universe" (2010, xi). The notion of an organizing force field recalls Ricoeur's idea that there is a "larger whole" against which we live out and apprehend stories as well as a background made up of the "living imbrications" of every lived story with every other lived story, now and in the past. Mindell's understanding of entanglement seems to complement Ricoeur's formulation. The notion of entanglement has a significant spiritual dimension for Ricoeur (see Hakker, 2004), as it does (in a different way) for Mindell. This can and should be open to critique (as in Faber's [1998] treatment of the Jungian concept of synchronicity); however, it is not necessary to make a metaphysical commitment to engage with the concept.

Being 'entangled in stories' is something that many of us have experienced as the common and shared urge to make sense of one's life and the story one is living, to live out a worthwhile story within the web of connections, storied and as yet unstoried, in which one finds herself, and in effect to pursue one's education (Connelly & Clandinin, 1995). The notion of desire has long been a taboo subject in educational contexts, but it is increasingly being recognized as crucial to the living out of a meaningful educational narrative (Garrison, 1997; hooks, 1994; Pryer, 2001). For Zembylas (2007), a 'pedagogy of desire' is a politically engaged pedagogy which might "open the space within which teachers and students are able to gain a new sense of interconnection and intersubjectivity with others" (344).

Electronic memory

With the advent of the internet, the everyday memory capacity of the average person has received an enormous boost. Personal memory obviously remains, like before, subject to the reliability of one's own efforts at storage. I still have some old journal notebooks, whereas much of my more recent journaling on the computer has been lost to the crash of hard discs. But the public side of our personal lives, events in which we participated with others, has become infinitely more accessible through the internet. In some ways, perhaps, we can now remember more than we need or want to know. Like many others, I imagine, when the internet first became available I tried to find people with whom I had lost touch; however, many of those I looked for could not be located, while those I did find were listed in obituary notices, and I soon gave up the practice.

And yet my memory continues to be enriched by information available on the internet. Some people I hadn't thought to look for have managed to find me. Some crucial information is available in on-line archives if one only knows where to look. My daughter was able to construct an extensive family tree for my father's family, to reconnect with some relatives and even to locate the graves of my paternal grandparents in Vienna (see Chapter 7). Further, I have been able to construct a wider understanding of my family story from internet searches; the ease of surfing the net means one can look up trivial details as easily as essential information, and sometimes it is the trivial, the marginal, the seemingly irrelevant, which serves as a trigger to comprehension, allowing one to link together disparate fragments of memory into a story.

Memory and trauma

Recently I returned from a dental appointment, made coffee and checked emails but without making myself really comfortable in front of the computer. Remembering the load of laundry done the night before, I took everything out of the dryer and started folding. When done, I was left with one red sock. I shook out the duvet cover which had been left to dry on a chair; inside were two more socks—unmatched, neither one red. Finally, the missing red sock was located and I cast about for something else to keep me busy: email again, a few games of Spider Solitaire, a reflective pass through the list of household repairs waiting to be set in motion, thoughts about some writing recently sent to me by students. Finally, behind everything else, waiting patiently like the red sock, I come upon my writing. Like a meditator coming back to awareness of the breath, like a distracted reader finding her place in the text, I return to consideration of writing. I decide not to delete this domestic digression: it stands in for all the wandering thoughts, the daydreams of vacation, the cups of coffee, the sandwiches when we are not hungry, and whatever else it may be that simultaneously keeps us from writing and keep us at it.

For months now I have been circling about, sometimes thinking about the writing and sometimes ignoring it, sometimes carefully editing a passage that is in no way final and may soon be scrapped just as it attains grammatical perfection. I reread the outline, look over some of the earlier writing that I plan to incorporate into the text. I collect more bibliographic references. I read, watch movies, and go to exhibits for inspiration. I talk about writing and read about it. A while ago I attended a conference on writing where I encouraged two young women in their writing projects, receiving wonderful advice and encouragement from them in return. In short, I've done everything but write.

This fear of writing is not my usual experience; typically I spin out words easily enough, though I may become a harsh critic of them later on. I have even become used to making brief forays into the personal without becoming paralyzed. But the current project is different. It is not primarily about memory as a theoretical construct, nor about memory as an experienced phenomenon, but about memories—mine, and those of others who have entrusted them to me. The memories I'm interested in are personal; some of them have lived in hiding for many years before being brought to the light of day. And many of them are not just personal but carry social, and cultural, and historical meanings not only for those who remember but perhaps more critically for those who do not. As Freeman (2002) suggests, "cultural texts and 'textures' become woven, often unconsciously, into the fabric of memory" (p. 193). Freeman coins the term "narrative unconscious," referring not to the more familiar concept of the psychological unconscious but rather to "those culturally-rooted aspects of one's history that remain uncharted and that, consequently, have yet to be incorporated into one's story." There are no set guidelines for charting this history, and one of the tasks of the present inquiry will be to fill in some of the unnamed and unacknowledged cultural aspects of my history and that of others.

My memories of schooling are readily available. I recall being given a mark of Unsatisfactory in a 3rd grade composition because I had written more than the 4 sentences requested (and bragged about it when I went up to the teacher's desk to have my work checked). I was used to being a good student, to pleasing my teachers but also to respecting their judgment even if they sometimes found me wanting. I didn't think the teacher's appraisal of my work was fair but neither did I think I had the right to question it. A few months later this teacher began acting strangely and soon left the school; the term "nervous breakdown" was used, a term not clearly defined, but it was enough at the time to restore to me my prior confidence in writing.

I remember doing a relief map of Australia in the 6th grade, enjoying the feel of the papier-mâché surface, the textures that represented forest, water and city, the bright colours of gouache paint with which I marked the different provinces whose names I remembered for many years after. In the seventh grade, there were heated discussions in the schoolyard at recess on the then-pertinent topic of "Better Red than Dead?" I remember leaning against the wire mesh fence in a corner of the yard, earnestly defending "Better Red." It seemed clear that anything was preferable to being dead, even the evils of communism, about which I then knew little (though admittedly I knew no more about being dead). In Canada of the late 1950s, the Communist Party was a legal but very marginal player in the political arena; Soviet communism was a different story: the Soviet regime was what prevented our having contact with my mother's family in Odessa. These events are not hard to remember, are even interesting to write about, despite a certain measure of angst carried by some of my recollections. I was a good student, I liked school, and it's not hard to understand why, as it turns out, I am one of those who never left school (Barone, 1989). These are not memories to be feared, nor do they reveal much about why the topic of memory is so complex nor why it has become the object of so much discussion in recent academic work.

The work I am avoiding relates to more difficult memories, brought forward in stories told by teachers and students, and in my case the memories that lie on the underside of my cheerful Canadian childhood. They are the memories of my parents who were born in Europe and emigrated to Canada—fled—my mother in 1925 during a time of pogroms in Russia, my father in early 1939, after being arrested in Vienna on "Kristallnacht," November 9–10, 1938. For me these are 'secondhand' memories, crafted out of the stories told by my parents, accounts that were already carefully edited and 'sanitized' versions of the terror they lived through; their stories were censored in order not to upset me but also in profound recognition that they were among the incredibly fortunate ones who got out in time while many members of both their families were murdered by the Nazis. These stories are what Hirsch (2001, 2008) terms "post-memory," to describe "the relationship that the generation after those who witnessed cultural or collective trauma bears to the experiences of those who came before, experiences that they 'remember' only by means of the stories, images, and behaviors among which they grew up" (Hirsch, 2008, 106). Constructed long after the fact by someone who did not directly experience the events, these stories are not *mine* in the usual sense: they are invented, fabricated out of the relics of others' actual memories; and yet they are powerful and they do belong to me. In the act of reconstructing memory, the individual adds to the historical record and makes the memory her own. Placing flowers on the graves of my paternal grandparents in Vienna in 2006, I was aware of making a small intervention in the historical record of a community with a long history, a community virtually wiped out in the Holocaust: "contradicting history with blue flowers" (see Chapter 7). As Benjamin notes:

> (…) for authentic memories, it is far less important that the investigator report on them than that he mark, quite precisely, the site where he gained possession of them. Epic and rhapsodic in the strictest sense, genuine memory must therefore yield an image of the person who, in the same way a good archaeological report not only informs us about the strata from which its findings originate, but also gives an account of the strata which first had to be broken through (Benjamin, 1999, 576).

In my experience of them, these stories are real, and even true, in some sense yet to be formulated. And it is only as "true stories" that they are likely to be pedagogically useful, to serve us in the ethical obligation to remember and care for our thick relations with others. I turn then to a discussion of the links between memory, history, truth and imagination.

Transformations of memory: History, truth and imagination

We have seen that both theoretical and empirical accounts of memory have a suspicion of the workings of the imagination in our efforts to recall the past. In their examination of the processes of aging from an interdisciplinary perspective, Randall and McKim (2008) acknowledge the ravages of time on memory, but at the same time they also introduce the fruitful idea of memory as a *compost heap* in which a series of ongoing processes take place: "laying it on," or the idea of memory as layered and thick with text after text; "letting it be," since "for memory to do its work…it needs fallow time, dreaming time, time for just sitting, time for settling quietly inside of us"; "breaking it down," which speaks to the inevitable 'decay' of memories which become fuzzy and tend to merge into composite events; "stirring it up," which takes place when old memories are triggered unexpectedly and brought to the surface; and finally "mixing it in," which is about the sharing of memories and experiences for the benefit of others and to foster their growth as well as our own." (147–8) This view of memory is one I would like to take on board, at least in part because it is a positive view of processes of memory decay that I am beginning to be aware of in my own life. However, one cannot endorse this view without also paying attention to the claims of history and historical accuracy.

Memory is often positioned in opposition to history: despite a diversity of epistemological positions concerning the nature of historical truth, despite the existence of competing narratives of given events, it is usually assumed that some consensus can be established about what happened, whereas there may be no way to confirm or refute the truth-value of particular memories, whether individual or collective. Steedman (1992), reflecting on the difference between writing history and writing autobiography, holds that autobiography is about inner experience while 'memoir' deals with "a series of external factors that is presented as dictating the narrative course" (1992, 44). As for history, Steedman takes up an ironic stance, holding that:

> Nothing can be said to have happened in the past until you have spent three years at it (three years at least), got on many trains, opened many bundles in the archives, stayed in many flea-bitten hotels. This is the craft-romance of historical practice, and I fall for it all the way. (Steedman, 1992, 45–46)

As a historian, then, Steedman argues that *Landscape for a Good Woman* (Steedman, 1986), her autobiographical account of her mother's life and its influence on her own working-class childhood, is *not* history: it is based on secondary sources, on memory and even on recollected dreams; no empirical research was done, no checking of facts. But Steedman hopes readers will reject her disclaimer, will say that it is indeed history; she wants to persuade us of the 'truth' of the story that she knows is both true and not true. Her refusal to call it 'history' stems from a critique of the romanticization that history inevitably operates: dealing with stories "made out of multiple poverties and real deprivations," she insists that "the life of many people in this society is not explained by the dominant forms that give expression to lived experience: novels, other literature, film, history" (Steedman, 1992, 46).

If, with Steedman and others, we remain concerned about understanding and explaining human lives, the lives of particular individuals and of the community, the notion of narrative truth offered by Spence (1982) as discussed above is a helpful one in identifying the processes by which the narrative inquirer and the writer of auto/biography (and perhaps also the historian) produce a coherent and persuasive text that creates meaning out of what was previously disorganized and incomprehensible. Freeman (2007) holds that the purpose of autobiographical memory is not to reproduce or resurrect experience but rather "to understand, to make sense of the past in the light of the present" (141), a task which he insists requires going beyond conventional language and forms, beyond culturally sanctioned genres and plotlines to convey experience in a way that brings out its uniqueness, its life, its relational and intersubjective qualities. Taking up this task fully calls for a more radical understanding of narrative truth, placing narrative and autobiographic inquiry at the intersection of art and science. And, as Hampl (1999) suggests, autobiography calls for a lyrical voice, for strange and unexpected detail, for the personal and the impersonal melded together, without which it would not be possible to convey "the immediacy of a human life moving through the changing world" (224), or understand the observation of poet Mary Oliver that "the black oaks along the path are standing as though they were the most fragile of flowers" (Oliver, 1986, 68).

Freeman argues for a "poetic science" that would support "not only the *epistemological* aim of increasing knowledge and understanding of the human realm but also the *ethical* aim of increasing sympathy and compassion" (2007, 142). With this, he brings us back to imagination, to the "story full of holes" with which this chapter began, to Bhatt's (2000) "broken narrative" and to Hirsch's notion of post-memory. If it is for epistemological and ethical reasons that we are attentive to the truth of narrative, it is for precisely the same reasons that we must draw on the resources of the imagination. As Morrison points out about her own work of conveying through fiction the experience of black Americans under slavery (e.g., Morrison, 1989), "These 'memories within' are the subsoil of my work. But memories and recollections won't give me total access to the unwritten interior life of these people. Only the act of the imagination can help me" (Morrison, 1995).

There is in recent theorizing a clear awareness of the blurred boundaries evoked by Steedman between truth and fiction, history and memory. Sturken (1997), distinguishing between personal memory, cultural memory and history, suggests that the relationship between them is (yet again) one of *entanglement*: "there is so much traffic across the borders of cultural memory and history that in many cases it may be futile to maintain a distinction between them" (5). Similarly, Rothberg suggests that memory cannot always be distinguished from either history or representation, yet "memory nonetheless captures simultaneously the individual, embodied, and lived side *and* the collective, social, and constructed side of our relations to the past" (Rothberg, 2009, 4).

In the context of traumatic historical memory, Hirsch suggests that "Postmemory's connection to the past is thus not actually mediated by recall but by imaginative investment, projection, and creation" (2008, 107). Likewise Stratton creates for readers a 'traumascape,' where his memories and stories create a link to the aftermath of the Holocaust (Stratton, 2005). Indeed, the stories I heard, that I now tell about my parents' experiences, are stories I have had to reconstruct and refashion, and I am well aware of the process of doing so.

postmemory…is a question of adopting the traumatic experiences—and thus also the memories—of others as experiences one might oneself have had, and of inscribing them into one's own life story. It is a question, more specifically, of an *ethical* relation to the oppressed or persecuted other for which postmemory can serve as a model: as I can "remember" my parents' memories, I can also "remember" the suffering of others. (Hirsch, 2001, 221).

Going further, Rothberg elaborates the important and productive notion of "multidirectional memory" according to which "Memories are not owned by groups—nor are groups 'owned' by memories. Rather, the borders of memory and identity are jagged; what looks at first like my own property often turns out to be a borrowing or adaptation from a history that initially might seem foreign or distant" (2009, 5). Rothberg's central concern in developing the idea of multidirectional memory is to open the possibility of a public sphere in which groups "actually come into being through their dialogical interactions with others." This is an important challenge to the prevailing understanding of memories as competing, a perception that is painfully in evidence in the Middle East where Israeli and Palestinian narratives of the same historical events seem irreconcilable, each side's suffering and grievances apparently denying or negating those of the other side (Gur-Ze'ev, 2001). I will return to this matter in Chapter 8; for now, I want to emphasize "memory's anachronistic quality—its bringing together of now and then, here and there," which Rothberg views as "the source of its powerful creativity, its ability to build new worlds out of the materials of older ones" (2009, 5).

I read theorists such as Freeman, Rothberg and Hirsch as opening a space in which it becomes possible to write about a past that I did not witness, to carry forward the voices of those who are no longer alive to tell their own stories, to do so even when I have no choice but to make some of it up, understanding that only in this way can we now remember those who suffered and in remembering forge solidarity across borders of time and space. This work is both personal and social, and it is essential for pedagogy, as can be seen in the work of Johnston (2011) and Attarian (2011) who both seek to remember and reexperience difficult family and personal histories. Greene (1995, 2000) speaks for the role in schools of imagination and the arts in fostering critical awareness, an enlarged view of the world and a sense of community and shared purpose. "Imagination summons up visions of a better state of things, an illumination of the deficiencies in existing situations, a connection to the education of feeling, and a part of intelligence" (Greene, 2000, 272).

In Chapter 2, I tell my family story, and in particular that of my mother, as a way of understanding my own life narrative and of making sense of the memories I carry. I focus on my mother because, like Diamant's character, the biblical Dinah, "I am not certain whether my earliest memories are truly mine, because when I bring them to mind, I feel my mothers' breath on every word" (Diamant, 1997, 89).

CHAPTER 2

"Firm on My Feet": My Mother's Story

The story begins with an ending, a leave-taking. It is 1905, in a small farming village, Kolonia Manshurova, not far from Odessa in Ukraine, then part of the Soviet Union. I picture the scene as dark and grainy, in black and white; the characters move slowly, as if reluctant to take the next step which will forever alter the family story. Sholem Ruvinshtein hugs his younger brother Efraim, who is about to leave for America. The decision was made quickly, as Efraim has been called to serve in the Soviet army, a terrible fate from which one must do anything to escape. Sholem is some years older and has given his papers to his brother so the authorities will be convinced the man leaving is past the age for military service. It is very early morning as good-byes are said.

According to Litvak (2006), the practices of forced conscription for a twenty-five year period were instituted by Czar Nicholas I in 1827, and called for conscription at the age of anywhere from 12 to 25; children, called "cantonists" would be sent to special training battalions, alongside children of soldiers, and would remain there until the age of 18 when they would transfer to the regular army to serve out whatever remained of their 25-year term. While adult Jewish soldiers were permitted to practice their religion publicly, child recruits were under strenuous pressure to convert. In the last years of Nicholas' reign quotas were increased and communities employed kidnappers to gather recruits; inevitably, wealthy Jews paid to gain exemption for their sons, and "the situation bred abuse to which the young, the poor and the marginal fell victim" (Litvak, 3). Nicholas died in 1855; his son Alexander I ascended to the throne, and the conscription decrees were abolished in 1856. But fear of military service lived on in memory and in the imagination through the reigns of three successive emperors, until the time of Nicholas II whose assassination in 1918 ended monarchic rule in Russia: Litvak records the prevalence in Russian Jewish literature of the theme of children snatched from their mothers' arms to serve in the army, long after the practice had been stopped, adding that "the literary construction of Eastern European Jewry has displaced the history of actual Jews who lived in a real place called Russia." (Litvak, 4) Indeed, Gray (1978) tells that her father injured himself to evade conscription to the Czar's army more than fifty years after the conscription decrees had been abolished.

In the once-real place called Kolonia Manshurova, Sholem almost pushes his brother out the door to the waiting cart. Efraim is leaving behind his young wife Toba and their infant son. Efraim had booked passage for Chicago, where his wife's relatives, the Manchefsky family, had settled a few years earlier; but on board ship he became friendly with another young man who wanted badly to go to Chicago but had been able to afford a ticket only as far as Montreal. When the ship reached port in Canada, Efraim exchanged tickets with his acquaintance and disembarked, perhaps happy to be independent and not have to answer to his wife's kin. In Montreal, Efraim found work quickly, menial labour for low wages, but he was lonely and glad to keep busy, saving as much as he could; within a few years he had a place to live and enough money to pay the passage for Toba and their son. Toba's goodbyes were said openly, to everyone gathered in the village pub run by her family. Pictures show that she was a delicate and pretty young woman; she was not running away but making the journey to join her husband, travelling on her own with a toddler in her arms.

At this point in my imaginary film, the scene lightens and turns to color as the couple is tearfully reunited on the docks of Montreal harbor; Efraim holds his son tightly in his arms and hires a carriage to take them to the tiny flat in the area, east of Mount Royal, where most of Montreal's Jewish community settled. They lived as did other immigrant families, a life of hard work on meager resources; yet four more children were born. Efraim was diligent and serious; his family always had food and a place to live, his children went to school, grew up Canadian, and prospered. In twenty years he would have the opportunity to repay his debt to his brother. Efraim, described by his family as someone who cared deeply for others, died of a heart attack in 1939. Never having met him, I take the liberty of storying him as the younger sibling, the beneficiary of his older brother's wisdom and guidance; his children and grandchildren (the cousins with whom I grew up in Montreal) might well tell his story differently. Indeed he must also have been a bold and adventurous man, the first in his family who dared to leave the terrible conditions to which his family and community were subject at the time. Efraim was one of many: in the period between 1881 and 1914, it is held that several million Jews left Russia, mainly for North America. But in the village scene, early in the morning of a day in 1905, Efraim Ruvinshtein is the singular hero embarking on a quest for a better life.

My mother, Bracha Ruvinshtein was born in 1907, not long after Efraim left for Canada. She was the fifth child of Sholem Ruvinshtein and his wife Frima Leah Wallach, followed by another sister and three younger brothers. She was around 7 or 8 years old when her mother took ill, was taken to a nearby town for medical treatment and died there. There was no explanation for her death; my mother remembered only that her father returned from the trip alone. Her maternal grandparents, the Wallachs, came to live with the family, to help care for the children. They were certainly poor, but my mother recalled a loving home. A wooden table stood in a corner, and on it were laid out bread and butter, a wooden-handled knife, and a large black radish; visitors were invited to help themselves.

My grandfather, Sholem, engaged in small scale farming and also worked as a sort of manager for a local landowner. Their village, Manshurova, was referred to by the name "Kolonia" because it was in fact a farming colony, one of numerous colonies set up on state lands between 1849 and 1852, and one of twelve in the Balta district alone in the southern part of the Podolia region bordering on the Black Sea (Chapin & Weinstock, 2000). Although these agricultural colonies were not fully cooperative villages, it seems that they later served as a model for the kibbutz movement in Israel. In 1858 there were 100 families in Kolonia Manshurova: 491 men and 382 women (presumably including children), living on 2181 "desyantines" or "desiatinas" of land; the desiatina is an obsolete Russian unit of measure equivalent to about 2 and a half acres, so the total area of the colony would have been around 5000 acres. The colonies ranged in size from 50 to 150 families, with similar parcels of land, making Manshurova about average in area and population. They grew potatoes, sunflowers (from which they made oil), beets and other vegetables, and kept cows and chickens. The religion of the colonists is not stated, but stories indicated that in Manshurova Jewish and Christian families lived side by side. There is no further information currently available in English about the village, its families and their means of livelihood, so I have had to draw on my imagination as well as on information provided by Chapin and Weinstock (2000) on the village of Letichev from which their families came.

Daily life was marked by uncertainty at best, terror at worst. The period after the revolution of 1905 was a time of political upheavals, and anti-Semitic pogroms swept the country (Smith, 2002; Klier, 1992). Of the three periods in which pogroms occurred in Ukraine, the worst period was from 1917–1921 during which, in Podolia alone, 213 pogroms were recorded, committed mostly by supporters of one of the various Ukrainian nationalist movements active in the region (Bickman, 1996). Because of the presence on the roads of the infamous Petliura gangs, Sholem was afraid to send his children to the school located in a nearby town. The villagers joined together and hired a local girl to teach the children in one of their homes. This worked for a while, but soon enough the teacher met a young man in the village and left her pupils to manage on their own while she chatted with her boyfriend. The teacher was fired, and formal education ended; somehow, my mother nevertheless learned to read and write Yiddish (which uses the Hebrew alphabet) as well as some Russian.

During pogroms, the family was given refuge at the home of a Christian neighbor, sometimes for several days at a time. My mother recalled that in order not to violate the Jewish dietary laws, they ate only boiled potatoes and eggs, cooked each time in a different pot. At one meal my mother saw that the food had been cooked in a pot that was also used for the baby's bath, and that day she refused to eat at all. But she remembered with great appreciation the family that sheltered them so many times. One of those occasions was during Easter, and the lady of the house had baked special loaves of bread for the holiday. Usually, on holidays the local priest made the rounds of all the houses in the village to bless the loaves of bread and wish his parishioners well. With her house cleaned and ready, her children on good behavior, this devout lady waited all day for the priest, but he did not come. In the late afternoon her husband told her gruffly, "He's not coming." He took her outside and showed her that the main door of the house had a large padlock on it. He had put a lock on the door to indicate that the family had gone away for the holiday, not wanting the priest to know that a Jewish family was hiding there.

On another occasion, however, my grandfather gathered all the children together and prepared to take them to hide in the forest. Perhaps word had got out that some of the villagers were hiding their Jewish neighbors, and it was no longer safe to stay in their homes. One of the older brothers, Eli, was ill with typhoid fever, and was too weak to leave the house; they left him in bed and ran to the wooded area on the outskirts of the village. Before they got to their intended hiding place, however, they turned around and came back. I still hear my mother telling this story: "My father stopped: we can't leave Eli that way, he said, and brought everyone back home." They found Eli wandering about the room delirious, his fever at a peak; he was put back to bed, and everyone gathered around their father to wait.

This story was told many times, but I never dared ask questions—what time of year was it? Was it raining, or was the weather fine? Did they rush to put on coats or sweaters, did they have boots, did their feet slip in the mud? How far did they go, how long was it before they got back home? And how long did they wait till there was a knock at the door?

When the knock came, Sholom opened the door and invited the group of thugs to come inside. He remained composed, despite the loud thudding of his heart; he offered the Petliura men food and drink, gave them whatever money he had, and then noticed one of the gang looking at his gold watch. He quietly removed the watch and offered it to the fellow, and soon afterwards the intruders left. The next day, they learned that villagers who had hidden in the forest had been found dead. And in the neighboring town it was told that in Kolonia Manshurova there had been only one man who had known how to speak to the Petliura men and show them respect.

Her father's example remained vivid for my mother; from him she learned how to keep fear at bay, and how to care for others unquestioningly. In 1923 my grandfather went to town to purchase wedding rings for the marriage of one of my mother's older sisters; on his return he was ambushed, robbed and killed. When my mother heard of her father's death she became mute and was unable to speak for several days. The perpetrator was caught when he attempted to sell the stolen rings, and it transpired that he was a Jew, and that he was crazy: that, it seemed, was the only way to explain the behavior of a Jew who killed another Jew in order to gain entry to the anti-Semitic Petliura gang. Even worse, the murderer was known to the family: he was a relative of the husband of one of my grandfather's sisters who had immigrated with her husband to the United States. After arriving in Canada my mother visited her aunt in the U.S.; she told me years later that the family there had pressed her for details about her father's death and she had been reluctant to speak about it, pleading that it was too difficult. In fact she was afraid of causing pain to her aunt and uncle if she told the story.

Distraught after the death of their father, my mother's older siblings feared they would be unable to provide for their younger sisters and brothers as well as their own young families. At this time the eldest brother, Yankel (Jacob), was already married to Chaika, and they had a son, Shunya. The oldest sister, Maika (Miriam), was also married and had two daughters, Nussia and Freema. They wrote to their father's siblings who had left some years before for the 'new world': Bessie was living in the United States while another sister had gone with her husband to Argentina, and by then Efraim, the youngest brother, had been in Canada for almost twenty years. It was said that Efraim's wife, Aunt Toba, "made the best offer," agreeing to take in three of her husband's nieces and nephews. Thus it was that my mother, her younger sister Esther who was 16 and her brother Itzik, aged 15, set off for Canada. Their oldest brother accompanied them by train to Riga, where they boarded a ship for England.

My mother did not mention many details, but according to online records they must have sailed to Liverpool, where they transferred to the *R.M.S. Alaunia*, a ship of the Cunard Line, for a voyage of almost two months landing in Quebec City on October 25th, 1925. The *Alaunia II* was a new ship that made its maiden voyage across the Atlantic in February of 1925. It weighed 14,000 tons, had one funnel and two masts, double reduction steam turbine engines, and a "service speed" of 15 knots. It was built to accommodate 500 cabin class passengers, and 1200 3rd class passengers. Over the years there were four *Alaunias* in the Cunard fleet: the first *Alaunia*, launched in 1913, had been sunk in 1916, while the *Alaunia II*, launched in 1925, ferried passengers—many of them immigrants—until 1939, when it was refitted as an armed merchant cruiser; after the war it continued to sail until 1957 between ports in the U.K., Africa and Asia. The *Alaunia III* and *IV* were cargo ships transporting fruit and other goods. It is not known who named this and other ships, but it appears that Cunard had been highly successful with an earlier poetically-named trio of ships—the *Andania, Antonia* and *Ausonia*—and later built three more, the *Aurania, Alaunia* and *Ascania*, the latter two designed especially for the Canadian trade. I wonder about the Cunard family, the shipping magnates who, figuratively at least, took my mother, my uncle and my aunt from the arms of their brother and ferried them across the ocean; I recall seeing the name Cunard in the news from time to time and note that this family is still in the business of cruising the seas, now mostly for pleasure.

The *Alaunia* itself, according to photographs, was a rather impressive ship, on which immigrants from many different countries travelled between England and Canada. There are records of some 500 immigrants arriving in Quebec city on the *Alaunia* in 1925, in three different voyages; given the capacity of the ship for close to 2000 passengers, this means that most of the passengers would have been Canadians returning from Europe, or British and European subjects travelling to North America on business or pleasure. Thus the portrait I had formed of huddled immigrant masses may not be accurate. The immigrants in that year came largely from Britain and Ireland, Scandinavia, Russia, Poland, and Romania.

Having spoken about the *Alaunia* itself and its business of moving people and cargo from place to place, having indulged in 'screen memories' to the fullest, I have to confront the picture that haunts me, hiding behind this wealth of information. It is a picture of three young people, children really—aged 15, 16 and 17—travelling on their own, while most of the other immigrants are in family groups, parents and children. They have dark hair and eyes and dark complexions; their eyes sparkle, but perhaps with fear and expectation more than pleasure. My mother and her brother are noticeably thin, while their sister Esther is a little plump; they are poorly clothed, and ill equipped for the Canadian weather. On arrival in Montreal their uncle took them to buy shoes almost immediately. When I picture them in my mind's eye it is hard to hold back tears.

The stories I heard about that period in my mother's life create a mixed tapestry. There was the excitement of the ocean voyage, the warm reception into their uncle's home on City Hall Avenue which, simple as it was, must have seemed luxurious to them, and the discovery of the big city where they soon found work in the clothing factories. My mother made many friends among her co-workers; photos show them having fun as young people do everywhere, swimming, picnicking, laughing. When my mother took lunch to work, her aunt always added extra cookies or cake for her to share with friends; many of my mother's friends and coworkers were young women who had immigrated to Canada on their own. My mother thought herself lucky to be living with family. But sometimes she and her sister would go to the park near their home, at the foot of Mount Royal, spread a blanket, remember their family in Russia, and cry.

Not being able to study was a great disappointment for my mother; schooling was expensive, and the cousins her age had already left school and were working to help support the family. Only one cousin, the scholar of the family, remained in school and became a doctor. But there was an education of sorts to be had in the encounter with people from many backgrounds: one of my mother's best friends was an Italian Catholic girl, Mary Gentile. There were arguments, too. My mother recalled a co-worker who came in one Monday morning scowling, and refused to talk to her; at lunchtime it transpired that she had learned from a sermon in church that the Jews had killed Jesus. Eventually, the two women found a way to remain friends. Working in the garment district, my mother and her friends were able to buy clothes inexpensively, and when I was a girl my mother regaled me with detailed descriptions of outfits bought for a dollar or two: the blue dress with the Chinese collar, the green dress with purple trim. My mother attended night school, until she was offered extra work at overtime pay, an opportunity that could not be refused; she learned to read English largely on her own and read widely, but being unable to write English well was her main source of embarrassment—or perhaps it was only an embarrassment to me that my mother could not write English?

One night when my mother was returning home after visiting friends, a man passed her on the sidewalk; she was bothered by the fact that he turned away and did not look at her: a man always looks when he passes a woman, to see if she's pretty or not, young or old, she told me. Immediately she was on guard, taking the handbag from her shoulder and holding it firmly in front of her, telling herself, "I have to be firm on my feet." Within moments she heard footsteps behind her and then felt a hand grabbing her leg; she spun round, brought her handbag with its metal clasp down squarely on the man's head and screamed with all her might. The man fled.

In 1943 my mother and her friends heard that a group of young Jewish men were arriving in the city: refugees from Europe who had fled to England before the war, were interned by the British as "enemy aliens" and eventually sent to Canada and Australia (to be far from the theater of war as they were considered dangerous). Given guarantees and offers of work by the local Jewish community, these refugees were gradually being released by Canadian authorities from the camp at Ile aux Noix in rural Québec where they had been detained; among them was my father. It was still wartime, but someone threw a party; my parents met and within a year they were married. My mother was 36, my father 41. In a photo taken on their honeymoon they appear very happy. Over the years their families got to know one another, and their stories intertwined in many ways. So it seems right that my father now appears, with his own story, as a major character in my mother's story.

My father was born in 1902 in a small town, Sloboda-Rangurska, in the Galicia region which, at the time, was part of the Austro-Hungarian Empire. His parents, Max and Fayga Luwisch, were first cousins; their fathers, Israel and Hersch Luwisch, were the sons (along with a third brother, Moshe) of Jacob Luwisch and his wife Chaya Hilsenrod. Max and Fayga lived in Vienna after their marriage but returned home to Fayga's mother for the birth of their first child. The family apparently had some status in the town of Sloboda-Rangurska: a wealthy aunt was the owner of an oil well in the region (still known for its oil fields), and my father eventually inherited a 16th part of this property although, by that time, the well was no longer productive. And his maternal grandfather, Hersch Luwisch, was co-mayor of the town, serving on alternate years together with a Christian mayor, with whom the relationship was less than congenial. In 1902, a year in which Hersch was not in office, he went to City Hall to register his grandson's birth, giving him the name Isidore, a common (and often mocked) name for Jewish boys at the time, resonating with his Hebrew name, Israel, the name of his paternal grandfather. However, the rival mayor intervened and inscribed a completely different name, Kasimir—the name of several Polish kings and a patron saint, a name never given to Jews. Once registered, the data could not be changed, and my father had to live with the name, which a school friend shortened to Kaly; this was later changed to Karl, and eventually, in Canada, to Charles.

My grandparents lived quietly in Vienna, where their second son, Emil, was born two years later (thus becoming the only member of the family to hold Austrian citizenship). I was told that later in life Max ran a tobacco shop and that earlier he had worked as a weaver in a workshop that produced prayer shawls. The story had it that he was instrumental in organizing a strike of all the Jewish weavers in Vienna for better working conditions; my father did not tell me exactly what the outcome of the strike had been, only that it had been reported on in the press. I confess that the entwining of a traditional Jewish occupation with a fight for social justice in my grandfather's story has always pleased me. But the family's life was marred by illness: Fayga suffered from diabetes, from which she died in 1909. In 2006, I visited Vienna and was able to find the graves of both my grandparents. About his mother, my father remembered only her illness: he recalled being chastised by family members for his bad behavior and made to feel that his actions were somehow responsible for his mother's suffering.

After his wife's death my grandfather moved with his two sons to Switzerland, where his sister Dora was living with her husband; they lived in Zurich for five years. My father felt at home there and remembered the school friend who gave him the nickname Kaly. After a few years they moved to Germany, to Reinfelden near the Swiss-German border. Eventually Max was remarried to Elsa Menaches, and three more children were born—Herman, Arthur and Lily. Their life together was not smooth; Max was drafted to serve in the army during the First World War leaving Elsa alone to care for the children, and in later years they lived apart. My father remembered his younger half-siblings fondly and saved some photographs of Lily as a child, taken in the country with her father. However, his stepmother was not warm to her stepsons, and was even suspected of having thrown away my father's Polish passport (something that had critical implications later on), but my father made a point of empathizing with her situation rather than blaming her.

My father attended school in Wiesbaden and later in Frankfurt, completed his compulsory schooling and started work as a clerk. He attended continuing education classes that were mandatory for young people of his age in Germany at the time; he dreamed of studying engineering but did not have the means of continuing his studies. In his spare time he joined a German-British Friendship Society and went with the group on a visit to England. In Reading they were hosted by local families, and my father stayed at the home of a young couple, Harry and Muriel Stevens, members of the local Quaker Society of Friends; a few years later Harry and Muriel visited Germany, and afterwards contact was maintained through letters.

On Hitler's rise to power in Germany, my father moved to Vienna as did his father and brother. He worked for a photographer and later as a salesman for a camera manufacturer; with the spread of Nazism his Jewish employers were increasingly unable to conduct business, and my father had less and less work. He and his brother Emil both applied to immigrate to the United States. Emil, as an Austrian citizen, received a visa fairly quickly and left Europe. My father held Polish citizenship, his family's petition to be recognized as citizens of the Austrian Empire having been rejected; but his Polish passport had been lost and his only official document was a "stateless passport," so his application for an American visa was delayed. On Kristallnacht in November of 1938 my father was arrested, together with his father; after a harrowing night they were released and ordered to leave Vienna.

Although he was still hoping to receive an American visa, my dad wrote his friends in Reading, with whom he hadn't corresponded for a while; "there had been nothing good to tell them, and in that situation I didn't want to write," he told me. He sent a brief note saying only that it had been a long time since they were in touch and he hoped they were well. Within a couple of days he received a reply: they were glad to hear from him, they too had been thinking of him. But Harry and Muriel went further than mere politeness required: perhaps he would like to visit them again in Reading? They would be happy to receive him, for as long a visit as he liked. If he needed money to make the journey, they would be glad to assist him. They did not have to spell out what they had obviously understood only too well: the lives of Jews in Europe were in mortal danger, and the Stevenses were prepared to do what they could to save his life. My father wrote back immediately: he did not need to take up their offer of money, as the Jewish community in Vienna was paying the passage of any Viennese Jews who had a destination to which they could escape. He did, however, need a visa to come to the UK; could they help with that? They could indeed, and within a short time my father had a 'trainee visa' which allowed him to enter the UK to work as an apprentice carpenter. My father was then 35 years old and since completing his schooling had worked as a clerk and later as a camera salesman, so it is apparent that Harry and Muriel had to tell some tall tales in order to secure this visa. The ethical awareness that this story highlights is particularly impressive against the background of the time: it was to be several fateful years be-fore the plight of the Jews in Europe was fully recognized.

My father went to England early in 1939 and stayed for a while in Read-ing, where he had little to do beyond giving a weekly German lesson to an elderly lady in the Friends' community in exchange for tea and pocket money. Shortly he made contact with relatives in London and moved there, working for a cousin in the maintenance of rental apartments. In 1940 he was arrested together with thousands of other "enemy aliens" (mostly German and Austrian citizens living in Britain, the majority of them Jewish) and sent, first to the Isle of Man and then to Canada (see Lederman, 2012, and Draper, 1985 for accounts of the story of some two thousand 'accidental immigrants' to Canada). After spending time in a series of internment camps, eventually he was released and met my mother as described above. They were married on June 20, 1944; there are no photos of their wedding, but I still have, tucked away in a drawer, the red lace bolero that my mother wore over a cream-colored dress. I was born just under a year later.

When I was two months old, my mother spent a few weeks at a small ho-tel in the country north of Montreal. My father came out on weekends, but during the week she was alone with me. One day she received mail from her family in Russia. Letters and photographs had been sent back and forth over the years, but during the war years contact was limited. In July of 1945, I imagine my mother's hands shaking as she opens the envelope. The war in Europe has been over for two months, and this is the first letter from her fam-ily since the end of hostilities. The letter is in Russian, and it says something about her sisters who lived with their families in Odessa. She struggles to read it, then rushes to the crib where I'm sleeping and lifts me up. "Your aunts are alive, your aunts are alive!" she repeats.

Later that day, my mother found another guest at the hotel whose Russian was more proficient than hers, and the letter was read to her word for word. It told her that her sisters, and their children, had been murdered by the Nazis when they invaded Odessa in October of 1941. Years later, we were told by family members still living in Odessa that Maika and Elka had remained in the city, refusing to be evacuated because their husbands were at the front, fighting with the Soviet army, and the two women feared that they would not get word from them if they left the city.

It is only recently that I sought out historical sources and tried to place what I was told within the historical record. Still, I do not know much. I do not know if they were sent immediately after being registered by the occupying army to the gallows or burial trenches that had been prepared within the city itself, or if they were taken out of the city to the Slobodka ghetto, to be shot at the edge of mass graves. Maika, I imagine, would have been with her two daughters, Nussia and Freema, then probably in their late teens or early twenties. Elka (whose wedding ring had been the ostensible reason for her father's murder in 1923) would have had younger children. Perhaps some of them survived the terrible conditions of the ghetto for a time until they died. Perhaps they were among those who were taken further away, towards one of the numerous small camps along the Bug River or those left to die of exposure and starvation in the countryside (Ehrenburg & Grossman, 1980).

Each time I return to the texts to read about these events, I discover new information; several times I've realized that I misread or misunderstood what I read previously. Repeatedly, I get the dates wrong. I am surprised to learn, and then forget, and then discover again that the occupiers of Odessa were not German but Rumanian troops who had joined forces with the Nazis. I am sure that everyone was killed soon after the invasion, then reread and learn that some people survived the appalling conditions until as late as 1944 and indeed, a few lived to tell the stories. The account of what happened in Odessa during the war takes up a mere fifteen pages in *The Black Book* (Ehrenburg & Grossman, 1980), yet it seems impossible to take it in, to get the information straight. As Audergon (2005) suggests, the experiences of wartime take on an unreal, almost hallucinatory quality, even for someone who experiences them at second or third hand.

When I was about two years old, my mother showed me a photograph of her sisters and told me they were "not here anymore." I asked to hold the picture, and to take it with me when I went for my afternoon nap. She told me the picture was important to her, and I promised to be very careful with it. When I awoke and my mother came to get me, she found the photograph under the blanket, torn into many small pieces. This story too was repeated during the years I was growing up, with only a faint edge in my mother's voice: I was little more than a baby, and she should have known better. "So we have to ask about historical losses, the ones that are transmitted to us without our knowing, at a level where we cannot hope to piece it together, where we are, at a psychic level, left in pieces, pieces that might be linked together in some way, but will not fully 'bind' the affect" (Butler, 2004, 97).

I have tried to find the places in my body where I must have locked away those fragments of experience: being grabbed from sleep, my mother in a state of excitement I had probably not experienced before; hearing a message repeated over and over, unable to fathom the notion of "good news," and later, being put to bed with hands that held the letter announcing death. Two years later I was old enough to understand something about an important photograph but not old enough to retain the memory of how that photograph came to be destroyed, deliberately and unwittingly by small hands. I do not know how a body takes in such events, much less those other events, horrific events I did not experience myself, and which even my mother did not experience directly, events conveyed to me in a gentle voice without reproach. Butler (2004, 99) suggests that "it is a registering and a transmutation that takes place in a largely, though not fully, preverbal sphere, an autistic relay of loss and desire received from elsewhere, and only and always ambiguously made one's own." These events form part of my 'narrative unconscious' (Freeman, 2002), allowing me to 'remember' something that is both less, and much more, than what I actually experienced.

In the experienced childhood that I do remember, there were many happy moments with my mother—going by bus to visit friends of hers, or shopping; eating lunch together at the kitchen table; helping her with baking—my job was to cut out the cookies with fancy-shaped cookie cutters. The body is present in these memories, indeed two bodies comfortable with one another. I know she held and hugged me when I was small (there are photographs), but later, I think, these gestures became ritualized: perfunctory hugs bestowed when I left the house for school, good night kisses on the way to bed. My lived experience is of being loved, cared for, and kept at a slight distance—as if she needed to be able to see me, to confirm that I was indeed alive and that my fate would be different. If I learned something from these stories about how experience is shaped by a social order, I could only have learned that it is not a loving social order, nor one that can be fathomed.

One of my earliest memories is of a dream: There is a war on, and we have to escape. Luckily our landlord, Mr. Masi, has a car (sometimes, we join the Masis on outings). I go outside to where the new black automobile stands at the curb; I wait and wait, but no one arrives, not my parents, not Mr. Masi or his wife. The dream ends as it began, with me waiting alone in the empty and deserted street. I assume the dream dates to the time of the Korean War, sometime between 1950 and 1953. I read about this war on the website of the Canadian veterans of the Korean War:

> On Sunday, the 25th of June, 1950, 135,000 troops of the North Korean People's Army slogged south through pre-dawn darkness and the wetness of oncoming monsoon rains. The main invasion thrust was through the Ch'orwon Valley, across the 38th parallel to the Ouijongbu corridor, the direct route to Seoul, capital of the Republic of Korea (South Korea).
>
> Korea, the Land of the Morning Calm, was now the crucible which turned the Cold War hot.
>
> By the time the civil war of the Koreas had halted, six million of their countrymen—civilian and military personnel—had perished. Nearly half a million Communist Chinese comrades-in-arms of the North Koreans, soldiers of the People's Liberation Army, were killed in action. To add to the bloodbath: The Americans who supplied the largest contingent by far for the United Nations Command suffered 103,284 wounded, 54,236 deaths including 33,629 killed in combat and 8,177 missing in action. Canada's casualties totaled 1,558 including 516 who died. The total number of UN Forces (including South Korea) killed, wounded or missing was 996,937. (http://www.kvacanada.com/canadians_in_the_korean_war.htm)

I am struck by the language and imagery of this account. The setting for the narrative is pastoral—the Land of the Morning Calm, the pre-dawn darkness and wetness of oncoming monsoon rains; but the war itself is described as a bloodbath, a crucible. The army 'slogged' southwards to death, killing and wounding. And the numbers, the numbers, so many killed, so many wounded, so many missing, and the final figure, *six million*—can it be possible? I try to imagine the effect this war would have had on my family, coming so soon after the Second World War which probably, in their imaginations, had not yet ended. In the early 1950s television broadcasting was just beginning in Canada, and my family did not yet have a television set, so I would have seen images of the Korean War only in the newspaper, but I must have heard news broadcasts on the radio. From my parents' stories war meant only one thing: the imperative to flee; but actually getting away was something I could not imagine even in a dream.

Once when my mother and I were shopping downtown, she met an acquaintance I didn't know, a tall angular woman who greeted my mother with a smile, said a few words to me and then asked about various family members and in particular about my mother's brother, Irving. Afterwards my mother told me the woman, whose name was Lea, was a Communist, had never married, and was, she implied, a little strange. Recently I learned that Lea Roback was a well-known Canadian feminist and social activist who had devoted her life to the struggle for social justice.[1] My uncle, who worked all his life in the garment industry, had been involved in the famous International Ladies Garment Workers Union strike of 1936, of which Lea Roback was one of the local organizers, and no doubt they knew each other from that time. Strangely, it never occurred to me to ask my mother if she too went on strike in 1936. I have no doubt that her heart would have been with the workers and that she supported her brother. But the photographs taken in the coat factory where she worked in the 1930s—the cheerful smiles of my mother, her sister and co-workers; the benevolent and paternal expressions on the faces of the factory owners; and indeed the fact that the bosses thought to gather their workers for a group photograph to memorialize their shared participation in the business of clothing the nation—all these only confirm what I already know about my mother: coming from the poverty of her early years in Russia, she felt lucky to have work, took pride in doing it well and was happy to be taken care of by her bosses. I can't imagine her going on strike. Communism for her at that time was less an ideology than a force, an almost superhuman power cruelly wielded by Joseph Stalin, which was keeping her apart from her family in Russia. She could hardly have thought of a woman like Lea Roback, who had rejected the comforts of family, had affairs but never married (although she did care for her immediate family members) and travelled on her own to Germany and the Soviet Union, as anything other than 'strange.'

Another early memory: I'm in the kitchen with my mother helping to make poppy-seed cookies. My mother makes the dough, rolls it out thinly on the kitchen table, and then I cut out the round shapes using a glass of just the right size (sugar cookies were given fancy shapes, but poppy-seed cookies were always just round). The news comes on the radio, and we hear the announcement that Stalin has died. It was March 5, 1953, and on hearing the news my mother tensed up; I don't recall her words, but she made it clear that one could only be glad of the death of this evil man. Perhaps now I'll be able to get in touch with my brothers, she said quietly, as if not quite daring to hope. In fact it took about ten years: the Cold War thawed a bit, Canada began trading in wheat with the Soviet Union, and my mother gathered up all the old letters and submitted the addresses to the Red Cross. Late one autumn afternoon in 1963 or 1964, I returned from university and found my mother in a state of high excitement: she had received a letter! It came from her brothers in Odessa and, once again, like the letter that had arrived not long after I was born, she managed to read some of it but was uncertain about the exact message until she went, later that evening with my father to have it read for her by a Russian-speaking friend.

This letter too contained a piece of sad news; one of her older brothers, Eli, the same brother whose bout with typhoid fever had probably saved their lives, had died a few years before (during Stalin's regime and, it was suspected, not of natural causes). But there were three brothers alive and well, all living in Odessa, married and with families, all of them sending us warm wishes and embracing us and sounding, despite the awkward rendition from Russian to English, absolutely overjoyed to renew contact. At that time, no member of my family had travelled outside of North America (or, in fact, much further than the triangle formed by Montreal, New York and Toronto), yet within the year my uncle flew to Odessa to visit his brothers. I remember the rush of buying gifts for him to take to the family, accompanying him to the airport, and waiting the three long weeks for his return. I remember the fear, which no one dared speak aloud, that the Soviet regime might regard him as a traitor to his birthplace, and not allow him to leave. On his return trip he had a layover in Zurich and phoned from his hotel to tell us he was on his way home. The relief was palpable. For weeks afterward we sat and listened to his stories every evening, pored over the photographs, and asked endless questions; I began to feel that I knew my uncles and aunts, and my new cousins, intimately.

When Irving arrived in Odessa—there was no phone link at the time, so I suppose he had sent a telegram informing the family of his arrival—he had been overwhelmed to find a huge crowd waiting for him at the airport, all bearing flowers—his three brothers, their wives and children, and various cousins and relatives by marriage. He had been obliged to pay in advance for a hotel room, all meals and the services of a guide and interpreter; needless to say, the family would not hear of his eating anywhere but in their homes. The hotel agreed to put his meal vouchers towards a festive dinner for the entire family near the end of his visit. He returned home with a suitcase emptied of its original contents, all of which he had left with various members of the family, and now filled with a different set of gifts: amber jewelry, a lacquered wooden box, silver spoons, and Soviet-style samovars of different sizes. All these gifts, we knew, had been purchased with weeks of work and after hours standing in line at government-controlled stores. I still have the lacquered box, and a balalaika, which I had requested, and on which a Yugoslav house-painter once taught me to play a single song.

This trip was followed by another about a year later, when my mother's sister Esther went to Odessa with her husband. While strolling in a city park, she saw and was recognized by a man from their village, Kolonia Manshurova, who had saved her from drowning in a local river when she was a child. My mother didn't make the trip, fearing that the emotional strain would be too great. However, in the fall of 1973 her brother Benchyk and his wife Frayda came to Canada for a month-long visit, an exciting and confusing time during which my mother spoke Russian to me, English to her brother and his wife, and Yiddish to my husband. I recall having a long conversation in Yiddish (which I understand a little but do not normally speak) with my Aunt Frayda. It was Saturday afternoon and everyone had gone to rest after a big dinner; although Frayda's Yiddish was liberally sprinkled with Russian and mine was more than half English, we were determined to communicate. She asked about my job, and I told her about my work in curriculum, hardly expecting to be understood. But I knew that we were communicating when she questioned how there could be ongoing work writing school texts: history, for example, was known, she pointed out, and the textbooks had been written already; why would the authorities pay someone to write another book? I managed to tell her something about the existence of different perspectives on what happened, as well as different ways of presenting it to children. As my aunt and uncle were then discovering how their country was portrayed on Canadian television and seeing that the decadent West looked rather different than they had been taught, it was a fertile context for a discussion of curriculum theory. Still, I am at a complete loss to explain how we could have accomplished this in Yiddish.

A few years later one of my cousins immigrated to Israel and my parents visited with him and his family there. My cousins Lola (who passed away recently in Israel) and Maya (who still lives in Odessa) and I each gave birth to a daughter in 1975; my daughter, like several of the cousins, is named after my mother's older sister Maika. In the years that followed I moved to Israel as did most of my Russian cousins. We are in contact, gathering for family occasions. I have conversations on Skype with Maya in Odessa, through the interpretation of her grandson who is learning English; when he's not there, Maya and I wave and smile and gesture in a kind of personal sign language. The family story is still marked by disruptions of various kinds, but also by a strong feeling of connection.

Writing the story

I notice that in telling the story of my mother's life my own voice frequently tried to interrupt. But academic discipline called on me to stay focused, to tell the story sparingly, avoid self-indulgence, seek theoretical usefulness (Bleakely, 2000). I should get on with it in the same rhythm that my mother used for housework, washing the breakfast dishes and making the beds promptly before going on to other tasks. When I sit too long over my morning coffee contemplating the day, there is always a background sense that it's wrong to waste time that way. But how can one stay focused when all the events, memories and images cry out for attention simultaneously? I recall the story of the encounter with the Petliura gang, told with pathos and now pictured in my mind in somber tones. Next an image comes forth of the immaculate white Canadian kitchen where I first heard the story told, with an odd mixture of feeling and detachment, over coffee and cake. Finally, I recall a painting in vivid color by the Russian Jewish painter, Ladizhinsky, which I saw a few years ago at the Diaspora Museum in Tel Aviv, depicting a ransacked house, in the aftermath of a pogrom by the Petliura gang. I came across the painting unexpectedly, and it held me transfixed for a long moment: the crazy array of broken and upturned furniture, boldly painted in the artist's naïve style, the harsh color of the scene, all seemed to confirm for me that the pogroms indeed took place, more convincingly than any of the historical accounts I had been reading.

"We are important and our lives are important, magnificent really, and their details are worthy to be recorded," says Natalie Goldberg (1986, p. 43), a Buddhist writer and teacher of writing. But I already learned this from my mother, from the way she attended to details: polished chrome and starched white cotton dresses. Perfect dough rolled out on the kitchen table. Smells of baking that rush to greet me at the open door. The body that holds itself just a bit stiffly, and yet creates for those around her a sense of warmth, order and safety, grounded in the earth, the picnic in the forest, the ship that sails to a destination where haven is promised. Safety in order, something I continue to search for. It was there in the cup of tea served on Saturday afternoons in her kitchen: everything carefully placed, the cake cut just so.

There should be a difference between memories of events I experienced, and memories of earlier events that originated in my mother's stories; but the pictures seem equally true to life. In fact, sometimes the pictures built up from my mother's stories are even more vivid, benefiting as they do from the active intervention of my imagination to fill in the colors, sounds and textures. I notice how my story sought a place for itself within my mother's story—with a childish impulse to curl up in mother's lap—even before I become a part of her story as a matter of chronological fact. Often I had to remind myself that I was not telling my story (or was I?), and that I was telling hers in order to learn about the place of body in narrative and in pedagogy. I also notice that the story is one of rupture, of repeated and ongoing separations from family, and of a necessarily incomplete yet also repeated coming back together. There are aspects of my mother's life that haven't found a place in this account: her many friends, her involvement with a religious Zionist women's organization, her love of reading, her delight in her granddaughter. Nor have I said all that might be said about my relationship with my mother, which was not always easy. My mother taught me a great deal about how to be a caring and generous human being, providing a model that often seems impossible to live up to; in other areas, particularly in learning to identify and express feelings such as anger and fear, wants and desires, I had to figure things out for myself as my mother, like many of her generation and time, spoke through actions and gestures rather than words.

Poststructural theory questions the constructed nature of identities, the role of language in creating representations of experience, and the possibility of attaining any sort of completeness in recounting events or lives. There is no methodology that can be called upon with assurance here because writing about one's mother is writing "from the darkest spaces of memory" (Cho, 2005, 50). And even qualitative description, if it involves attaching labels to experience, risks emptying personal experience of its unique meaning for the individual as well as trivializing the experience of a social group.

However, while growing up I would have been grateful to have a convenient label to describe my mother's experience, as existing designations did not apply to either of my parents. Both left Europe before the Second World War (my father just in time), so despite the losses in their families, the term 'survivor' did not apply to them, and likewise the term "second generation" as usually under- stood doesn't apply to me. When my mother went to Canada in 1925, despite the fact that she was escaping horrific pogroms, she and her siblings had the status of immigrants and not refugees. Ordered to leave Austria in 1938, my father travelled to England on a "stateless" passport with a trainee visa; the British interned him as an "enemy alien" and shortly there- after sent him as part of a large group of Jewish internees to Canada under the ignominious designation of "prisoners of war," an absurd but clever move designed to persuade Canadian authorities that accepting this group would be a contribution to the war effort—removing dangerous persons and potential spies from the theatre of war! Eventually my father and the other members of this group were officially reclassified as "refugees from Nazi oppression," but upon release from the internment camp my father left be- hind the string of labels to become an 'ordinary' immigrant. By the time I was old enough to be aware of these matters, both my parents had received Canadian citizenship which seemingly "erased" the traces of their history and the circumstances under which they had come to Canada. And yet it is im- possible for me to understand my mother, my family, or myself without ref- erence to the Holocaust.

Seidler (2000) writes about his experience growing up in England as a child of refugees, and many aspects of his story resonate with mine. Seidler's parents, like mine, had lost many family members in the Holocaust and had left behind cultural worlds full of meaning; yet they raised their children to be "like everyone else," to be English. The importance of fitting in, of being like everyone else, led in my family to an anxious concern with politeness and acceptable behavior: I recall the discomfort I saw on my mother's face when I was asked, at a family gathering, which of two desserts I would prefer, and I gave the only 'wrong' answer: "I want both!"

Seidler felt he owed it to his mother to be happy and to sustain the myth of a happy childhood; he points out that "it was difficult to name what had been passed on to us, for it was often difficult to separate emotionally from parents who we wanted to protect because 'they had suffered enough'" (2000, 152). I too felt that my happiness was an obligation owed to my parents, and I still remember a happy childhood that faded away with the onset of adolescence. However, it never occurred to me to think of my parents as refugees, a designation that no doubt would have offended them. Refugees, in my childhood, were different from us: they were the newcomers who had arrived in Canada after the war with heavy accents and strange clothes; some of them had numbers on their arms. The arrival in Canada of survivors and refugees from Europe in the post-war years no doubt motivated my mother to teach me *never* to ask people personal questions, implying that one could never know what wounds one might be reopening; for many years this teaching retained for me something like the force of a moral prohibition.

Looking back, my mother's story as it came to be written here seems both fragmented and coherent, hanging on a few key episodes yet implying a linear progression. I'm surprised to notice that the story has no real ending: in fact my mother died in 1978, after battling cancer for a year, and my father died in 1984 after joining my family in Israel. But I did not want to end my mother's story there. It seems that my voice takes over her story at the point in my mother's life when I reached the age at which I began to have opinions of my own. This may be a clue to the inherent coherence of the story, and the reason, perhaps, that it does not end with her death: for my mother, making sense of the loss and trauma that marked her early life could only come through a generative focus. She cared for her family as well as for her friends, but she needed my arrival in her story to mark the fact that the story would indeed continue to another generation. This implicit narrative coherence explains how my mother could be a source of support and encouragement to those around her and also raise her daughter in hope.

Writing even a partial and incomplete version of my mother's story still seems an impossible task, even when I look at the pages already written. Cosslett (2000) discusses the move by feminist scholars to construct a 'matri-lineage,' drawing on the imagination to reconstruct stories of mothers and in particular of their subjectivity; she finds that there is something essentially 'unknowable' particularly about narratives of mothers who are unable to tell their own stories. Still, this writing responds to "the ancient imperative to care for the self" (Gannon, 2006, 480; Margalit 2002, 37) by eliciting the connections of past, present and future, and listening to the multiple voices that echo through the story. As Ellis and Bochner argue, "the narrative text refuses the impulse to abstract and explain, stressing the journey over the destination, and thus eclipses the scientific illusion of control and mastery" (2000, 744–745). The present chapter constitutes a journey back in time to retrieve my mother's story and bring it forward into the present (Strong-Wilson, 2008). Telling the story has enabled me to recover memories and gain new understandings about my mother as well as about myself and the sense of purpose in my work. However, there are limits on what we can come to know through narrative research: researchers, like participants, con-tinue their lives, and in the process stories are changed and reinterpreted. New meanings emerge as the journey continues. To my surprise, this is no less true for the story of my mother which, in calendar time, came to an end over thirty years ago. And as Cosslett concludes, "to have an intersubjective bond with someone unknowable and full of new possibilities is an exciting idea" (2000, 151).

Within a postmodern view of writing, Gannon insists that "the authority for the story begins with the body and memories of the autoethnographic writer at the scene of lived experience" (2006, 475). In the next chapter, I continue the journey in a different way, by exploring my own and others' stories of mothers, bodies and teaching in relation to the literature on moth-erhood, embodiment and pedagogy.

Note

1. http://www.fondationlearoback.org/home.htm

1. The Wallach grandparents, seated; behind them, my mother's older sister Maika (Miriam), her older brother Yankel, and her Aunt Devorah.

2. Aunt Toba, with her son Joseph, on arrival in Canada in 1907–8.

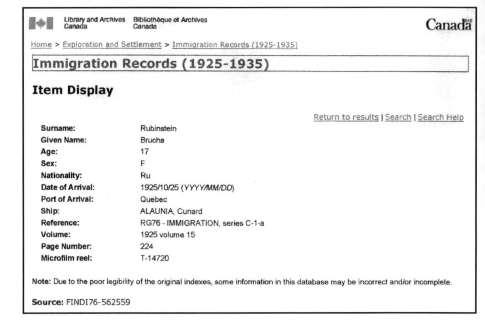

3.   Canada immigration record of my mother's arrival in Montreal on
     October 25th, 1925.

4. Nussia and Freema, my mother's nieces, the daughters of her sister Maika; the photograph was sent from Russia to my mother in Canada.

5. My mother in Montreal, with a group of friends, seated in front,
    on the right, around 1930; one of many photos taken in the same
    spot on top of Mount Royal.

6. My parents outside the home of Aunt Toba in Montreal, not long
    after their marriage.

7.   My mother and I (around age 2).

8. My mother and I (age around 10), taken on vacation, probably in Burlington, Vermont.

CHAPTER 3

Mothering, Embodying, Teaching

The purpose of this chapter is to make sense of the complex relations that obtain among the three terms that make up its title—mothering and teaching as two practices central to society, and embodiment as a crucial feature of both. These three terms figure centrally in my own life story as they must in the stories of other women in education. Holding together the multiple concerns reflected by the three terms is a difficult task. As Pillay (2008, 1) reminds us, there is a clear distinction between "being mother, traditionally associated with nurturing, love and emotion, and being academic, traditionally associated with reason and logic." There is a parallel disconnect between our everyday experience and understanding of our bodies and the ways that the academic world has at its disposal to take account of embodiment. And similarly, the theoretical understandings of teaching as a practice and a profession, and of pedagogy as a subject of inquiry, are not so commonly linked up to either mothering or embodiment. And yet understanding and telling forward my own story require an examination of these terms in concert.

Trusting that a story which demands to be told has shaped who I am and still has much to teach me about being an educator and scholar, I decided to begin the inquiry of this book with my mother's story. Chapter 2 stands as a first effort to write about my mother, to quiet the voices urging me for many years to write about her. The need to write about my mother is connected to memory, of course, and to the desire to remember someone who died too soon. But it goes beyond that: it is tied to the ongoing need to feel the juices of creativity flowing in my work, to reconnect to the "prima materia" of my life, to my origins and history, and also to feeling and imagination, to the life of the body, to the basic impulses that move me —in short, to everything that makes up an awakened life.

The diverse connections between mothering and embodiment, between the body and lived experience, and between all of these and teaching, have been the subject of theoretical inquiry, of course, but to do the work of uncovering the connections that exist among these terms and forging new ones, I begin with lived experience and with memory. I am aware that what I live, remember and understand in the moment is already shaped by my reading of theory, and even before that by participation in a given society and the discourses it makes available. In exploring these complicated connections, I seek to learn more about the possibility of retrieving and telling a life through auto/biographical narrative. And since the impetus for the exploration is located in my work as an academic, a student of teaching and a teacher educator, the present inquiry raises and questions the pedagogical implications of these explorations, in particular for an understanding of what it means to be present as a teacher.

The discussion in this chapter is structured in a seemingly linear progression, looking in turn at mothering, then at embodying, and finally at teaching, along the way bringing the terms into relationship and introducing other related terms. However, my approach will be to weave together stories and theory, to bring the lived experience of mothers and teachers into connection with the words of theorists many of whom are also, of course, mothers (or fathers) and teachers. To really hear the many voices of mothers, to feel their breath as Diamant (1997, 89) puts it, calls for breaking through existing conceptualizations behind which real flesh and blood mothers as subjects seem to be hiding. Drawing on what Franke (1995) calls "lateral citation," theoretical ideas are offered to resonate with story rather than to analyze or explain events, threading theory through the account not to call into question the authority of the personal but to dialogue with it (see Gannon, 2006).

Mothering

A Jewish saying holds that "God could not be everywhere, and therefore he made mothers" (quoted by Erlich, 2009, p. 44). In Islamic law, a famous hadith enjoins the listener to "stay with your mother, for Paradise is at her feet." Common to both these expressions is the sense that mother is not just a person: mother is actually a *place*; mothers, unlike God, are able to be everywhere, and wherever they are, there is Paradise. These traditional sayings put forward an expansive view of the identity of mothers as persons who can transcend the usual limitations of space, can make room for and contain their own children and perhaps all children.

Historically, however, the conception of motherhood has more often been a restrictive one: the image of a good mother is of "a person without identity except for her motherhood" (Hager, 2011, 36). Telling about her personal experience of motherhood in contemporary Tel Aviv, Hager recalls that "it was expected that I, a person with pains, feelings, desires, and aspirations, would set myself aside for an unlimited period of time, diminishing myself, disappearing, becoming obliterated" (2011, 36). Noting that conceptions of mothering have been, and continue to be influenced by historical, social and cultural circumstance (see Badinter, 1981; Ribbens, 1998; Rich, 1997; Ruddick, 1995), Hager mentions the widespread practice during the 17th and 18th centuries in Western Europe of sending infants to be raised in the countryside, where conditions were thought to be more favorable for their health and development. Our current conception of the 'good mother' as someone who could not bear for her infant to be raised by another woman is traced by Hager to the Industrial Revolution at the end of the 18th century, when the family ceased to function as a center of production, and the definition of the mother's role changed: mothers were now expected to create a warm and supportive home for husbands returning from their labors and for children.

While the image of the good mother seems to evolve over time in response to changing social conditions, the 'story of mothering', as it is named by Andrews (2002), remains one of the dominant stories of patriarchal culture and provides a 'language' that has profoundly influenced pedagogy (Estola, 2003; Grumet, 1988). Even today, a view of motherhood as involving suffering, sacrifice and devotion to the care and welfare of one's children is still prevalent. In Israel, as Hager's (2011) personal story suggests, in both Jewish and Arab cultures mothers are appreciated and even revered; they are storied as loving, caring individuals who readily put aside their own needs for the benefit of their children.

This view of mothers is also evident in our everyday understandings, as indicated by the writing of prospective teachers in my classes. For many years, as part of a course on multiculturalism (see Li et al., 2009) I introduced an assignment asking students to write the life story of a person who had influenced them. While students chose many different people—relatives, friends, siblings, cultural figures, sometimes even teachers—as the subject of this writing, quite often they wrote about their mothers. Mothers were chosen by students from all backgrounds, but particularly by women students from the Arab/Palestinian sector and by male Jewish students whose mothers were divorced or widowed and had raised them alone. Female Jewish students who chose family members more often wrote about their grandmothers.

In reading these life stories of mothers, I find the approach of Ruddick (1980, 1989) helpful, as she seeks to understand motherhood and mothering in terms of the concrete work mothers actually do. For Ruddick mothering is a social practice that gives rise to a particular way of thinking, which can be described in terms of three central features: 1) preservative love, which orients mothers to act in ways that protect and safeguard the life and health of the child; 2) fostering the child's growth and development; and 3) social training, or raising the child to behave and to be acceptable within the given social milieu. This view grounded Ruddick's contribution to a feminist peace politics based on the common interests of all mothers in preventing war (Ruddick, 1989). Ruddick's approach has been criticized for seeming to universalize mothers, ignoring the effects of race and class privilege on mothering, as well as making an unstated assumption that all children are alike, ignoring children with illnesses, handicaps or learning disabilities (Bailey, 1994). With these limitations in mind, a practice-based approach to mothering is useful in reminding us to look closely at what mothers (and by extension teachers) actually do, and what forms of thinking, feeling and understanding result from their work. Some brief examples from the writing of students will illustrate.[1]

Stories of three mothers: Munira. Reem wrote about her mother, Munira, who was her parents' first child. Reem notes that her grandfather had hoped for a son, but when he saw the glow on the infant's face he was glad, naming her Munira which means light. A good child who helped take care of her three younger brothers, she was pretty and curly-haired like her mother, clever and hard-working like her father. When she was only 9, Munira's father, a heavy smoker, died of cancer. It was a "black day" for the family; although relatives and friends helped at first, Munira's mother, a widow of 30 with four young children to support, had to manage on her own. She moved the family from their village to the city, where it was easier to find work; at 16 Munira left school and worked at two jobs to help support the family. She had been a good student but, her daughter notes, there was no one to pay attention and worry about her future: Reem implies that traditionally, this should have been the responsibility of the girl's father. When she was 21 Munira married and a year later Reem and her twin brother were born. Munira stayed home with her children at first but later went to work as a secretary. Reem remembers her parents' pride when the twins graduated from high school, something neither parent had been able to accomplish. Munira is described as someone who always encourages her children (all now studying in higher education). Reem says "I am the product of my mother, when we sit and talk—and we love to talk together —we have the same thoughts; I seem to be one of the few people my age who can really communicate with her mother. Life without her would be life without light; she is more than a mother, more than a sister, more than a friend." In Ruddick's terms we see that Munira was focused on preservative love, working to help support her children and provide them with the advantages she did not have in her own childhood; in terms of fostering growth and development, she was concerned about their education and took pride in their accomplishments. And her daughter's comment that she can really communicate with her mother suggests that Reem has been raised as an 'acceptable' member of society.

Sylvie. A very different story was told by Mark, whose mother Sylvie was a Holocaust survivor living in Europe, and Mark interviewed her via email. Sylvie, the youngest child of a well-off Jewish family, remembers the day that her own mother cried and hugged her repeatedly, packed a small bag for her and kissed her goodbye. After several lonely and difficult moves from place to place, she lived out the war years with a small and loving family, attending kindergarten in the local Church; she was warned not to tell anyone she was Jewish and to participate in prayers like the other children. The family took pains to tell Sylvie that her prayers could be directed towards the synagogue; this devout family never tried to make their 'foster daughter' adopt their religion. As the war continued they often had to sleep on the floor during bombings, and sometimes Sylvie was sent into the forest with food parcels for members of the Underground. Finally after three years, the war ended. One day a stranger arrived—Sylvie's father—the man who had saved her life refused to accept compensation and wept that he had been unable to save her mother and siblings as well. At that moment Sylvie understood that only her father had survived the war. At first he was unable to care for her and had to place her in an orphanage; later he remarried and brought her to live with him and his new wife. But both worked long hours and had no time for her; her stepmother was cold to her and Sylvie could only wait until she was old enough to leave home. She married young, to a survivor like herself with his own problems; the marriage did not last. She suggested that "like after an earthquake there are smaller shock-waves, so too my life was made up of quakes of different intensities."

Mark wrote that he cried often while writing his mother's story and that he learned much although he had assumed he knew the whole story. He wondered why she deserved this cruel fate and questioned whether he would have been able to survive what she did. For him Sylvie is a heroine, like Job, a small creature set against a world in which there is little pity or justice, who received no glory or public recognition yet struggles still to live her life. Interestingly, Mark says nothing about his own upbringing or about Sylvie's qualities as a mother. However, the very fact that he chose to write about her and to pay homage to her life's struggle indicates that she must have contributed significantly to the sensitive and aware person he has become.

Sarah. Tami wrote about her grandmother Sarah who was born in Yugoslavia in 1927, the youngest of four sisters. Sarah's father was a cantor in the synagogue of a small town and the family lived quietly until the Germans entered Yugoslavia in 1944. The family was rounded up along with all the Jews of the town and sent by train to Auschwitz. Sarah and her sisters passed the selection, were made to shower and numbers were tattooed on their arms; their heads were shaved, they were given a dress, shoes and a blanket and sent to Block B. Sarah and her sisters at first worked as seamstresses but were soon transferred to work in the munitions factory; conditions were 'fair' as long as they did their work: they witnessed other workers being shot for trying to sabotage production. One day, they were made to line up outside and were marched for three days in the cold to a railway station from which they were sent to Ravensbruck, where conditions were even more difficult than at Auschwitz. On the way Sarah's sister Bella became ill, and she died soon after; the three remaining sisters had no choice but to carry on. They were transferred yet again, and Sarah became ill with typhoid fever and meningitis. By this time, the war was nearing its end and the Russians took over the area; Sarah was sent to hospital where she recovered. Returning to their home town, she and her sisters found a Serbian family living in their house; they learned that their parents were no longer alive and that only 15 people remained of the town's Jewish community of 200. They decided to go to Palestine, and made their way to a Jewish center near Budapest where Sarah met her future husband. In 1948–49 both of them went to Israel where they were married; their son was born in 1952 and their daughter, Tami's mother, in 1956. The family is close-knit, meeting every Friday for a meal cooked by Sarah. Still very active, Sarah volunteers with many community organizations, and when a cleaner comes to work in her apartment she prepares by moving the furniture herself to make it easier for the cleaner. A positive and hopeful woman, Sarah is still angry at the world for being indifferent to the plight of the Jews, and she steadfastly refuses to travel outside of Israel.

Tami appreciates her grandmother for her strength and optimism; whenever Tami is upset or in difficulty she can count on her grandmother's encouragement. Sarah's experience helps Tami to see her own life and problems in perspective, to struggle for what she wants, and to remember to live fully and enjoy life. Sarah's story—like Sylvie's—is that of a woman who was deprived of her mother, yet in her own family she managed to put into practice the 'preservative love' described by Ruddick, something she still lives out as a grandmother within her extended family.

McAdams (1988) suggested that there are 5 'generic plots' that can be identified in life stories, regardless of genre. These plots as he defined them are 1) establishing or consecrating a home; 2) engaging in a contest or battle; 3) taking a journey—a physical or psychological voyage; 4) enduring suffering; and 5) pursuing consummation, or seeking transcendence, liberation or self-actualization. Typically, the students' narratives about mothers (and grandmothers) were elaborated around the plots of establishing a home, engaging in a battle or struggle of some kind (often for physical or economic survival), and enduring suffering. This is not surprising, given that these plotlines seem to accord both with the traditional "story of mothering" (Andrews, 2002) as caring for others and with the practices that Ruddick suggests are most central to the work of mothering. But if the stories are somewhat predictable when viewed in social and cultural perspective, it does not make them uninteresting as narratives. McAdams suggests that in mid-life stories are likely to combine several of the generic plots, making for more complex stories and hence more interesting ones; this is indeed the case for the present stories. Reem's story of her mother, for example, is elaborated around the main plot of establishing a home. It is a hymn of praise to the person who gave the writer life, made a home for her and her siblings, supported her and provided a model of ideal behavior to be followed; however, this story also includes a minor plot around the suffering that followed the death of Munira's father, and the struggle to support the family. Mark's story of his mother Sylvie was told as a story of struggle and suffering intertwined, describing the difficulties undergone by the mother during the war and the legacy of suffering that began with her separation from her own mother and which she continues to live out. Tami's story of her grandmother Sarah seems also to be elaborated around two main plots, this time following one another in sequence: struggle during the war years and the establishment of a home after coming to Israel.

I can recall only a few examples of stories in which mothers were associated with either taking a journey or self-actualization. One student wrote about a grandmother who spends most of her time traveling from one place to another to spend time with her children and grandchildren who now live around the world. Some stories did focus on women seeking self-actualization, including some who happened also to be mothers, but I remember only one example in which the subject was the mother of the writer, a woman whose fulfilling career as a nurse was an inspiration for her daughter. Thus, overall, the stories of mothers written by these student teachers tended to reinscribe a traditional view of mothers as associated with home-making, with struggle and with suffering. While living out traditional plots, these mothers were portrayed as powerful and influential individuals whose lives could inspire others; but still, perhaps, they were storied less as women with an inner life, with conflicts and decisions to make, in short—less as subjects and authors of their own stories. Perhaps the mothers themselves chose to tell their stories with an orientation to the present and future, focusing on outer struggles and glossing over uncertainties and difficulties.

The tendency of theory in various fields to view mothers as "not quite subjects" has been noted by feminist theorists. Palgi-Hacker (2009) shows how psychoanalytic theory in particular has failed to view the mother as subject. Benjamin (1995) illuminates the psychological connection between the self-sacrifice enshrined in the traditional view of motherhood and the difficulty of viewing mother as subject: if one gives up on the self in order to care for others, it seems that one cannot really care for others in the way that one intends. As Benjamin notes, "Intersubjective theory postulates that the other must be recognized as another subject in order for the self to fully experience his or her subjectivity in the other's presence" (1995, 31).

Walker (1998) attends to a more specific phenomenon, the silencing of women within philosophy. In an effort to view the mother as subject, she focuses on theorizing of the maternal body, citing Irigaray's reading of Plato which suggests that woman is the "unacknowledged place or grounding substance from which the masculine subject draws his reserves or resources" (Walker, 1998, 12). This highlights a conceptualization of 'woman as place' that resonates with the folk sayings about mothers mentioned above. To remedy the absence of women's voices from philosophical dialogue, Walker imagines a symposium of women speaking with one another, a multifaceted discussion among theorists such as Kristeva, Irigaray and Cixous, and between them and Freud, Lacan and others. With Kristeva, Walker sees the mother's body "as the site of a disruptive refusal of paternal/Oedipal logic" (144–5) and encourages us to "explore maternity for its wealth of repressed material" (148). She highlights women's writing on the body, such as Cixous' view that women should "express themselves" by writing in the "white ink" of mother's milk (1976) and Young's (1990) moving phenomenological account of her own pregnancy. Such work "performs a serious displacement of traditional Western constructions of the mother as the silent term in relation to the son" (181), and as such, perhaps allows for understanding mothers and mothering in radical new ways.

Feminist theorists also point to the fact that the effort to understand mothering differently is a task that calls for going beyond familiar methods. Ribbens (1998) explores the difficult task of separating her actual feelings as a mother from the feelings she knows she is 'expected' to have. Cho (2005) worries about the meager sense that conventional statistical methods would make of her mother's story, saying: "I write you from a place that cannot be domesticated by the disciplining methods of social science…I write you from the darkest spaces of memory" (Cho, 2005, 50). Cho sees her mother's story as the starting point for her own academic story, recalling how she came to critique the conventional research methodology which would have labeled her mother, reducing her difficult experience to a statistic about a denigrated group of women abused in wartime. Theorists who have taken the step of writing about their own mothers, looking critically at their own upbringing, include Steedman (1986), Scott & Scott (2000) and Cosslett (2000).

Perhaps it is even harder to subject one's own practice as a mother to public scrutiny as did Hager (2011). Abbey (1999) who carried out collaborative research on the mothering of daughters and sons, talking with the daughters and sons of the three co-researchers, reflects on the difficulties and concludes that "If we are to encourage authentic stories of mothers and mothering, we will need to find ways to honour and validate multiple or contradictory realities that do not necessarily adhere to conventional forms of discourse" (53). And Sotirin (2010), exploring her own experience as a mother, calls for a "rhizomatic practice of autoethnographic writing and reading that works creatively within, upon, and beyond personal narratives... creatively dismantling the affective relations defining the institution and experience of motherhood" in order to learn something new.

While my students' writing was sometimes disappointing in the limited extent to which they challenged received ideas, there was also something compelling about their stories, conveying as they did that the mother was indeed someone important, unique, and dear to the writer, someone whose caring inspired them to be caring teachers, someone who believed in them and held them to high standards, modeling the person they might perhaps become for their future pupils. Reading my students' work, although I understood that I could easily fall into the same traps, nonetheless I too wanted to write about my mother, to give her a place on the page, and especially to begin to understand how her stories live on in many small places in my body, posture and movement and in how I live in the world.

From the theoretical ideas briefly presented here I draw a number of suggestive directions to explore. First, as Cho (2005) points out, to understand mothering, and no less the notions of embodiment and teaching which will be taken up shortly, we need to risk drawing on unconventional methodologies. Taking Benjamin's ideas seriously, it seems that in order to understand mothers (and I will suggest the same holds for teachers) as subjects, the intersubjective dimension is crucial, hence the importance of Walker's creation of a dialogic space. Women as subjects need to speak to one another, in safe places where they are able to relate to one another on many levels: to bring up repressed memories and share the attendant emotion, to argue and challenge received ideas, to explore and question idealized images such as that of the 'good mother,' the 'good teacher,' the 'ideal woman,' and to risk sharing what they may perceive as failures to live up to those images. Much has already been written, yet more is still needed not only to challenge the familiar images but to dream and offer new ones. And it seems clear that relating to the body is crucial for an understanding of women and teachers as subjects. I turn now to focus on embodiment and on how bodily habits shape lived experience.

Embodiment

There is a need to understand the body not just because it is there, but because it conditions and shapes our lives and understanding from the beginning; as Sarbin (2001) points out, "emotional life is *embodied*. Not only is the participant in an emotional drama engaged in living out a story, his or her engagement is embodied" (218). Particularly in situations that involve conflict and trauma, attending to the body may be essential for understanding (Elbaz-Luwisch, 2004a; Fine, 2002; Rothschild, 2000).

Post-structuralist theorists since Derrida (1967, 1976) have taken it as a central task to deconstruct the familiar binaries of mind and body, reason and emotion, male and female, and to imagine the construction of knowledge in new ways that do not reinscribe these binaries (see Burkitt, 1999). From the beginnings of feminist writing, research and pedagogy, feminist researchers in particular have worked to go beyond the mind-body split and to valorize the body as a site of both experience and knowledge (e.g., Grumet, 1988; Haug et al., 1987; Somerville, 2004). According to Grosz,

> By body I understand concrete, material, animate organization of flesh, organs, nerves, and skeletal structure...it is indeterminate, amorphous, a series of uncoordinated potentialities that require social triggering, ordering, and long term administration. The body becomes a human body, a body that coincides with the shape and space of a psyche, a body that defines the limits of experience and subjectivity only through the intervention of the (m)other and, ultimately, the Other (the language- and rule-governed social order) (1994, 104).

And as Peters (2004) points out, drawing on the work of Merleau-Ponty:

> The body is not an 'object' in the objective sense through its spatial properties and
> its location; neither is the body limited to cause and effect descriptions. Rather, the
> body is the subject of action: it is essentially a practical, pre-conscious subject in the
> lived world that possesses both 'intentionality' and 'knowledge. (20)

Thus body defines the limits of experience, but it can do so only within and under the auspices of society—the "language- and rule-governed social order"—whose first representative, the first 'other' encountered by the infant, is mother. Postmodern social science views the body as a site of discursive formation, arguing that we know the body only through the lens of a given language, a discourse which allows us to speak and write about the body, whether it be the gendered body, the physically fit body or the body in illness, the body clothed and decorated, the body marked, scarred or mutilated, and so on. In much of the writing on the body, the concern is not with the actual physical body, skin and bones, muscles and inner organs, but with the textual body—the body as written about by theorists. Barnacle (2009, 23) comments that "while discourse on the body continues to proliferate within and beyond feminist inquiry, the body itself is rarely afforded more than a very limited agency."

It is interesting to notice just how little social science in fact deals with the body of our everyday experience—that annoying one that eats too much, feels tired, limps or has high blood pressure. Somehow, social science is telling us that bodies as such—the 'real' bodies we meet in everyday reality—cannot really be contained in theoretical discourse; something about bodies will always escape our understanding. Perhaps bodies are too dangerous, too fragile, or too messy to deal with; better to focus on how bodies are spoken about, written about, discussed or ignored—by academics, for the most part. But however we ignore the experience of the 'real' body, it is always there, even when not actually "causing trouble" by illness, accident, or simply by refusing to do what we expect of it. Freeman (2002) suggests that some of the understandings and practices that orient us in our everyday lives in the world remain implicit, unthematized and not subject to thought. These implicit understandings give form to ways of standing, sitting and moving; they shape our ways of arranging objects in space, and of performing daily tasks. They become the habits and practices of everyday life, and even, as Connerton (1989) suggests, become part of the ground for the construction of social memory. Yet body habits remain largely invisible and perhaps are most easily identified when violated, in situations of conflict or strong emotion, in ways of coping with surprise, trouble or illness.

One way of approaching these implicit understandings is through Mindell's (1982, 1998) conceptualization of the "dreambody": a level of experience that is quite familiar to most of us yet plays out just outside our everyday understanding, coming to us through night-time dreams but also in daydreams and reveries, in fleeting images and strange thoughts that cross our mind, in bodily symptoms, inadvertent gestures and movements, as well as in chance or accidental events. Mindell interprets Jung's work to say that "the psyche was not necessarily a pathological phenomenon but a meaningful realm of events with its own inner structure and flowing processes" (1982, 7), and he goes on to offer a variety of ways to work (both in a therapeutic context and on one's own) with dreams and with symptoms and bodily processes to expand awareness and gain meaning of one's personal experience (Mindell, 1984). Mindell's approach informs much of my thinking about embodiment and bodily processes. I will focus here on how bodily habits shape lived experience and how body and memory interact with the work of the imagination.

In my mother's story it was apparent that keeping silent, holding one's fear tightly at bay, in one's clenched fists and at the bottom of one's stomach, are habits and skills she must have acquired very early. The 'habits' of worrying about others, caring for all the members of her family, being loyal to her clan, were unquestioned. Showing respect for authority, doing what was expected of her, avoiding trouble, also seemed to come 'naturally.' My mother refined these skills when she came as an immigrant to Canada at the age of 17, and I acquired some of the same habits, in the telling and from the transmission of my mother's body to mine, from the felt tension of muscles and a particular way of holding one's body. I also learned to appreciate the importance of saying the right words, with the correct degree of polite deference; speaking to people in positions of power involved a particular posture and a way of holding the head at a slight angle (see Connerton, 1989). I saw this during childhood when my mother came to school to speak with my teachers. Words could not merely avert danger but actively shape one's destiny.

My own experience of immigration, however, took me —at least to some degree—in the opposite direction. Israeli culture seemed to be more open and relaxed (or is this largely a stereotype, a surface impression?) and to allow for a different way of living in one's body than I had become accustomed to in Canada. In my first year in Israel, working as a volunteer teacher in an elementary school serving a population of children of immigrants from North African countries, I developed a repertoire of formats for teaching basic English vocabulary and grammar: "This is my right hand! This is my left hand!" I would lead the 5th grade children in my class in reviewing the terms for parts of the body, shouting out the statements in a loud voice, my clear enunciation accompanied by exaggerated gestures and movements. The children loved these drills, and I loved them too as they got me through at least half of each class without discipline problems; I also enjoyed the rare opportunity to be loud and dramatic, a way of being that did not have much space in my everyday life.

My mother's way of organizing life involved a careful orchestration of movement and stillness which, I imagine, served in an imperfect way to confine the remembered horrors to the margins of her lived experience, leaving her body to carry the traces of memory faithfully and silently. I think of my mother as embodying a frozen stillness, the stillness of fear, of a child hiding in the forest with her family, a child hidden by the neighbors, staying quietly in the background in a house full of children and noise. But then, my mother was also movement—always busy, cleaning or cooking. She was quick in her movements and quick to observe—your eyes look funny, do you feel all right? This observation usually meant that I would be sick the next day with fever and a sore throat and have to stay home from school. You bring me breakfast in bed on a wooden tray with a picture of geese; a pretty napkin, my special plate, triangles of toast with my soft-boiled egg. You take my temperature and then check the thermometer with your soft hand on my forehead; you turn my pillow. I braid the woolen fringes on my plaid blanket.

Reflecting on my mother's story of how she confronted an attacker on a dark Montreal street, I remind myself that my mother was small—barely 5 foot two (158cm) and weighed less than 50 kilos—she certainly had no training in martial arts. I wondered if I would ever have the courage to react as she did. The need to be "firm on my feet," as she put it, is something I am keenly aware of, especially as I get older; a few years ago I had an attack of sciatic pain and discovered to my shame that when pain forced me to walk bent over, I stayed at home rather than suffer the injury to my pride of appearing in public in what I felt was a humiliating posture.

Body and imagination. Cornell (1995) has worked to theorize the embodied nature of the imaginary domain, which "is the moral and psychic space we need to become a person in our own way through language and with the heritage and culture into which we are thrown by birth and circumstance" (Cornell & Dean, 1998, 176). The imaginary is one of the layers in an understanding of the body that is multilayered, combining lived experience, legal constructs, and "projected fantasy." All these constrain who we might become, but Cornell's formulation is open ended, and she suggests that the imagination may "break open the intelligible to create new forms of intelligibility" (187–88). Language offers not only conceptual tools but also the power to express, paint verbal pictures and evoke feelings and impressions. It remains true that because the mother has been storied in Western culture as "the abjected other," the only way the daughter can—and perhaps must—identify with her mother is in the role of one who will sacrifice everything for her children and family. Yet the imagination provides the possibility of taking those same materials given in experience and putting them together differently, inventing new ways of understanding.

I imagine my mother, eager to learn in a tiny makeshift schoolroom, the main room in one of the village homes in Kolonia Manshurova. She would have had the neatest handwriting and been the quickest student in the bunch. What if there had been no pogroms, no violence on the roads that kept her from attending school, no efforts to hold back Jewish students? I imagine her in a bigger classroom, in a Soviet school in a nearby town, taking in every word, doing all her assignments, obeying the party line but remaining quietly skeptical. What if, later in Canada, there had been no prejudice against immigrants, no financial worries, no assumption that it was too late for a 17-year-old to begin again in a new language and to go as far as her abilities would take her? I see my mother in a Canadian schoolroom where immigrants are learning English, enjoying her growing mastery of the language, becoming comfortable with the more relaxed atmosphere, beginning to allow herself to dream. Given her culinary talents, it is easy to imagine her setting up a catering business, providing the wonderful food she prepared for us to more and more customers, hiring young women who needed a break and helping them to become independent. I can imagine her completing a high school diploma, continuing on to university, perhaps studying social work or psychology and turning her natural skills as a supportive listener into a profession. In fact she worked in a coat factory, doing the fine hand-sewing of buttonholes and loops, attaching fancy labels to the finished garments. I think of her hands. I remember watching, learning and eventually helping to make particular shapes out of dough for particular holidays: I was helping to cut out poppy seed cookies when we heard the news of Stalin's death on the radio in March 1953. I remember how everything was ready on time for the evening meal, perfectly seasoned, nothing ever burnt or underdone. Thinking of my mother's firm but delicate touch, remembering her carefully coordinated movements, it is not such a big leap to imagine my mother wearing green scrubs, carefully washing her hands, putting on rubber gloves and entering an operating theatre.

Poetic language allows us to become familiar with mothers from distant places as if they were our own. When Sujata Bhatt's mother puts on her sari (2000), "her right hand is firm and fast, and moves like a fish (90)." Agi Mishol finds nighttime comfort in being able to fulfill one of her mother's last wishes, "to lie on your side with your knees bent," to dream in "your brown angora sweater/soft as love/simple as a peanut" (2006, 25). If the language of poetry makes it easier to approach the everyday, it should be no surprise that we need such language even more to understand what is truly urgent and fateful in life. Referring to the chant of the women in Toni Morrison's novel *Beloved* (1989), Cornell (in Cornell & Dean, 1998) points to the evocative power of language, the need for ritualistic forms of recognition, and for new forms of solidarity, all of which might allow us to go beyond the more common cognitive understandings. Gurevitch (2002, 405) describes this going beyond through writing as a moment of 'transfiguration': "an act of writing through, transfiguring the personal, the lived through, as well as the world into the objectivity of poetry." Israeli poet Eliaz Cohen also points to the possibility of going beyond ordinary understanding, telling us that "Something will yet arise from all this blood" (2004; my translation); he repeats the line over and over at the beginning of each four-line stanza of his poem, setting up a hypnotic rhythm.

After my paternal grandmother died in 1909, my grandfather took his two young sons to Switzerland for a few years, later moving to Germany. At the time there could have been no way of knowing that it would have been worth making every effort to remain in Switzerland. *The fires that burned my cousins, the earth that buried the others alive.* During the war some thirty thousand Jews were given refuge in Switzerland (Seidler, 2000), while an equal number were turned away.

A few years ago, attending a seminar on the work of Marion Woodman in Einsiedeln, a small town in Switzerland, I found myself gazing at softly flowing green hills and listening to the constant chiming of cowbells. One morning we visited the town's cathedral famous for a statue of the Black Madonna; although I tried to feel into the spirit of the place, I was unable to see this small figure dressed in elaborate silks and brocades as a symbol of feminine strength, of cultural transformation and the valuing of diversity (Woodman & Dickson, 1996). There are no rational grounds for the feeling of threat that came over me in those moments, but I was beset by sights and sounds of war: *The gunpowder, the bombs, The attacks from air and sea.*

I remembered one of the first films I saw about the Holocaust, on television when in my early teens; it portrayed a small group of Jews being led through snowy forests to the Swiss border. Most of the group made it to safety, but two members of the group were slower than the others—an elderly man and his young granddaughter. Shots rang out and the grandfather was killed. I left the cathedral, sat outside and opened my notebook. *This happened before I was born, it happened last week, it is happening now in my brain, in my stomach, in my toes, arms, liver and spleen.*

Writing with the body, in time with the breath, there is an unexpected vehemence; images appear from different places in memory: from my mother's stories, from books and films about the Holocaust, from television news broadcasts of terror attacks and recent wars. Lining up, one after another like soldiers heading into battle, the images seemed to belong together, to share an easy and terrifying camaraderie. Or perhaps, like refugees hoping to escape, they line up and cling together with a different kind of tension. The images are on no one's side and require no explanation beyond the shared trauma to which they bear witness. It is in response to the persistent nature of such images that Israeli poet Agi Mishol (2006, 9) invokes her muses, asking their forgiveness

> *for disturbing you with our history*
> *repeating itself*

For Cornell, "aesthetic ideas allow us to integrate our experience in ways left contingent by the abstract system of nature based on the understanding and elaborated by reason" (1998, 187–188). Such integration is described by Duarte Esgalhado (2001) who "began to feel deeply, in my body, mind, and sex, that which I had long taken for granted in the casual exchange of language among family members" (253); in a life story marked by immigration, loss of a culture and mother tongue, and a return home to the greenery of Portugal and the convivial table at which her family gathered to eat, sexuality comes up readily. What a relief, after trauma, to be able to talk about sex.

According to Cornell, the imaginary domain is "necessary for us if we are to shape a person out of our sexual identifications, including what feminine sexual difference is going to mean in a life-history" (Cornell & Dean, 1998, 176). In the time and place that I grew to adulthood, sexuality was not a topic of direct conversation; I remember only flashes, like the twinkle in the eye of my mother's cousin Elka, as she told slightly off-color jokes with great flair. And there was a childhood game in which a few of us girls sat under a blanket on our balcony (my mother was in the kitchen and *never* came to check on us) and took turns showing body parts not fit to be seen in public; we laughed and giggled before and after this game, but the showing itself was done silently and with great seriousness. There was gossip too: about the girl down the street who "went in the bushes with men" and about babies born "out of wedlock"—terms I barely understood. Almost forgotten, these memories and the language of the time in which they were formulated, now appear readily as I write, as does my mother's barely concealed embarrassment when the topic of sex came up. Writing about these memories "enriches the text with the body" (Esgalhado, 2001, 254), but it also enlivens the body itself.

Teaching

The study of teaching has been enriched in recent years by approaches which take up as a matter of course many of the themes that have been examined in this and earlier chapters, themes which scarcely found a place in earlier cognitively-based process-product studies of teaching. As indicated in Chapter 1, attention to memory is implicit in narrative and biographical studies of teaching which understand that teachers can only teach who they are and that early experiences in school and at home have a formative impact on teacher development (Bullough et al., 1992; Cole & Knowles, 2000; Elbaz-Luwisch, 2005; Kelchtermans, 2009); teacher-student relationships live on in memory (Uitto, 2011). Recent work joins the interest in memory with a concern for multiculturalism and social justice (Li et al., 2009; Mitchell et al., 2011; Strong-Wilson, 2008).

The theme of mothering has been explored both directly and indirectly and in a variety of ways in relation to teaching (see Casey, 1990; Galea, 2005; Grumet, 1988; Pinnegar et al., 2005). Mothering is invoked in work which attends to the relational aspects of teaching and in particular to the notion of caring (Goldstein, 2002; Noddings, 2005). Teaching and mothering (Estola, 2003) are intertwined, embodied practices as are teaching and parenting (C. Simon, 2005). Doll (1995) makes these links apparent by weaving stories of her mother's life and death through a series of essays on teaching.

Miller (2005, 221) pointed out that it is not common for teacher-educators to "encourage future or practicing teachers to address issues of, say, sexuality, the body, the unconscious, or desire in relation to conceptions of what constitutes an 'effective' or 'good teacher'." Yet increasingly, studies reveal the work of teaching as embodied (Dixon & Senior, 2011; Elbaz-Luwisch, 2002; Estola & Elbaz-Luwisch, 2003; Golden, 2004; Uitto & Syrjälä, 2008; Zembylas, 2007). Narrative studies of teaching in particular point to and evoke the body, for, as Johnson pointed out, "Narrative, too, is a bodily reality—it concerns the very structure of our perceptions, feelings, experiences, and actions. . .[I]t is what we live through and experience prior to any reflective 'telling' of the story in words" (1989, 374–375). Swanson (2007) reports on an incident where she was required to perform the morally and practically impossible task of dividing up the contents of an inadequate food parcel sent from a privileged white South African school to her class-room of 50 poor black students. Providing vivid accounts of the children's bodies pressing up to receive something from the bag of food, or of one child physically bullying another in the schoolyard, Swanson demonstrates how "embodied approaches contest the dualistic way in which the body is conventionally conceived...rendering embodied ways of knowing and 'coming to be' as crucial to learning and living" (69). The centrality of embodiment in the practice of teaching and the diversity of its manifestations are highlighted in the collections edited by Bresler (2004), Weber and Mitchell (2004) and Springgay & Freedman (2007). Springgay (2007, 2008) seeks to teach and develop curriculum together with and through the bodied subjectivities of young people, holding that "to be a body is to be 'with' other bodies, to touch, to encounter, and to be exposed"; she suggests that embodied encoun-ters in the classroom "produce intercorporeal understandings and in doing so imagine an intimate curriculum that is vulnerable and hesitant" (Springgay, 2007, 192).

Theorizing the embodiment of teaching as a form of practice, Griffiths (2006) points out that practices "are relational and formed...as a result of particular human delights and terrors. Teaching is intensely personal and corporeal" (395-6). Griffiths' analysis is a radical one, showing that em-bodiment is not a fault, nor is it a limitation peculiar to women who are inca-pable of separating the personal from the professional. Rather, embodiment is inherent in the very conceptualization of practice as such: practice is some-thing we could not engage in without bodies, without a personal point of view. Further, Griffiths sees practices as "fluid": diverse practices influence one another and have permeable boundaries. "The practice of teaching leaks into the practices of mothering, fathering, managing, facilitating, counseling, and philosophizing—and vice versa" (Griffiths, 2006, 394–5).

Miss Law was an English teacher who came into our 8th grade classroom one day to substitute for one of our regular teachers. She was tall, with long dark hair tied back at her neck, wore a tweed suit and probably would have been called 'handsome' at the time; I thought she had style. She handed out some mimeographed sheets, sat on the teacher's desk and proceeded to read to us from the early poetry of Yeats. Her rich voice captivated my attention utterly. It was the first time I'd heard poetry read *as poetry*, resonant musical sound that conveyed meaning through tone and rhythm, not just through the arrangement of well-chosen words on paper. The class was silent and seemingly receptive, so perhaps I was not the only one who later read and reread the poems until I'd memorized them. I especially loved "The Stolen Child," about a child spirited away by faeries. At fourteen, I did not think for a moment that the poems might be about me. Only now, as writing mysteriously brings the words back, do I realize that at the time I was, indeed, a child, one of many children who were entrusted—too soon—with stories of "a world more full of weeping than you can understand" (Yeats, 1961, 20–1), demanding stories that lived and waited in my body until they could play themselves out in the classroom and in writing.

Looking more closely at how embodiment plays out in teachers' stories, we find teachers taking up a "position of presence" (Estola & Elbaz-Luwisch, 2003) in front of students. As Paula, an elementary science teacher in Israel, said, "In those moments when I am in front of the class, I am the figure that they copy, that they watch. I am the person, the adult that is present in front of them" (in Estola & Elbaz-Luwisch, 2003). Rodgers and Raider-Roth (2009) define presence as "a state of alert awareness, receptivity and connectedness to the mental, emotional and physical workings of both the individual and the group in the context of their learning environments and the ability to respond with a considered and compassionate best next step" (266). Miss Law gave us little direct attention—she didn't introduce the poetry, explain it or even engage us in discussion about it; possibly, having to substitute was an imposition she resisted, passively, by spending the hour reading her favorite poetry aloud to us. But she was alert and aware, and in bringing the work of Yeats to our class she took us seriously as people who could understand and care about poetry; to that extent she did indeed connect with the class in the context given.

In addition to the qualities highlighted by Rodgers and Raider-Roth—and perhaps it's just another way of saying the same thing—I suggest that presence requires the teacher to be herself, as fully as possible in the moment: body and mind, feelings and desires, past memories and imagined future, all the strands coming together. But is presence in this sense really possible? A wide range of studies call into question the idea that merely being present as a teacher can be anything but fraught with difficulty. As Rogers illustrates,

But it wasn't simple at all to come into my body in that room. Over the next thirty minutes, Kristin had me perform a "three-act play." "Here is how it goes," she said, "Act I: I am, Act II: here, Act III: in this room." Stomping on the carpet in bare feet, pounding the walls with my hands, whispering, shouting, I cajole and finally convince myself, Kristin, and my small audience of my presence in the room (Rogers, 1993, 284).

By all accounts schooling is a highly regulated and organized enterprise in which teachers play a role as representatives of the state, charged to implement official programs designed in conformity with policy mandated from above. Leaving aside for the moment critical views of the school's reproductive function (e.g., Bourdieu & Passeron, 1977, 1990), many have noted the extent to which teaching is a performance. Eisner (1994), discussing the idea that teaching may be considered an art, points out that "teaching can be performed with such skill and grace that, for the student as well as for the teacher, the experience can be justifiably characterized as aesthetic." Sarason (1999) offers an extended analogy with the performing arts, claiming that "the teacher willingly and internally defines a role with characteristics intended to elicit in an audience of students a set of reactions that will move them willingly to persist in the pursuit of new knowledge and skills" (51); the teacher as performer thus models for students what it means to be an engaged learner, involved with learning and with subject matter that is personally meaningful. These formulations do not carry any criticism of teachers for being "on stage" in what might be thought of as a self-serving way. However, both Eisner and Sarason are critical of schools and teacher preparation programs, for failing to enable teachers to work, live and develop in ways that would enable them to carry out the role of teacher as elaborated by these theorists.

For critical and feminist studies, however, the criticism goes deeper, as "performance" has become a central category in the social sciences and humanities, influenced in part by the early work of Goffman (1959) who portrayed social life as a performance in which persons act to manage the way that others see and judge them through "a potentially infinite cycle of concealment, discovery, false revelation, and rediscovery" (Goffman, 8). In postmodern explorations this cycle may become a playful one that is productive of multiple meanings. For example, in an examination of the personal in pedagogy edited by Gallop (1995), the notion of "impersonation" serves as a focal point. Otte (1995) looks at the difficulties faced by writing teachers with the notion of "authentic voice," which seems unattainable and even impossible to define; he advocates dropping any pretense to authenticity in favor of teaching students to take up and master the different voices available in academic discourse, which he terms "in-voicing." Grumet (1995), working with autobiographical writing in the setting of a course in philosophy of education, chooses to focus her students' attention on "the contradictions, the inconsistencies and the leaks" (43); she cheerfully sends up her own performance by describing the soft and comfortable, slightly tatty green robe in which she writes, a robe which makes present the disheveled and often disowned underside of proper academic demeanor. Miller (2005) explores the possibility that teachers' autobiographical writing can exemplify performativity by producing accounts that are open, that reflect changing cultural identities, that call into question normalized accounts of teaching and of being teacher.

Simon (1995) presents his sometimes tortuous efforts to bring his Jewishness into the classroom; as an important part of his identity, 'being Jewish' had the potential to brings him and his students "face to face with alterity" in an immediate way. Simon's reflections remind me of my own encounter with anti-Semitism in the person of a student at a Quebec university. Wanting to be present "as myself" with students, and not suspecting the complexities that might ensue from inviting students to confront alterity with and through me, I had spoken briefly about my background and about the years I had spent teaching and doing graduate study in Israel. Several students thanked me for this, including one student who had visited Israel, taken part in an archeological dig, and come back with positive impressions, and a T-shirt on which "Coca-Cola" was written in Hebrew. However, some months later the same student, while serving on a program review committee, made some offensive comments about my teaching and added a vague and indirect qualifier which could be understood only as a reference to my being Jewish. My first reaction was laughter at the roundabout and almost clever way the student expressed himself; in retrospect it seems I recognized his way of speaking as a form of "Jewish humor." Later I was upset and angry if not outraged, as were several colleagues who insisted that a student who spoke this way should not be allowed to become a teacher. Other colleagues, however, saw him as young and thoughtless and felt that no more than a reprimand was warranted. It took months to resolve the situation, and during this time I suffered from a painful stiff neck. Once the episode was over, the pain vanished. Looking back I realized that the symptom was the almost inevitable result of two strong and conflicting urges to movement: on the one hand I was angry and wanted to fight back, and on the other hand, I held back because I had been made aware that it was not in my interest to publicize this kind of conflict with a student. It was fine to be Jewish, but not fine to make a public issue of it: I was expected to "leave my difference at the door" (Simon,1995, 100). As a result of the experience I actually left much more than difference at the door when I walked into that classroom: not feeling very friendly towards the group as a whole, I taught the rest of the semester in what must have been a very formal and stiff manner.

Thus both the literature and personal experience demonstrate that presence in teaching is not something to be taken at face value. Clearly, presence is structured by the history and politics of the institutional setting in which one is present to others, and of the wider society that legitimizes the institution. It will not do to ignore this structuring effect as it can make a significant difference to what people experience and how they interpret their experience. However, what passes between a teacher and a student, or a group of students, whether at the university level or with children in compulsory schooling, is not historical or political ideas or understandings (though that may be made a focus when appropriate) but the stuff of human interaction: communication, feeling, sensation, physical touch, eye contact, recognition. What makes for presence is the same regardless of the historical and political conditions under which teaching takes place: a complicated mix of "self-knowledge, trust, relationship and compassion" (Rodgers & Raider-Roth, 2009, 266). And as already suggested, what is present is a body, the teacher's body standing in front of the class.

Conclusion

The exploration of ideas and experiences around motherhood, embodiment and teaching opens up many directions of inquiry. However, the discussion also leads me to a simple conclusion: it seems that writing about my mother, intentionally and with purpose, can be seen as an ordinary and unexceptional part of the academic practice of making sense of my experience as a researcher and teacher educator. I now see that as a researcher, the choice of narrative as both method and phenomenon in my research is interwoven almost invisibly with the need to answer the demand that my mother's stories be told and, with them, the stories of others who have not been heard. My interest in using stories to foster dialogue across cultural, religious and political boundaries (Elbaz-Luwisch, 2001; Li et al., 2009) has its roots in the stories told by my parents of their relationships with people from other communities and of the courage and generosity of non-Jews who saved both their lives. How I enter the classroom is partly shaped by who my mother was: her sporadic attendance at a village school in Russia, and her acute sense of what she had missed in not being able to study; the way she dressed me for the first day of kindergarten (navy blue pleated skirt, white sweater with a pattern of deer on the yoke), and her concern to raise an "acceptable child" (Ruddick, 1989). Whatever presence I might have as a teacher can make sense only through attending to the presence my mother had in her kitchen, the place where she was most at home and comfortable in her body. The details could have been otherwise, and they are, of course, different for each of us; but specific details are essential to understanding how any teacher comes to be who s/he is in the classroom. When I invite students and prospective teachers to write about a person who influenced their lives, I hope that in writing and sharing their stories, they will be present—to themselves, to one another, and to their future students.

Note

1.   The work of students in these courses is described and discussed in Li et al., 2009. The focus of my research then was on the interaction and dialogue among students based on their written stories. Students were informed that the work of the course was being documented for research purposes, and I requested to retain copies of their group work. Some individual stories were resubmitted as part of the group projects, and it is on these stories that I draw here, changing all names and identifying details. Hence the stories were not chosen to be representative but rather to illustrate some of the insights I gained from this project.

CHAPTER 4

Retrieving Memory, Shaping Teaching:
Stories of Teachers

After beginning with the family stories that shaped my own life and identity, I now turn to the life stories of educators from the diverse communities that make up contemporary Israeli society. I wonder what their stories might have in common. How do they differ? What makes the difference? How does place matter—in particular, living on 'contested ground'? What of time—lived time, historical time, the sometimes hallucinogenic time of violent conflict? Do the teachers' narratives embody closure and self-protection, as one might perhaps expect, or are there openings within them to dialogue and criticism? To look more closely at these issues, in this chapter I examine the life stories narrated by a group of teachers who are graduate students in education; in Chapter 5, I will examine the life stories of colleagues, teacher educators in Israel and abroad.

As already noted, the students at the University of Haifa are a diverse group in both age and background. The university does not provide official demographic information about the student body, but it is usually held that roughly eighty percent of the students are Jewish (most of them born in Israel, about a third immigrants—mainly from the former Soviet Union). Around twenty percent of the students belong to the Arab/Palestinian community; by religion they are Moslem, Christian, and Druze. Some of the students are religiously observant or traditional, others secular. They have been educated (and those who are teachers now teach) in a school system that, with the exception of a small group of bilingual schools (see Hertz-Lazarowitz et al., 2008), is largely separated by language: by choice of both communities, the Jewish schools teach in Hebrew and the schools in the Arab sector teach in Arabic[1] (see Al-Haj, 1995; Kalekin-Fishman, 2004). The Jewish schools are also divided in terms of religious observance (there are separate systems for the secular, religious and ultra-orthodox populations). In the university context where Jewish and Arab students meet, often for the first time, most of the students interact easily enough on matters relating to their studies, and more guardedly when it comes to personal or political issues; overall, it seems that students define their identities in diverse ways both within and across communities (Hertz-Lazarowitz et al., 2007; Li et al., 2009). Beneath the surface, of course, lie significant differences of opinion on the contentious matters of Israeli public life (as will be discussed further in Chapter 8).

It is often suggested that postmodernity produces identities that are problematic, fragmented and non-unitary (Bloom, 1996; Giddens, 1991; Goodson, 1998). Given that culture, religion, history and politics all influence the ways selfhood can be elaborated, and do so simultaneously but often in different directions, the expectation of fragmentation makes sense. This is perhaps especially the case in a setting like Israel which is characterized by diverse cultures, divergent identities, and competing memories and narratives of the past (Caplan, 2009), giving rise to a range of overlapping conflicts: between Jews and Palestinians, between religious and secular Jews, between Jews of European origin and those from Eastern (Sephardic) backgrounds, and between the socialist ideology of the founders of the state and current capitalist and managerial perspectives. In recent years a previously taken-for-granted and unitary view of Israeli identity, shaped by Zionist ideology, has been slowly giving way to a diversity of conceptions (see, for example, Kemp et al., 2004). These conceptions seek to take account of the actual diversity of Israeli society, which comprises native-born Israelis, Jewish immigrants from many countries, a significant minority of Palestinian Arabs (Moslem and Christian), Druze and Circassians, as well as foreign workers who are granted few civil rights. The conceptual diversity incorporates recent scholarship carried out from critical (e.g., Kemp et al., 2004), feminist (Abdo & Lentin, 2002; Lentin, 2000) and post-Zionist perspectives (Silberstein, 1999). In my work with Israeli teachers and student teachers from diverse backgrounds, however, it seems that while identity is indeed multi-vocal, it may be less fragmented than the repertoire of diverse views and identities would lead one to expect (Elbaz-Luwisch, 2005; Griffiths, 1995a; Kalekin-Fishman, 2005). The present chapter explores these issues through the autobiographical writing of Israeli teachers engaged in graduate study in education.

Methodology

In this chapter I examine the writing of 7 Israeli teachers who participated in a Masters' level course in narrative research. The teachers represent the diversity of Israeli society: out of a group of 20 in the course, 16 were women and 4 men, about half Jewish and half Arab/Palestinian. Three of the Jewish teachers were born in Israel, 5 immigrated (most as children) to Israel from the former Soviet Union, and one emigrated as a young adult from the United States. Of the Arab teachers (all born in Israel), seven are Moslem, one is Bedouin, and three are Christian.

Early in the course the students submitted a piece of autobiographic writing, a task for which they were given minimal guidelines; it is this 5–10 page assignment which I analyze here. The course focused on life story interviewing and "responsive listening" (Brown & Gilligan, 1992) to the stories of others, as well as on different ways of analyzing life story material; the autobiographies, as well as later interviews (conducted by the students in pairs) served as shared material for analysis and interpretation. Attention was paid to voice (Bakhtin, 1981; Goodson 1992), to time and place (Conle, 1999; Casey, 1992) and to the effects of power on life narratives in education (Davies and Gannon, 2006; Phelan, 2001). The contrasts between the narrative interviews and personal writing draw attention to the fact that all of us have multiple stories of our lives. The course, which I have taught regularly over the years, sometimes prompts an ongoing inquiry, for example, on the process of group interpretation (Elbaz-Luwisch, 2010c). In the session discussed here, I focus on how culture, history, place and background come into play and shape the life stories narrated by the students.

In interpreting the life stories I draw on diverse modes of narrative analysis (e.g., Clandinin and Connelly, 2000; Brown & Gilligan, 1992; Conle, 1999), paying attention to the time continuum of the narrative, to place (cultural, historical, geographical and experiential—see Casey, 1993), and to the relationships of the teller to others in her setting and to herself. The process of interpretation is holistic and draws attention to the way the stories are told and to salient themes they bring forward. My intention is to honor and give room to the personal while at the same paying attention to the ways that culture, history and politics shape the narratives (Goodson, 1992), providing a critical distance from which to read.

The students whose writing is discussed here volunteered to make their work available to me for research purposes. (I occasionally refer briefly to the writing of other students in the course, without quoting directly from their work.) The participants (all pseudonyms), as they described themselves at the time of writing, are:

- **Lily** — in her late 20s, married, a teacher of literature now working as director of a community centre; Jewish, born in Israel.

- **Eliana** — age 40, married with 2 children, a teacher of high school physics; Jewish, born in the former Soviet Union, immigrated to Israel at age 10.

- **Andy** — in his mid-20s, single, teaches English as a Second Language; Christian Arab, born and lives in an Arab city in the north of Israel.

- **Marie** — in her late 20s, married, teaches English as a Second Language; Christian Arab, born and lives in Haifa.

- **Lisa** — in her mid-20s, single, trained as a teacher of English as a Second Language; Jewish, born in the former Soviet Union, in Israel since age 8.

- **Niveen** — in her mid-20s, married, trained as a teacher of mathematics; Moslem Arab, born and lives in the north of Israel.

- **Ella** — late 20s, single, teacher of history in an alternative school.

Unsurprisingly, all the writers talk about their childhood and adolescence and about their education. They discuss the choice of a career in education, which often follows from a combination of motives: for women, particularly in the Arab sector, teaching may be an obvious choice (Al-Haj, 1995; Eilam, 2002); but at the same time many express a sense of vocation (Estola et al., 2003). They talk about important persons in their lives (including teachers), about their choice of a life partner, their children, and sometimes the death of a parent or other close family member. They mention hobbies, travel and other activities. Those who were immigrants to Israel invariably give some account of this experience (see Eisenstadt, 1995; Golden, 2001; Lieblich, 1993; Elbaz-Luwisch, 2004b). Although it would seem difficult to ignore the volatile political situation in Israel, and politics can often be detected just beneath the surface of their narratives, the teachers hardly mention history or politics in their life stories—an omission to be considered later in the chapter. Usually their accounts are roughly chronological; they make sense and give the reader an understanding of who the person is and what is important to her. These superficial similarities may seem trivial, but they indicate a degree of shared culture and common understandings about what makes up a life, or at least, a life story. There are other similarities and differences, of course, yet equally, each account is absolutely unique.

This chapter will present the analysis and interpretation of the teachers' narratives in two main sections: first, I look at the prominent themes that recur in many of the life stories, all of them falling under a general heading of "journeys of personal development." Then, I will examine the way that the stories are put together and told, paying particular attention to what I term "origins and outcomes." In both sections, I try to stay close to the stories themselves, juxtaposing the voices and stories of the teachers to highlight the multiple connections, common threads, divergences, silences, echoes and disharmonies that can be found in the stories of people who all live in the same small area of the north of Israel. I aim to produce a weaving together of their stories that does not override any of the voices. As suggested by Amitava Kumar, an Indian writer, poet and academic living in the United States, "The personal voice...achieves the greatest critical purchase when it expresses a complexity that would otherwise remain beyond the reach of the traditionally academic commentary" (Kumar, 2000, 145). Kumar attains that complexity through poetry (his own and that of other postcolonial poets), photographs, and reported conversations, woven throughout his autobiographical narrative. In what follows I juxtapose the narratives in ways that allow them to be heard clearly while also making it possible to question and go beyond them. In the final section of the chapter I will venture some further reflections on the narratives and their meanings.

Themes in teachers' stories: Life as a journey of personal development

Lily says, "After much thought, I decided to try and set out on a 'journey to myself'...to go back in time to those significant moments that are stored in memory and that have influenced, and will continue to influence my life." The journey is an apt metaphor for many young Israelis such as Lily, who has lived in different regions of Israel and travelled in South America. The journey has a number of stages that virtually all the writers visit: childhood, adolescence, and their current life as young adults and (for most) married couples with young children. I will explore the main themes and then examine the underlying discourse of personal development through which these themes are elaborated.

The happy childhood. A common theme in virtually all the autobiographies, and the starting point for the life journey, is a happy childhood, surrounded by family and friends and busy with diverse activities. Lisa comments, "I always felt that my sister was my best friend…we were always together in games in our neighborhood, and went to the same kindergarten." Andy reports, "I had no less than a perfect childhood…my father exposed me to different kinds of sports, such as swimming, karate, and boxing. He also had me take music lessons, and I learned how to play the oud and the guitar. I lacked nothing as a child." They also tell about trips and special occasions. For those who grew up outside Israel, trips usually involved the whole family. Lisa recalls her family's visit to St. Petersburg with its white nights, fountains and grand palaces, while Eliana remembers 'driving' with her father through the night on family trips to Odessa on the shore of the Black Sea. They don't fail to mention the magical scenes of winter, the glitter of frost on windowpanes and the crunch of snow underfoot. For Ella, who grew up in a small farming community (a 'moshav'), the first significant trip was not a family event but a camping trip with the youth movement: "it's hard to describe the excitement of a girl in the fourth grade who goes for the first time, completely on her own, for a trip of several days to an unknown place."

For the most part, childhood is seen as a protected time during which mistakes are forgiven and achievements are praised lavishly. This is given more emphasis by some striking exceptions. For example, Eliana at age 8 was required, according to local custom, to be part of an 'honour guard' standing for long hours beside the open casket of a classmate who had died. And Lisa experienced the negative side of being Jewish in the Soviet Union: in first grade, she suddenly found herself surrounded by a curious circle of children as one of her classmates shouted at her "Jew!" Lisa had hardly heard this word before and did not know its meaning; she felt insulted and hurt until one of her teachers assured her that it did not mean anything bad. Notably, no one suggested it might mean something positive. From this day on, Lisa gradually began to be aware of being different; she noticed that her grandparents sometimes spoke in a different language (Yiddish, she learned), and when her grandfather spoke too loudly her grandmother would remind him anxiously that the neighbours might be listening. Not long afterward, Lisa's parents began to organize for their emigration to Israel.

Some of the teachers wrote about being given responsibility for younger siblings at an early age. As Lily tells it, "Everyone called me the 'latchkey child'…the regular routine was to pick up my brother, buy something to eat on the way home (I always got pizza or just sweets, and my brother always got falafel), at home we'd do our homework, watch television and go to our after-school activities, and in the afternoon mom would come home and spend time with us."

School was important for all of the teachers, and they were encouraged by their families to do well; as expected of a group of teachers, most report that they were good students (see Lortie, 1975). Marie says

> In elementary school I was always one of the first in my class, I say 'one of the first' because there were always competitors. At the end of the fourth grade I was chosen along with 5 or 6 other pupils to take an entrance exam for a new program, a school for the gifted, which I attended from the 5th grade once a week on Sundays, the day when the Arab schools in Haifa don't have classes.

Eliana remembers her first day at school in vivid detail:

> I woke up very early, all excited, and got dressed in the brown school uniform with white lace at the collar and cuffs and a white apron over the dress. Mother combed my hair and tied a big white bow, there were flowers, and a school bag…I remember the teacher, short and thin with a hairdo tall as a tower. On the first day we were taught to sit properly on the chair, to raise our hands properly, to sit with a straight back.

Eliana's description highlights bodily discipline (Estola & Elbaz-Luwisch, 2003; Davies & Gannon, 2006) as a central ingredient of schooling which, in different forms, transcends time and place. Most of the teachers were not just good students but also 'good children' who earned the approval of their elders. Discipline, physical and intellectual, seems to have come easily to them; only one talked about having learning difficulties in the early years of schooling.

Teenage angst. Many of the writers mention painful episodes that marked their teen years. For Andy, "As a teenager, growing up in a conservative Arab society, my life was full of social boundaries that I was not allowed to cross. Any attempt on my part to go against the social code was met with repression, punishment, and ostracism on the part of my family." Those who were immigrants found adolescence particularly difficult: still in the process of adapting to a new country, they were unequipped to deal with issues of belonging to the social group that is so crucial during adolescence (see Lieblich, 1993). Eliana sums up her experience, "I was a new immigrant from the Soviet Union, a bookworm, good at science, and my study of piano and long hours of practice all put me definitively in the 'out' group."

Niveen was a happy, active child and socially dominant, but "after age 10, I started to hear all sorts of comments from my family that were strange to me: "Why are you behaving that way? Why do you think you're better than everyone else? Look at your sister who is so quiet, worried only about her studies. You should behave according to what is accepted." At first Niveen didn't understand; her family had always encouraged her lively behaviour and admired her assertiveness—"Why now are you asking me to be 'not me'?" Thus began a long process of reflection: "It was the first time in my life that I had to deal with questions about the ambivalent attitude of society towards myself and towards my brother who was a year younger than me, how social norms (regarding dress, manner of speech, games, going out) were valid for girls and completely irrelevant for boys who didn't have to make any concessions to society." In junior high, Niveen began learning more about Islam, particularly as her father became more religious; she was especially influenced by a teacher who taught her that a religious person could "combine his own needs and concerns with concern for society, and could fulfil the religious commandments without sacrificing his own uniqueness."

Although Niveen felt that her brother was exempt from the social restrictions placed on females by Arab society, Andy's story suggests that boys also encountered obstacles:

> In the eleventh grade, I got to know a girl from my own town who was three years younger than I was. We had been chatting online for a long period of time, when we eventually decided to meet face to face. I can still play the video of our first meeting at a local restaurant in my head….we continued to meet in secret every now and then, and we used to talk for long hours on the phone… However, no sooner had our relationship come into being than it was doomed to end…her parents found out about us, and they took away her cell-phone. …As to my family, I remember being sent for by my dad, upon receiving the phone bill of the last couple of months; he showed it to me as if it were a warrant for my arrest. The figures in the bill were so high that I wished the ground would open up and swallow me.

For the Arab Palestinian teachers, adolescence seems to end with the end of their schooling: some worked for a time before beginning their studies, while others went directly to university; all of them seemed to be fully engaged in starting their adult life. For the Jewish teachers, military service came after high school, bringing a kind of moratorium but also the opportunity to prove themselves: Lily worked as a teacher in a small community in the south of the country and later as a coordinator for all the teacher-soldiers in the region. Lisa was "a personal assistant to an officer and received two certificates of excellence; I was full of motivation to contribute to the State of Israel and carry out my duties in the best possible way." For the Jewish teachers, the transition to adulthood does not seem complete without a period of travel and adventure: like many other young Israelis, Lily spent 6 months after the army backpacking in South America. Ella postponed the trip abroad for almost ten years to take advantage of work opportunities but finally took time off to trek in the Far East. Eliana still regrets that when younger she did not have the means to take a long trip.

Family life. Israel is considered to be a very 'familistic' society (Fogel-Bijaoui, 1999; Lavee & Katz, 2003), and family is indeed central to all the stories. For members of the Arab community, the influence of family extends to many areas: some parents gave advice regarding choice of a field of study and career, while others influenced the decision about whether to study at university or closer to home in one of the teachers' colleges. Many of the teachers continue to live near their families, sometimes even in the same building, as is customary in Arab towns. And mothers are there to help with the grandchildren, making it easier for women to continue their studies and pursue a career. The Jewish participants tell their stories in terms of a more independent lifestyle—they are less likely to mention the influence of family members on their decisions about education and career, for example, and "leaving home" is a transition to be managed at some point in their story, not related to marriage. However, family figures prominently in the Jewish teachers' stories as well. Ella, one of the most independent-minded participants, recently returned to live near her parents in the small agricultural community where she grew up, enjoying the family closeness (and her mother's home cooking) while continuing to chart her own course in life.

The influence of family is most critical when it comes to choosing a life partner. For the Jewish teachers, this is the fortuitous end of a period of dating and usually living with one or more partners before deciding to marry.

For the Arab/Palestinian teachers, it is a process that is carefully watched over, if not directed, by the family. None of the teachers described a strictly arranged marriage, and some met their partners at university, outside the family setting, and dated for a while before deciding to marry; but living with a partner before marriage is not accepted in the Arab community. Their stories reflect the changing nature of courtship in the Arab community.

Marie's narrative illustrates these changes. Marie worked in her father's stationery store for a while after finishing her studies, and customers would regularly inquire as to whether she was interested in meeting someone; she usually refused these offers until finally her father began to tell customers, "She is a salesperson here, not for sale." Marie went on to university, and "met boys looking for a serious relationship and it did not work, it became a matter of routine that I would meet people and it would not work out; my parents didn't have a problem with this, they trusted me and knew that I was looking for the best for myself." Finally, she was set up with someone, something she never thought would succeed, but it did. Like quite a few other stories, this is one of a loving and supportive partnership: "married life is a continuation of the recognition, appreciation and love."

The Jewish teachers often met their partners during their military service or while studying at university. Lily's husband had been her brother's commander in the army; another Jewish teacher met her husband on the kibbutz where she came as an immigrant from the United States. Despite differences across the diverse cultural backgrounds, and one unusually candid story about a difficult marriage, most of the narratives are very positive about the beleaguered institution of marriage and tell the story as one of agency in creating a relationship with the right person; this is the case regardless of how the tellers actually met their partners and what influence their families had in the matter.

The discourse of personal development. In reading the teachers' stories, an individualistic and largely psychological understanding of the life course stands out clearly. It is hardly surprising that a group of educators would take up a psychological perspective: teacher education in Israel as elsewhere is still conceptualized primarily in psychological terms, and programs typically provide a significant load of courses in psychology. The culture of personal development and self-help that is put forward in popular literature (both in local versions and in translations from English into Hebrew and Arabic) no doubt also heavily influences the teachers' writing. Furthermore, while our course was titled, "Narrative Approaches in Multicultural Context," and included some readings that explicitly put forward social and critical perspectives (Bloom, 1996; Marsh, 2002) as well as giving attention to the influence of society and culture on life stories and in the conduct of narrative research, I would have to admit that I did not make special efforts to question the individualistic bias of much that is written about life stories.

However, while an individualistic view of childhood is certainly evident in the psychological literature, this literature hardly suggests that a happy childhood is an everyday occurrence (e.g., Miller, 1980). Statistics show that child poverty in Israel grows from year to year, being more pronounced in the Arab sector, and neglect of children is also found among wealthy families. The happy childhood is hardly the norm, and childhood has undergone radical changes in postmodern times (Aviram, 2010). But for most of the writers, perhaps under the spell of a certain nostalgia, the fact of a happy childhood is not something to marvel at—though many of them do express gratitude to their parents—but simply something to be noted. Whether, and to what extent they might be engaging in a rewriting of the past cannot be determined from their accounts. Most of them do point to at least some negative events from childhood, which suggests that they are seeking to provide an accurate account of the mostly happy childhood as a factual matter rather than an idealized portrayal. Possibly this has something to do with Zionist ideology which—particularly in the kibbutz version—believed that in Israel's new society, children would be both protected and free, growing up in a healthy child-oriented setting where all their needs were met. In time it became apparent that these "children of the dream" (Bettelheim, 1969) merely grew up with a new set of problems, but perhaps the dream of a happy childhood for all has carved a place for itself in the imaginary of many Israelis, even those with no affiliation to Kibbutz ideology.

The assumption that adolescence is, and should be, a period of problems and difficulties does accord with western psychology (e.g., Erikson, 1959/1980), and this assumption seems to be widely accepted by the teachers, including those from the Arab community. The degree of rebellion varics, as docs the degree to which adolescent problems are seen as personal: in fact, most of the stories, like those of Niveen and Andy mentioned above, attribute the difficulties of the teenage years to the need to adapt to society and conform to its dictates. This has a particular emphasis in the stories of those who were immigrants to Israel: Eliana, for example, comments that her parents were much too busy trying to survive in the new country to understand what she was going through as an adolescent. Lisa, on the other hand, seems to suggest that once she learned Hebrew well enough, only her own motivation and determination to do well mattered. Interestingly, Zionist ideology had offered a solution of sorts to the problems of adolescence: from the early years of the state, almost all children belonged to youth groups (sponsored by different political or cultural organizations) which organized after-school and holiday activities for children and adolescents and also provided the opportunity for teenagers to develop leadership skills: everyone belonged, and everyone (in theory at least) had a place. Ella's narrative described her intensive participation in such a youth group. Today, although youth groups still exist in both the Jewish and Arab sectors, their influence is marginal as the global youth culture, mediated by television and internet technologies, has overwhelmingly captured the interest of Israeli youth. Thus the teachers' stories reflect the fact that adolescence has become a time to struggle through on one's own.

The way that the teachers write about family life seems to invoke new myths—that of the happy family and the supportive, loving marriage. Here again the statistics tell a more complex story. Family continues to be of central importance in the life of Israelis of all backgrounds: Israel has higher rates of marriage, lower rates of divorce and a higher birthrate than most industrialized countries. However, the rate of divorce has been increasing steadily, even (albeit more slowly) among Moslem, Druze and Christian couples (Fogel-Bijaoui, 1999). Family violence is reported in the news with disturbing frequency. However, with only one exception, the narratives of the group of 20 students scarcely entertain the possibility of marital discord; they stress the support, communication, mutuality and love that they find with their partners, and those who are not married tell of growing up in stable homes with loving parents. Perhaps the writers are an unusually fortunate group, but whatever their lived experience in reality, it seems that despite the different patterns of experience of the Jewish and Arab teachers, all the teachers maintain a belief that marriage can work and that family life can support the well-being of all its members.

Erdreich (2006), who studied Palestinian women university students in Israel, noted a language which privileges relationships and intimacy, a discourse in which the women narrate themselves as subjects but, in her estimation, thereby also participate in a discourse of bourgeois individualism which reproduces the hegemony of the nation-state. In the context of a clearly psychologised view of interpersonal relationships, courtship and marriage, this point is difficult to contest. However, from reading the teachers' narratives as texts each with its own integrity, not overwritten by theory, a different understanding emerges: each of the stories demonstrates the working out in practice of this discourse of love, intimacy and family. Sometimes the stories glide over the difficulties but they are there: Lily talks about having too little time to spend with her husband. Marie mentions the heavy weight of responsibility for her newborn son and recalls the terror of living in Haifa under rocket attack during the Second Lebanon War in 2006, just weeks after her son was born. The stories show the working out of identities through narrative in ways that are quite similar across the diverse stories. There is no doubt that a belief in the possibility of maintaining love and intimacy is useful in the context of a society where war and violence are ever-present, and the support of family and close relationships are essential in coping with the stresses of the wider context. The teachers, even if they are secular, also retain a strong sense of connection to tradition.

Telling the stories: From origins to outcomes

To understand how the writers manage to produce their narratives, drawing on what sometimes seem like fictions and yet remaining closely tied to the realities of life, I turn now to the question of origins and outcomes: how do the writers understand where they came from and where they are headed, and how does that help their stories 'hang together'? I will first consider how the writers begin their stories, and will then look at how they move on from the origin or starting point of the story.

Beginnings. Almost all the teachers chose to open their autobiographical writing with the basic information one expects to find at the beginning of an autobiography: details about the date and place of their birth, their place in relation to siblings, and information about their parents and other family members. Most provide some reflective commentary on the situation of writing one's autobiography and the difficulties of doing so. A number of stories go back in time to the meeting of the writer's parents and to the hopes and plans entertained by the parents for the birth of their child.

> My parents met on a bus when my father turned to my mother and asked if her name is Lisa (actually, her name is Anna)…at the end of the trip he insisted on accompanying her home, and during the walk to her house they checked out various details about one another, including the fact that both of them were Jewish…my mother tells me that my father courted her in a very charming way, he even read a book on etiquette to make a good impression. As a result of my father's opening line, they named me Lisa…I love the story of my parents' meeting because in the middle of the bustle and rapid pace of everyday life on a crowded bus, a story of true love was created that has accompanied them all their lives.

The opening of Lisa's story highlights the dilemma of the writer of an autobiographical text: in order to tell a story that captures the reader's interest, the autobiographer must begin in a way that is sufficiently familiar to allow the reader to connect but at the same time must offer something that is unique, to warrant the reader's time and attention. For Lisa this is accomplished by her parents' meeting in a completely ordinary setting, but one in which her father won her mother over with a clever pick-up line which eventually gave Lisa her name. As we shall see, all the autobiographies describe the writer's origins in a way that balances the everyday with the special in one way or another: in each story there is something unique but also a sense that the story also has something quite ordinary about it.

Viewing one's life story as following a 'normal' order and having a familiar or 'natural' point of origin seems to be a common format which may have an underlying political motivation: written into the discourse of both the Jewish and the Arab communities in Israel is the need of each community to establish that we are here, we have always been here, and our presence is not open to question; the collective narratives of each side typically do this work in a way that negates the legitimacy of the other side's account (see Gur-Ze'ev, 2001). Here, despite the fact that the stories are personal, and the writers' intentions were also personal, presuming a 'natural' point of origin for one's story reflects the political work accomplished in these autobiographical narratives. How then do the stories continue from these natural points of origin, and what motifs organize the telling?

Andy and Lisa: The sense of vocation. Andy and Lisa are at the beginning of their careers as teachers of ESL, and both are still single; their stories are similar in the way they are put together. Both began by talking about their parents and about the happy homes in which they grew up, homes that seem to anchor their sense of self and allow their stories to be told. Both had some difficult experiences along the way: for Lisa it was the difficulties of being Jewish in the former Soviet Union, while for Andy the "perfect childhood" described above ended rather abruptly at adolescence. After some struggles, however, both Lisa and Andy seem to have found their place in society. And both conclude their stories in an open-ended way by focusing on their hopes and plans for the future. Lisa notes that she chose her profession in part because of several Israeli teachers who served as models for her; she would like to ensure that her students avoid some of the negative experiences she had as a child, and she hopes to educate them to become contributing members of Israeli society. Andy concludes his autobiography by mentioning that he always enjoyed English language and literature and is proud to have attained a degree in English; he is working to attain near-native proficiency in the language so that he can be the best possible teacher for his students. For both, their sense of vocation as teachers (Estola, Erkkila & Syrjälä, 2003) serves to orient their narratives toward the future in a hopeful way.

Niveen: The search for authenticity. Niveen begins her story by saying "I was born to a well-off family as the second daughter, a pretty, active, friendly and intelligent child with a great love of life." In what follows, she provides little direct information about either her family or the place where she grew up but rather writes at length about the development of her personality and about the conflict between her individuality and what society expected of her. Niveen uses quotes from the literature to help explain her personal development, drawing on Krishnamurti and Kierkegaard; east and west, these two writers seem to be equally distant from the setting, and cultures, of the Middle East, suggesting that Niveen wants her story to be seen as universal rather than parochial.

After describing her happy and active childhood and the rude awakening to society's dictates, Niveen tells that she became a serious student, quiet and dedicated to her studies, and also began to lead a more religious life as a Moslem. She completed a college degree, married a man she loves, and gave birth to a child. Along the way, however, she feels that "I lost Niveen who was active, dedicated, strong, interested in others. ...I feel nostalgia for the spontaneity, the activeness, the sense of wonder...it seems that in making efforts to adapt myself to social and educational expectations, I gave up on my authenticity." But as she looks forward, Niveen is hopeful: in writing her life story, she began to see how one event led to another and what the overall process had been; she expects that "I will continue to experience things and to change, but today I feel more mature and able to find my way." Although Goodson (1998) suggests that "The ideal of the authentic self is everywhere in retreat...it simply has been rendered obsolete by history," in the context of dynamic change in the traditional and collectivist Palestinian culture, the notion of the 'authentic self' seems to do the job of holding Niveen's story together, at least in the moment.

Lily: Journey to myself. Lily begins with a reflection on the difficulty of writing her autobiography: obviously she will not tell the whole truth, and it would be better to make it up, create an interesting fantasy. She decides to try to conduct a 'journey to herself.' And then she begins with an opening that seems to surprise her with how much it reveals.

> My childhood seems to me like an ordinary period, an attempt to live a routine life in a small family with a mother who was a single parent and a brother two years younger than me. My father died when I was eight years and seven months old, on the eve of Passover—the Seder night. To this day I remember the phone call from the hospital that instantly cut off the holiday celebration.

This story raises many questions: Lily calls her childhood 'ordinary' and 'routine,' but her language indicates that living a routine life was not a given but "an attempt." She immediately tells of a very extraordinary event in the life of an eight-year-old, her father's death. She was much too young for this to happen: exactly eight years and seven months old, and only the very young count their age in months. The night of the Passover Seder, celebrated by religious and secular Jews alike, is a time for family unity and happiness, not a time for death. Lily remembers little beyond the precise moment of the phone call followed by her mother's rushing to the hospital. In contrast with Eliana's story, Lily and her brother were considered too young to attend the funeral.

I remember that everything returned to normal at a very fast pace: the routine life of studies, friends, school, after-school activities...family visits, birthdays and more...life without a father at home seemed routine, completely normal. My mother who immediately took on both roles tried with all her might to try and fill the lack, and in truth I never felt anything was missing during my childhood...when I grew up I started to feel his absence and to imagine what life would have been like if...

After such a traumatic experience, life does go on, but the decision to carry on as normal, "business as usual," seems to be a typically Israeli way of managing after a tragedy. How one copes under such circumstances is not a matter that Lily questions directly. However, her story seems to be exploring different ways of conducting 'normal' life. She was fascinated by the small development town where she did her army service; she eagerly absorbed impressions during her travels in South America. Today she contrasts the busy, convivial life of the working-class suburb where she grew up to the pastoral quiet of her life in the north of Israel where she lives with her husband. The north always seemed to Lily green and peaceful, yet Lily comments that she enjoyed the friendliness of the neighborhood where she grew up; she easily slips back into the habits of her childhood when she goes to visit there— calling across to a neighbor from the balcony, being involved in other people's lives. She now lives with her husband in an urban setting where Lily hardly knows her neighbours. Looking to the future, Lily hopes to live one day in a "moshav" (a small rural community) in the Galilee. This imagined future is quite different from the past, and yet perhaps it also functions as a kind of return to the peaceful, simple childhood that Lily remembers (or perhaps only imagines) before her father died.

Ella: The parachute jump. Ella's story begins with the words, "At 13 I parachuted for the first time." Parachute jumping is not something one does by chance, not a natural event that just happens, yet the matter of fact way that Ella tells about her desire to jump, to touch the sky, makes of this almost the natural point of origin that characterizes many of the other stories. Ella grew up on a moshav, the youngest child with two older brothers. One wonders if her brothers were involved in challenging sports, if she sought to emulate them; she doesn't reflect on this, telling a story in the first person emphasizing her own agency. Jumping is something she wanted as a child, and it has become a way of life: not just as a sport that she continues to practice, even competing at one stage, but as an attitude. A few years after her first jump she jumped in another sense: deciding she was bored at school and wanted a change, she transferred to a democratic school. She took on a leadership role in a youth movement, gaining early experience of being a mentor for others. In her army service she found herself posted to the military radio station where she hosted a news program, a job she felt was perfect for her: "action, phone calls, living with your hand on the pulse. ..." After the army she moved to the big city (Tel Aviv) and worked in commercial television, but at the same time she began studying in a new teacher education program for teachers in democratic schools. Towards the end of her studies, "a new dream began to take shape: to set up a democratic school. To learn more before giving it a try, I signed up for an MA program." Ella also moved back to live on the moshav, in the house that had been her grandparents'. This is a story of quick decisions and dramatic changes, but it is intertwined with a softer strand as well: Ella tells about learning to read sitting on her grandfather's lap as he read the newspaper and later accompanying him in his decline due to Alzheimer's. She mentions that "the year is divided...according to the fruits that ripen, each in its time: fall belongs to the guavas, and winter to the oranges." She concludes by saying that the democratic school movement and parachute jumping together have made her the person that she is today, someone who is assertive and serious but also a dreamer who tries to make her dreams come true.

Marie: I am from Iqrit. Marie's autobiography begins simply: "I was born in Haifa in July 1980." She goes on to talk about her attachment to her childhood home, a small apartment where she shared a room with her sister and brothers. Marie stresses that her parents "worked hard and did not earn much" but always managed to provide their children with what they needed. Only in a conversation at the end of the course, when we were discussing "what is not told" in a life story, did Marie volunteer, almost by accident, an additional piece of crucial information: her family hailed originally from the village of Iqrit in the Galilee, an Arab village of about 500 residents that was evacuated in November of 1948 by the Israeli army along with a neighbouring village, Bir'am. The residents of both villages were told that they would be able to return after the hostilities ceased, and they left their homes almost intact; subsequently the military refused to allow them to return and destroyed most of the buildings. A petition to the Israeli High Court in 1951 was successful, but the army repeatedly blocked the return. Marie's father was only 5 years old at the time, but the family continues to identify with the village of his birth. Marie talked about participating as a child in visits to the site of the village, in picnics, demonstrations and other activities; the former residents of this village, and their descendants, are in a sense a part of her family, and of her identity, to the extent that she says "Actually, I am from Iqrit."[2] Rereading Marie's story after hearing this 'postscript' in class, I began to notice in her narrative a recurring theme of confronting injustice. First, Marie described her parents as working very hard and earning little, implying that something in the situation is not right. Later, she recounts an episode from the eighth grade: in her French class, Marie wrote a composition which was entered in a competition, the winner of which would win a trip to France. Marie was named a finalist along with two other girls, one of them the daughter of a judge. ("What can one say about the daughter of a judge who contributes financially to a private school run by nuns?") At first, the third girl was declared the winner; the next day, the girls were informed that a mistake had been made. The winner was in fact the judge's daughter, but since the other girl had already been notified of her good fortune, both girls would be sent to France. The teacher promised Marie that she would go to France the following year; "I not only felt, but saw and heard, the falseness in her words."

For Marie this was one more instance of ongoing discrimination against the children of poor families in the school; she felt sorry for the rich kids because "only the teachers liked them." Another episode of injustice marked Marie's final year of high school. It was time for the long-awaited graduation ceremony, and Marie had a beautiful new white blouse to wear with elegant black slacks and high-heeled sandals. The class assembled on the school steps, "very excited, laughing, shouting, and waiting" for the photographer to take their picture on their last day together. Marie lifted her arms to hug two of her friends, when she felt someone pulling her blouse down. It was the school principal, a nun whom everyone feared; she told Marie in English that she could not go on stage to receive her diploma in the blouse she was wearing because if she lifted her arms her stomach would be exposed. Marie tried to show that the blouse was perfectly modest, but to no avail; she was forced to change into a borrowed blouse. On stage when she received her diploma the principal whispered "Excuse me," but Marie was not to be consoled until the end of the day, after a family celebration she hardly remembers, when her father suggested she write a letter to the principal telling her exactly what she thought and felt. Some years later, as a newly qualified teacher, Marie returned to the school from which she had graduated, and one day she found herself alone with the principal in the photocopy room. The principal asked if she remembered "their fight" and told her that only after receiving Marie's letter had she realized how much she hurt her; the principal had not forgiven herself for offending one of the best pupils in the school.

These episodes show Marie paying close attention to moral issues: she "sees, hears and feels it" when something is not right. There have been a number of experiences of unfairness and injustice in her life, some larger and some minor; sometimes amends are made and sometimes not. The episodes are significant points that move her narrative forward, but Marie's story begins and ends with family: at the close of the story she describes herself preparing for her classes while her infant son sleeps. She sums up her life in the present by saying: "it's not easy, but it's fun, it's beautiful, it's love, it's warmth, and it is what it is."

Eliana: At a crossroads. Eliana's story seems to deconstruct its origin even as she tells her story in the most 'natural' way possible.

> I was born in a small town in a far-off country that no longer exists. The place is there, of course, but the 'bosses' were replaced, the name changed, the house destroyed, and in its place high-rises were built—everything changed. In 1968, at the end of the mythical 60s, in one of the republics of the Soviet Union…it's not clear how in the heyday of the Iron Curtain, and from where, they found my name.…It's a familiar and even common name in other parts of the world, which were then closed to my parents—Italy, Argentina, perhaps Spain. I asked many times, but they could never explain to me how they chose the name. They just told me that for some reason they were supposed to give me a certain name…and this name (starting with the same letter) was prettier.

This story apparently refers to the European Jewish custom of naming children after a deceased relative, as a way of keeping alive the person's memory; but if indeed this was the reason, her parents followed the custom without being able to explain it to their daughter. The story seems to constantly question itself in the telling: Eliana indicates the point of origin of her life very clearly in both time and space but then adds that nothing is left and the place has changed completely. The time—1968—now seems lost too, no longer a specific year but "the mythical 60s"; all has disappeared in the mists of cultural and political upheaval. The child is given a name that sounds and feels like it belongs elsewhere. Eliana later explains that her parents had wanted to immigrate to Israel but were held back by the objections of her mother's parents; when she was 10 both grandparents died within a short time, and the family was able to leave. Eliana is an uncommon Hebrew name but sounds like it might belong in the Mediterranean: perhaps this name expressed the parents' desire to be in another place in a way that would have been acceptable in the Soviet Union at that time, whereas a name that was obviously Jewish or Hebrew might have caused difficulties.

Later in her story Eliana tells about further moves, with her family to a different town in Israel (where she had to adapt once again), then leaving her family home, and later moving with her husband to a distant city where he found work. Finally, a few years ago they returned to Haifa, "back to my family and friends and the city I love." But in her inner life Eliana seems still to be searching, and she says that "today…I stand at a crossroads in many respects. The teachers' strike last year opened my eyes to the lowly status of the teacher in our society, and to the indifference of government." There is in this story a sense of a 'paradise lost,' always beyond reach; finding her place seems to be an ongoing quest for Eliana, but she goes about the search with increasing confidence: "I believe that a period of big changes and new beginnings is ahead of me. I feel that I've changed a lot over the years. Today I look with relative calm at the various events, I'm enjoying my studies and hope for good things in the future."

While Eliana and Marie tell very different stories, each one is in some way a story of 'displacement'. Marie grew up in a very stable setting to a family that had experienced displacement long before she was born, but the loss of the family's home and village continues to shape Marie's life even while she is making a new home with her husband and son. Eliana experienced the displacement of immigration and seems to be continuing to live out the immigrant's search for belonging. Taking a cue from these stories, the other narratives can also be read as involving various forms of displacement and of the search for place and belonging. Lisa, like Eliana, was also an immigrant to Israel who had to make her place in the new country. Andy grew up in a stable family and in a town where his family has long roots but has found it difficult to make his peace with the traditional Arab culture; his town has also been a site for the enactment of political dislocations (Rabinowitz, 1997; Abdo, 2002). Niveen is still engaged in a search for her authentic self. Lily's early loss of a parent shapes a dynamic narrative as she too looks for the right place to make her life. Ella returned to live in her childhood home, giving up what seemed an exciting life in the big city working in the communication industry to find her place in education; she had just become a teacher in a democratic school and had her sights on becoming a principal, and eventually on setting up a new school. These stories are not directly representative of all the teachers' stories, but it could be said that most Israelis have in their background a story of internal or external displacement. The search for place, for a sense of home and peace, for justice, for belonging and comfort—all are familiar themes. Although they share a certain preoccupation with displacement, the narratives reflect diverse ways of beginning, or of conceiving of one's origins, as well as different ways of putting together a story that connects beginning and end, albeit imperfectly. The stories of Andy, Lisa and Ella seem to be at peace with their origins, pointing to the future. Lily's story and Eliana's narrative both embody an ongoing process of searching. In Marie's account there is a loss of home that was not in fact narrated in writing, and while she still seems to be concerned with putting things right, Marie's story ends with a statement that is firmly grounded in the here and now. The narratives illustrate the creativity of the teachers in storying their lives in useful and productive ways. I now turn to some reflections on what might be learned from going beyond these narratives.

Place and displacement, change and continuity

After exploring the teachers' narratives in depth, I find it significant that teachers from such diverse cultural backgrounds, with not just different but competing versions of history, tell stories in which there are so many 'family resemblances.' Memories of home in diverse settings, longings for family warmth, the joy of bringing children into the world, the agony of fear for their safety, the sense of purpose and vocation of teachers, the love of learning, the desire for justice, the sadness at the loss of loved ones...all the teachers' narratives play with these elements (hence their inevitable coloring of nostalgia). The narratives also follow similar storylines, all more or less invoking a psychological view of the life course and of personal development. The diversity of cultural background and conflicting political views notwithstanding, as individuals the teachers understand their lives in similar ways.

There are many postmodern influences on life in Israel (rapid technological change, globalization of the economy and so on), and each of the narratives can easily be seen in terms of Giddens' (1991) notion of a postmodern reflexive project of the self': one clearly sees the work of the narrator in shaping her life story, confronting a range of options offered by society. The Palestinian women teachers in particular have access to many possibilities not available to their mothers' generation—study, work outside the home, equality in family decision-making. The Jewish teachers also speak about the options of travel and have more freedom in choosing a career and deciding where to live. All the life stories are characterized by a certain openness; none reads as though the writer is living out a preordained sequence of events. According to Giddens (1991, 46), "The idea of the "life cycle"... makes very little sense once the connections between the individual life and the interchange of the generations have been broken." However, despite their postmodern characteristics, the stories of these Israeli teachers do remain very strongly connected to the "interchange of the generations." It seems likely that the different communities' sense of history, on the one hand, and the fact of living under constant threat of war and violence on the other, may be what anchor the teachers' lives and their stories in the sequence of generations. Jewish Israelis remain committed to remembering the Holocaust, while for Palestinian Israelis remembering the 'Nakba' (catastrophe) of 1948 is tied to the ongoing struggle for Palestinian statehood. These existential commitments to preserve the memory of one's community and work for its future, although they are hardly expressed directly in the stories, can still be detected as part of the taken for granted assumptions behind the stories; and they seem to keep at bay some of the pressures of the postmodern temper.

Rogoff (2000) calls for paying close attention to the contradictions and conflicting desires that produce, mark, distort, confuse or hide behind most understandings, both the everyday kind and the theoretical formulations, of identity in the Israeli as well as other contexts. In the narratives presented here, we find many layers of contradiction: The fondly remembered home in the former Soviet Union was also a place where one was humiliated for being Jewish. The school where one acquired a love of learning discriminated against poorer students. The society that invests in and supports women's learning still expects them to be good wives and mothers first of all, with well-disciplined bodies. The most obvious contradiction, perhaps, is that of the silence in most of the stories about the political situation which shapes all of life in Israel and the region. However, in the immediacy of their accounts, the concrete detail that describes precisely the taste of one's favorite child-hood dish, there is always something that goes beyond nostalgia, calling things into question. The narratives are not encapsulated accounts of the past but open-ended 'works in progress' which make visible the task of shaping useful, worthwhile and even hopeful lives under conditions of periodic vio-lence, unfairly distributed resources, unpredictable discrimination and rapid cultural and global change.

Much of this work is, as always, women's work, struggling for empow-erment while trying not to burn dinner. The teachers' autobiographical narra-tives do not have the status of 'critical personal narrative' (Burdell & Swadener, 1999), but they are open to critical reading, thus contributing to a critical perspective on the lives and work of Israeli teachers. And in practice, as the teachers read one another's life stories and learn more through inter-views, something more often comes about. In the course reported here, for example, two students—Palestinian Israeli women—decided to do an inter-view study with an elderly couple who are neighbours in Haifa of one of the students; the couple is Jewish, and both are survivors of the Holocaust. The curiosity that is born from writing one's own autobiography and reading those of one's colleagues should not be underestimated nor should the com-passion.

Notes

1. As Al-Haj (1995) explains, the division according to language was established in the early years of the state according to the preference of both the Jewish and the Arab com-munities, but has given rise to persisting inequalities in educational provision, although the situation has improved since Al-Haj's work almost 20 years ago. In the Arab sector, many of the schools are semi-private schools run by various Christian denominations but open to students from all religions. Small numbers of Arab students study in the Jewish

school system, and there is also a recent movement for bilingual schooling which has established a half-dozen schools attended by equal numbers of Jewish and Arab students. See Kalekin-Fishman (2004) for a comprehensive and penetrating account of the education of minorities and immigrants in Israel.

2.   The legal case of Iqrit and the neighboring village of Bir'am remain unresolved even after 60 years. The residents refused compensation and have insisted on their 'right of return' to the village. Although the High Court ruled in 1951 in favour of the residents, in practice they were not allowed to implement this ruling. In 2003, a renewed petition to the High Court was turned down; this time, during the Second Intifada, the court ruled that the return of the residents would constitute a problematic precedent; the court even suggested that if the political situation changes the petition of the residents of Iqrit might be received differently in the future.

CHAPTER 5

Retrieving Memory, Shaping Teachers: Stories of Teacher Educators

Introduction

> The thing that made me very enthusiastic about teacher education is just this, some-
> thing I like to quote that Dylan Thomas wrote to Caitlyn. He wrote her, "Thank God
> writing poetry gets more and more difficult."…thank God teaching gets more and
> more difficult, I never found it possible to use the notes from last year, to do the
> same thing this year, I never found a formula for anything. (Devorah, 2nd interview,
> March 2012)

Having been engaged in teacher education for most of my working life, I was moved on hearing the quote from Dylan Thomas that Devorah brings to describe her experience as a teacher educator. Although I have had some wonderful experiences working as a teacher educator and learned a great deal about myself and something about teaching, I never felt confident about knowing "how to do it." Yet despite my own questions and the discomfort that sometimes accompanied the questioning, I always appreciated the fact that teaching teachers was interesting, puzzling and challenging work (see also Clandinin, 1995).

In the policy environment, however, the puzzling and problematic nature of teacher education is not typically viewed with such approval. The education of teachers has been widely critiqued and found wanting (see, for example, Fullan et al., 1998) as has the research on teacher education (e.g., Wideen et al., 1998). One of the main directions proposed for the advancement of teacher education has been the establishment of a knowledge base for the teaching profession (Murray, 1995; Raths & McAninich, 1999; Shulman, 1987). While still being developed (e.g., Darling-Hammond & Bransford, 2005), the nature and purpose of such a knowledge base remain a contentious issue: increasingly, there is discussion about how to build the knowledge base of teaching in a way that is not divorced from teachers' experience and understandings (Cochran-Smith & Zeichner, 2005; Hiebert et al., 2002). Cochran-Smith (2003, 25) emphasizes the importance of taking an inquiry stance and "conceptualizing the education of teacher educators as a process of continual and systematic inquiry wherein participants question their own and others' assumptions and construct local as well as public knowledge appropriate to the changing contexts in which they work."

Sarason (1982) pointed out that while teachers are expected to foster an interest in and excitement for learning in their pupils, schools typically are not places where teachers find opportunities to explore their own interests and to keep alive their own passion for learning. For teacher educators, it would seem, the situation is a little different: according to Asaf et al. (2008), who studied teacher educators working in teachers' colleges in Israel, "It is possible that the college, the work environment to which the teachers belong at this stage, enables and encourages reflective processes, and provides, as characterized in the literature, a knowing environment, as opposed to the school environment, which is characterized in the literature as a doing environment." However, the "inquiry stance" advocated by Cochran-Smith should not be reduced to "reflective processes" alone, and it is still important to question whether the universities and colleges where teacher educators work indeed provide the opportunity to continue to learn and grow and in what ways.

These concerns were addressed by Weber (1990) in one of the first narrative/biographical studies focussed on teacher educators. She conducted repeated interviews with two experienced teacher educators, inviting them to tell "the stories within the stories" of their lives and engaging in a dialectic process of analysis and interpretation in order to understand the meaning that events had for them, seeking thereby to learn more about the process and structure of their professional knowledge. She concluded that her participants viewed teacher education as "a culturally generative mode of being, a primary way of seeking meaning and confirmation in their own lives by creating or protecting a legacy of pedagogical thought, theory, and action." Both teacher educators spoke about their deep commitment to teaching and to learning, and they seemed to entertain the hope "of indirectly touching the lives of children by influencing the practice of future teachers, thereby making schools better places for children to be." (Weber, 1990, 156)

Weber pointed out the lack of studies focused on the lives and experience of teacher educators up to the time of her work, published in 1990. Since that time, some studies of the experience of teacher educators have been carried out (e.g., Acker, 1997; Cooper et al., 1999; Ducharme, 1993; Ducharme &

Ducharme, 1996). Many teacher educators have taken up the challenge of becoming researchers of their own practice: the field of self study of teaching and teacher-education has burgeoned, generally focused on a deeper under-standing of teacher education practice itself (see Kosnik et al., 2006; Loughran et al., 2004) but also examining the personal experience of being a teacher educator (Clandinin, 1995; Craig, 2010; Vagle, 2011), questions of teacher educator identity (Lunenberg & Hamilton, 2008), and teacher educa-tors' knowledge and professional development through writing (Shteiman et al., 2013). This work provides much-needed portrayal and fine-grained analysis of the practices of teacher education from the point of view of prac-titioners (e.g., C. Simon, 2005; Smith, 2009). In some ways, however, We-ber's call for a better understanding of the lives of teacher educators has still not been sufficiently addressed. Asaf et al. (2008), for example, hold that the professional development and career stages of teacher educators have not been studied extensively. And while the self-study literature is rich and illu-minating, the concern with developing the pedagogy of teacher education, its programs and curricula, seems to privilege reflection on professional prac-tice, giving less attention to the personal experience of teacher educators as they live out their pedagogy within the institutions where teacher education takes place (see Loughran, 2011; Turley, 2005; Zeichner, 2005). Thus, the present chapter seeks to enrich our understanding of the lives and work of teacher educators, continuing Weber's exploration through examination of the life stories of a group of women educators in the specific context of teacher education in Israel.

Methodology

The process of inquiry in this chapter is similar to that described in Chapter 4, although the setting and prompt for the inquiry were not a specific course but rather my ongoing work in a faculty of education engaged in teacher education among other tasks. My questioning of the lives of people who teach teachers began some years ago when I interviewed a colleague, the late Lia Kremer (who had herself studied the experience of teacher educators: see Tillema & Kremer-Hayon, 2005). At the time I did not have a specific research question in mind; my request grew out of simple curiosity and interest in the life story of a valued colleague. Unfortunately, the computer I was using crashed, and the transcript of what I recall as a fascinating conversation was lost.

In 2005, I began a research project with the title "Memory and Pedagogy"[1] to study the intersections of life story and teaching in a multicultural society; one part of that study involved setting up a circle of women educators who met monthly to tell our stories and discuss our lives in the complicated context of Israeli society. (The same study also followed the processes of writing and sharing personal stories by pre-service teachers; a sampling appeared in Chapter 3, and the process will be highlighted in Chapter 7.) At each meeting of the women's group, one member told her life story in a format of her choosing; the sessions were recorded and transcribed. These meetings have been written about and the development of the group analyzed (see Elbaz-Luwisch et al., 2008; Simon & Elbaz-Luwisch, 2010), but the life stories told by group members were not studied in depth. The members of the original group (eleven, including myself) were diverse in many respects: age and years of experience, roles in the school system (teachers, mentors of teachers, teacher educators), cultural and religious background. The label "women educators" reflected the desire to bypass traditional hierarchies of position and power and to shape a diverse group interested in reflecting together on our work, and in this I believe we succeeded. Although at some time most of the group members had worked in various kinds of mentoring relationships vis-à-vis other teachers, I focus here on the stories of four group members who were involved, full or part time, in formal teacher education during the life of the project.

In addition to these stories which were told in a group setting and transcribed, I also conducted individual in-depth "interviews-as-conversation" with two colleagues, emeritae who had been deeply involved in teacher education at the university level, as well as in various projects focused on the multicultural nature of Israeli society. I reflected at length as to whether my own story should be included here, particularly as it inevitably colors my understanding of the stories of my colleagues. In fact the story I told in the women's group said very little about my work in teacher education, perhaps because the group members already knew about it, and several were involved in the project in which pre-service teachers were engaging with stories. I decided to leave my own story in the background in order to focus more clearly on the stories of the others.

As Hamilton et al. (2008) have demonstrated, diverse methodologies may be called for to shed light on teacher educators' lives and practice. In interpreting the life stories here, as in Chapter 4, I draw on diverse modes of narrative analysis and pay attention to time, place, and to the relationship of the teller to others in her setting and to herself. The process of interpretation is holistic and draws attention to the way the stories are told and to salient themes they bring forward, foregrounding the personal while also paying attention to the ways that culture, history and politics shape the narratives (Goodson, 1992), providing a critical distance from which to read.

The teacher educators whose stories feature in this chapter are Iman Awadieh, Hiam Nasseraldin, Fany Shimoni and Chava Simon (members of the women's group, each of whom had also been my students at some stage of their graduate studies), and my colleagues Rachel Hertz-Lazarowitz and Devorah Kalekin-Fishman. I originally wrote a brief sentence for each participant, giving the usual demographic details: age, place of birth, area of study and employment. However, a request by one of the women to make corrections in this description led me to reconsider the practice and to see its reductive nature. I decided to forego the typical flat descriptions and to present the women as far as possible in their own words in the sections that follow.

The women's stories were told in two different settings which undoubtedly had some impact on the stories told. The women's circle had been formed deliberately as a multicultural group; the stories told there were very personal, usually beginning by situating the teller in terms of her family and community and only later referring to her work. These stories were told informally, often accompanied by photographs and objects brought by teller, with questions and comments from the group throughout; the recording and transcription reveal these accounts to be less orderly and linear than is the case for the stories told in interviews. In the interviews, my opening question to both Devorah and Rachel was much the same: I asked them to tell about their involvement in teacher education and multiculturalism and to trace the sources of this work in their lives. Rachel began by telling me about the various programs and courses in which she had been involved at the university and only later, at my request, went back to talk about her early life and her family of origin. Devorah on the other hand began by asking "Where should I begin, with childhood? My mother's pregnancy?" She then told her story in largely chronological fashion beginning with childhood, reflecting on her parents' history and tracing her education and the different stages of her working and family life. Two of the women's group members, Iman and Hiam, also told chronologically organized stories, while Fany ordered her story around important people in her life; Chava's story was non-linear as she spoke about her recently completed doctoral research and its meaning in her life. Despite these marked differences in organization and sequencing, the stories told by all six women were varied and rich in detail, highlighting many different themes; all of them spoke about where they came from, their families of origin and communities, about spouses and children, about their education and work. Reflections on education and teaching, and on the relations of research and practice, came up in many of the stories. I focus here on four central topics that were important to all the tellers as well as to my own inquiry in this book: origins and place; how purposes are played out in teaching and teacher education; being the first generation in one's family to attain university education; and the diverse interactions of research and practice in their lives.

Origins and place

Devorah comments, "I came from New York and was very conscious of that; to grow up in New York is a gift for your whole life—it was so rich, there was no limit to how rich it was." The richness of the city was defined by the cultural and educational opportunities it provided for Devorah, who was encouraged by her teachers to take the entrance exams for a prestigious high school where she had excellent teachers and was well prepared for university. She also studied music, as her mother was able to buy a piano for a minimal sum; these advantages contrasted sharply with the deprivations of the home in which she grew up. Her parents had emigrated to the U.S. from Ukraine, although in response to my insistent questions (as my mother's family had come from the same area), Devorah told me with a laugh, "I never was interested in where they came from. As a true-blue American I didn't want to hear any stories." Devorah feels that her parents "struggled all their lives" but, like many immigrants, they were ambitious both for themselves and for their children, despite the fact that "all they had was night school for learning English. And they spent their lives not really belonging." Devorah refers to her own "not belonging": "I had polio when I was 2, and I grew up not belonging." As a child Devorah was unable to do many of the things other children did yet "grew up in denial": she took part in folk dancing in the youth movement and learned to put aside her difference. However, "what all this comes down to is a sensitivity to the fact that there are people who are out of place." Later in her story Devorah speaks about living in Jerusalem in 1949 and the privations and opportunities of the early years of the state; about her years on a kibbutz; about the town of Kiryat Shmona, where she became deeply engaged in the teaching of English to children of immigrants, and about Haifa where the family moved in the 1960s partly so that she could pursue graduate studies. All of these places are described mainly in terms of the human and cultural landscape they provided for Devorah and relationships that she formed.

Chava who was born in Jerusalem says nothing about her own childhood there but tells at length about her father, whose own father died when he was young. His mother kept the girls at home but, presumably for economic reasons, sent her two boys to an orphanage, where he grew up in difficult conditions, often coming home covered in bruises. But another family story told how her father had come home to find his sister exhausted from sewing; he sent her to bed and stayed up all night to finish the work and brought it to her employer in the morning. Chava mentions that when her daughter was seven, they took her to Jerusalem, and "after we had seen the Jewish Quarter of the Old City, where my father was born, we went to the Tower of David…and there's a spot there that I had never visited before, where the First President of the State used to sit and study Kabbalah at night, echoing my mother's stories about my grandfather who studied Kabbalah at night with the Chief Rabbi…there's something special about Jerusalem, its spirituality."

Rachel tells about growing up in Haifa in the years prior to 1948:

> When I was born we were tenants to an Arab landlord in a mixed neighborhood, in what to this day I think is one of the most beautiful architectural projects in Haifa, although over the years it has become a slum. Living with the Arabs, up to 1948, there were pools with fountains—lions spouting water from their mouths, jasmine blooming in every corner, and wonderful parquet floors, and railings that had been

brought from Spain. And when the Arabs left in 1948...everything became neglected and dilapidated...so I come from a place where the term "Arab" refers to a
beautiful setting, to wonderful celebrations, and all my childhood, after they left, we
tried to maintain the gardens so that they would continue to bloom, and I organized
the children to do that, for years.

She adds, "I still have an emotional connection to the Haifa of that time,
which had Arabs, and Oriental Jews, and the British, all living there...at one
point my grandfather and grandmother had a shop in the Talpiot Market, so
it's clear that I feel good there, and I still go to the stores where my grandmother shopped." She adds that she agrees with the claim that the "Nakbah"
(catastrophe) of the Arabs in 1948 is also the "nakbah" of the Jews: "I have
my own 'nakbah', because the magical garden, and the wonderful house, and
all that beauty, have been lost...and it doesn't matter that I saw the first boy
killed by an Arab sniper in 1948 in the yard of our house. We lived right on
the seam between the Jewish and Arab parts of Haifa." Rachel adds that although her parents were religious, they lived in a mixed neighborhood where
good relations prevailed among neighbors regardless of religious beliefs or
lifestyle. As a pupil, Rachel found it difficult to accept authority without
questioning; eventually she gave up religious observance and married a man
who, she suggests "has a different religion, the religion of the Left and of the
socialist youth movement." Rachel lives out a complicated dance within an
extended family most of whose members remain orthodox, and with whom
she takes care to maintain close connections and a sense of family unity.

Fany was born in Chile and recalls growing up near the home of her maternal grandparents which had "a long corridor linking several rooms and we
used to play hide-and-seek there, running from room to room." In 1970,
Fany's parents decided to immigrate to Israel; at first the grandparents stayed
behind, saying they were too old to start over in a new country, but within a
few months they were overcome by loneliness and also immigrated. The difficult political situation in Chile at the time is mentioned in passing as part of
the background to the family's leaving. In Israel the economic situation was
not easy: "I remember my mother leaving for work at 5 a.m., they left us an
alarm clock and sandwiches to take to school." Fany's parents were very sensitive to the needs of their children and managed to give them whatever they
could despite economic struggles; she still remembers the much-wished-for

bicycle that she received as a present on her 12th birthday. The family is a close one, and Fany makes an effort to keep it that way, inviting the extended family to holiday and birthday gatherings; the closeness is not something she takes for granted, rather it is something to work at, "a training for the soul" to maintain lively connections with all the in-laws and with more distant family in Chile.

Iman comes from an Arab city in the lower Galilee where her family is well known. She had a sheltered childhood, but in the 7th grade began attending a private school in Haifa run by a Christian order of nuns (affiliated with the elementary school she had attended). She describes this as the point when she started coming out of a bubble, and her mother claims that "since then, you do whatever you want." Iman has three sisters and parents who have always given her a great deal, supported her and made it possible for her to live an independent life that is not typical for her community. Her story emphasizes her personal development and comes to focus on place only when she talks about taking part in a prestigious program for educational leaders from the periphery. Each member of the group took the participants on a tour of her own setting, and for Iman it was important to take the group to visit the Church where she had been introduced to prayer and a form of meditation, and to the community center where she has been active in organizing varied cultural opportunities.

Hiam grew up in the Druze community, where her father is a respected religious leader. Her story centers on the customs and practices of the community which, for women, was a sheltering and closed space; she tells of the gradual process by which she came to quietly challenge and go beyond it. Higher education for women was not considered acceptable, especially for the daughters of a religious family. As a child Hiam had wanted "to study computer engineering at the Technion" like her older brother, but this was not possible at the time. Attending a teachers' college in the city, for which a precedent was set by Hiam's older sister, was possible only because her father drove her there and back. As a young woman Hiam had two main goals, besides marriage: to study for a Masters' degree and a driver's license, but "both were impossible as long as I was not married...I myself understood that the social pressure on my parents, especially from religious leaders, would be too great." After she married, with her husband's support, Hiam learned to drive and began graduate study at the university, which she describes as an "empowering experience" especially because she had "dreamed of it and waited for it for so long."

All the tellers mention the places where they were born and grew up with some fondness, and they intertwine stories of family with stories of place. The stories of Rachel, Devorah and Chava particularly emphasize what is special and unique about the places where they were born. It might almost be said that New York, Jerusalem and Haifa are characters in their stories, the source of important values and perspectives that continue to mark their lives even though Rachel is the only one of the three who still lives in the city where she was born. Fany talks about the warmth of South American culture as a defining characteristic in her life, but it is clearly her family, rather than the country or any particular city which constitutes her origin. The stories of both Iman and Hiam relate to place in a more indirect and perhaps ambivalent way. Both of them are close to their families and very much a part of their communities, yet each of these women in her own fashion has carved out a life that is oppositional in some ways, to the norms and traditions of their communities of origin, to family expectations and sometimes to the women's current place within the educational system. This opposition is reflected in the ways that the tellers speak about their work and about their purposes as educators, to which I now turn.

Purpose in teaching

As already mentioned, the women's stories were told in two different settings, and as a result the women educators' stories centered on the personal, while references to their work were more anecdotal, whereas both Rachel and Devorah spoke directly about their involvement in teacher education (partly but not only in response to my questions). However, in all the stories there are statements about the teller's views on and sense of purpose in teaching which follow, usually quite clearly, from the personal story.

It's also interesting to note that half of the women came to teaching, and to teacher education without formal training. Devorah came to Israel in 1949 when the state educational system was just being reorganized; she met other recent arrivals who were attending a three-month teacher training course in Jerusalem but at that time she was uninterested in becoming a teacher. Later she had to chart her own path, going to talk with experienced teachers who gave her the benefit of their experience; eventually, she felt that her lack of training was an advantage: "I had no teacher education, so nobody got to me in time, I guess, to make me toe the line." Chava was a teacher of special education, completed a master's degree abroad and became a teacher in a college; at the time she told her story she was participating in a course for teacher educators which would grant her, finally, the teaching diploma she had never had need of and which she now required only for pension purposes. Iman studied French and Education for her B.A. and was hired as a French teacher immediately on graduation, as French teachers were in short supply. All three women found it important to mention their lack of teacher training, while the other women did not speak at all about their experience of teacher education. Thus it seems fair to assume that their perspectives on teaching and on teacher education were formed largely from early experience, the "apprenticeship of observation" and on the job.

Fany's story begins with a recent experience of giving feedback to a student teacher whose work had not gone well: "I told myself, I have two possibilities here, either to crush her or to help her grow. I hope that, from her difficulty, she will go forward." This anecdote sets up a polarity which underlies and shapes the story: Fany speaks at length about family members as well as good friends who gave her support and encouragement but also highlights negative events which she remembers because they helped her to grow. One such event concerned a teacher who "hopefully did not destroy too many children along the way": Fany and her family, recently arrived in Israel, had just moved to a new town, and she was "an 11-year-old girl who knows Hebrew but still has some difficulties." The teacher said Fany's name was not a Hebrew name and must be changed (a not uncommon practice in line with the "melting pot" policies of the early years of the State). Fany "stood in front of her and said, 'My mother called me Fany, that's my name and you have no right to change me.'" In the second event, Fany worked in a kindergarten where one class had to be closed because of lowered enrolment; Fany did not want to move to another location, but had no choice because the other teacher had seniority. However, as a result of the move she had more opportunities to take initiative and advance in her work. These negative events resonate with the opening anecdote about the student teacher: one en-

counters difficulties, is empowered by dealing with them and grows professionally as a result. Fany chose to conduct research for her Masters' thesis
(Shimoni, 2004) in a college where she was hoping to work eventually, and
she considers herself lucky that a position opened up there at the right time.
She comments that she enjoys her work, particularly when she teaches students she knows well. It is this combination of closeness, support and family-
like solidarity, combined with a metaphoric kick in the pants when needed,
that Fany wishes to provide for the pre-service teachers with whom she
works.

Chava has worked for many years as a teacher educator in the field of
special education; the completion of her doctoral dissertation (C. Simon,
2005) led her to new reflections on her work. The participants in her study
were teacher educators like herself, "pedagogical counsellors" (a unique
function in Israeli colleges of teacher education) who accompany student
teachers throughout their studies and particularly in their practicum place-
ments. In her study Chava found that all the teacher educators she interviewed saw parenting as a central aspect of their work: "as soon as you are
involved in education, all of them are your children." The male participants
saw fathering as particularly important and raised the themes of care and
"consolation" (Ricoeur, 1969), emphasizing it as a powerful but often tacit
quality in adult fathering. In Chava's estimation these are sensitive topics
and to speak of them openly is "like putting your hand in the fire." She
speaks with feeling about her father, who did not receive much care and attention from his own parents yet was able to give love and care to his sister,
his mother, and his own children as well as offer support to the extended
family. She says she was a rebellious teenager and was emotionally rather
independent, but over the years she came to appreciate the devoted and loving quality of the parenting she received. Chava mentions having two deep
and meaningful conversations with her father, the first one at age 14 and
again when she was 20, becoming deeply aware of her father as an orphaned
child and recognizing the importance of fathering through the imprint of its
absence or loss. From living with her own parents, and from the stories of
her research participants, Chava concludes that the centrality of the complex
theme of adult parenting (fathering as well as mothering) is applicable and

relevant to the pedagogical process. This is the main message she wishes to bring to teacher education.

Iman has been a teacher of French, and has worked in a regional teacher development center and as a researcher in a research institute. At the time she told her story she had been teaching in a college program for the retraining of academics. This work brought her up against a number of difficulties. First, the students are in their first year of studying education, and she feels it is too soon for them to be taking her course, the topic of which is teacher research. Second, there are language problems: although Iman is teaching in her first language, Arabic, her professional vocabulary is almost entirely in English and Hebrew. "Once I used the word 'dichotomy', and I was in the middle of a sentence…and one of the students stopped me…he said, you just said the third word in a row that I don't understand." Iman points out that the setting is an academic one and she could simply come, give her lectures and leave, but "this is not me." Referring to Vygotsky's theory of the social dimensions of learning, Iman feels that she should adapt herself to the setting and find ways to bring about meaningful learning.

Alongside her work, Iman has been socially engaged in her community from an early age and is a leader in a community organization that provides informal education in art and music, which would otherwise not be available in the city. In her professional capacity as well as her social involvements, she is concerned with expanding the cultural resources of her community, with equality of opportunity, and with gender equality in particular. She has chosen a steady path of personal and professional development that is not the norm for her society in which women are expected to marry early and devote most of their energies to their families. At the end of her story Iman speaks about wanting to expand her skills as a researcher, and it might seem that her career in teacher education will not continue for long. However, regardless of the particular job description under which she may work, it is clear that Iman's purposes are those of an educator.

In the early years of her academic career, Rachel was asked to teach large compulsory courses in adolescent psychology, developmental psychology and so on, and "as a psychologist I felt obligated to teach about Piaget and Freud and Bruner…but it became obvious that these traditional courses didn't allow us to meet the teachers where they are, and to take them where they want to go." Rachel was involved for some years in an innovative field-based program and later developed a course on the topic of teacher professional development which enabled significant work on the social, cultural and personal issues brought by the students. But, she adds, "it took me a long time to change my discourse openly; I did it tacitly for many years...but I was still committed to the idea that students should study the literature on stages of teacher development." Rachel cites many influences that gradually changed her work: the influence of narrative studies, the attention to context, to novels and fiction; gradually she became more interested in the 'softer' aspects of education and began "meeting the students in new places." What emerges from the story is a focus on giving students the academic tools to understand classroom practice, getting to know students on their own ground and helping them to meet one another across difference, and facilitating critical dialogue in the university classroom and beyond.

Hiam works as an English teacher and mentor of other teachers in English and in the integration of computers in the classroom; not long after she told her story to the women's group she also began working in a teacher education college. Her story highlights several themes that relate to her purposes as an educator: feminist awareness, an active and creative approach to teaching, and the importance of fostering a sense of belonging, not just to Druze society but also to the wider Israeli collective. Hiam recalls that she was exposed to feminist perspectives in a course she took in her first year of the Master's program (taught by Rachel!), and she hasn't looked back; for her thesis she studied Druze women educators who had attained positions of leadership and their conceptions of success (Nasseraldeen, 2006). In telling her story she reflects on the gradual process of change in her community, where until recently women had not been allowed to study outside the community at all. She also considers the costs of women's empowerment in her community: she notes that men may not fully accept the changes taking place for women, and conflicts in the home may be an unintended result of women's new roles and aspirations. Hiam describes how becoming a parent influenced her teaching: "I had one daughter at home, and I felt that I had another thirty children in school; that was my experience, I was totally there." She made home visits to all the families, and her close knowledge of where each child came from served her well, particularly in working with the children who had difficulties. For Independence Day one year Hiam developed a project in which her class wrote letters to soldiers ("in Arabic, Hebrew and English") and sent them drawings and sweets for the holiday. Men in the Druze community serve in the Israeli army, and Hiam wanted the children to experience care for the soldiers and a sense of connection to the holiday, a day on which there are no special rituals; "there is Memorial Day, but I didn't want them to be connected only to loss and death." Hiam's students received letters of thanks from the soldiers, and she received a certificate of appreciation from a high-ranking military commander. The school had provided no support for her efforts, and after the fact there was no recognition either, only criticism that the project had been conducted in the name of her class and had not gone forward in the name of the whole school.

Devorah tells how, after a year in Jerusalem, still intending to return to the States, she went north to visit a kibbutz where she'd heard there was a group of Americans. She spent a month on the kibbutz, met her future partner, began teaching music, and stayed. When their son was born, Devorah hated the way that babies were cared for communally; she convinced her partner to move to the nearby new town of Kiryat Shemona, where she started teaching English in the high school. The school, she comments, was the centre of social life for the young people, and "teachers were so important...there was a common purpose, and coming from New York my mission was to bring the big world to them." Devorah speaks with tongue in cheek and a dose of self-criticism about her ambition to bring culture to her students, acknowledging that in those years, she had "no consciousness that these people had their own culture. There was no consciousness of that in the country and I was not contaminated by it either. Arabic was not something people spoke, coming from home they were supposed to be ashamed, as I was ashamed when my mother came to school." However Devorah made no judgements about her pupils' ability or what they might be capable of achieving. Her face lights up when she speaks about the pupils she taught in Kiryat Shemona: "they were wonderful children."

In 1968 Devorah and her family moved to Haifa so that she could continue her studies. She began teaching in one of the local high schools where she was asked to replace a retiring coordinator of English. She found herself teaching three 12th grade classes, "a full time job with a lot of responsibility, not sure I realized how much responsibility I had...for each class I had to prepare differently, I thought, so it wasn't boring." The principal of the school wanted uniformity and control, expecting all the teachers in a given grade level to give identical tests, but for Devorah this expectation did not take account of important differences among students; she "enabled each teacher to put in questions for her own class. So these were the 'standardized' tests." She adds that her position wherever she taught was usually "to be the underground, I was always doing things I wasn't supposed to do." After a few years, the principal of Devorah's high school moved to the university, where he became involved in teacher education, and he invited her to work as a mentor, accompanying student teachers into schools and analyzing lessons with them; later she taught courses and seminars in the didactics of English. She also played a central role in a project which incorporated a workshop on "coexistence" for all students in the teacher education program and developed a highly successful project in which Jewish and Arab student teachers worked together in pairs to develop a unit of study in their subject and to teach it jointly in their two schools.

Attaining university education

I was surprised to notice that, like myself, all of the women belonged to the first generation in their families to attain higher education. Research suggests that first generation college students tend to be less well prepared for academic work, to take longer to complete their studies and to be less persistent in staying the course (Tym et al., 2004). Clark/Keefe (2006) highlights the particular difficulties of first generation students coming from working class and poverty-class backgrounds. These studies, however, do not seem to reflect the experience of the six women whose stories are presented here.

First, it is important to note that all the women expressed respect for their parents, for their diverse abilities and talents as well as their struggles, quite apart from the level of education they had attained. Rachel appreciated the open-minded and tolerant attitude of her mother, a deeply religious woman who said of her early years in the country: "we grew up with people who were wealthy, and others who had less, some were poor, and Moroccans, and Arabs. . .and we all got along, they all were human beings." Chava mentions that her father was self-taught in many areas, including teaching himself to play the violin and calligraphy. Devorah's father was the secretary of an immigrant organization for which he kept the minutes "in his beautiful handwriting." Iman's parents are practical and successful people, respected in the community, who have given her whatever she needed and supported her in following her dreams. For Hiam it was important that her father, a religious leader in the Druze community, had been willing to bend the traditions and redefine the norms of the religion to make it possible for his daughters to study at a college outside their town. And although they had not attended higher education themselves, some of the fathers had attained a high level of religious education.

Most of the women came from families that had experienced financial struggles at some point, and while this certainly influenced them, it did not appear to be a limiting factor in their access to higher education. Fany remembers her parents keeping a strict record of all their expenses in a notebook and telling her and her brother, "Our big legacy to you will be your studies; we didn't have a profession but you will." Similarly, Devorah also emphasizes that her parents expected her to study: "it's not as if they accepted being less, they didn't accept it for themselves, they surely didn't accept it for their children." As distinct from accounts of multigenerational poverty and its impact on school achievement (e.g., Pemberton, 2012; Sharkey & Elwert, 2011), mobility seems to be almost taken for granted in the women's stories. What makes the difference is probably the fact that all of the women grew up in a time and place, whether in the diverse ethnic/religious communities of Israel or in Jewish communities abroad, where difficult economic conditions and individual struggle were common, but there was communal support and respect for anyone who engaged in study in order to make a better life.

Further, all of the women enjoyed the support of their families in their quest for higher education. Chava describes telling her mother about her dissertation research in detail, when her mother was already on her sickbed but still interested in following every word and offering encouragement. Hiam and Iman both comment that their mothers, in particular, expressed some reservations about their academic ambitions, but have supported them nonetheless. In fact it was Hiam's mother who began the process of making higher education possible for her daughters:

When my sister worked in a local factory after finishing high school, my mother felt that this work was not good enough for her daughters. With my father's agreement she started to study in a teacher education college...the college had a program for women only, and this enabled my parents to defend themselves against the severe criticism under which they came, as religious people, for allowing their daughter to travel to study outside the town. After this my older sister, who was already married with two children, joined her at the college and then it was natural that I and my sister who is a year and a half older than me also went to the same college after 12th grade.

The stories allow us to view women's advancement in higher education in the specific context of Jewish and Arab cultures in Israel. Although differences are still to be found, it seems that the expectation that women can and will study is now largely shared by members of all the communities that make up Israeli society. But access to higher education is still influenced by one's background and culture, impacting the decision to study at a university or a teacher's college and perhaps determining whether the woman will go as far as her abilities allow or will stop after attaining a first or second degree.

The participation of women from the Arab/Palestinian community in higher education has received considerable research attention in recent years (Erdreich, 2006; Gilat & Hertz-Lazarowitz, 2009; Gross, 2012; Hertz-Lazarowitz & Oplatka, 2009), and portrays a complicated picture of considerable advancement alongside persisting inequalities and limitations. Alayan & Yair (2010) suggest that despite significant advances, many of the educated Palestinian-Israeli women who took part in their study of key educational experiences still expressed "heteronomy and submissiveness to external figures of authority"; they caution that "expansion of educational opportunities has limited effects on personal subjectivity, largely because a cultural habitus is slow in changing" (Alayan & Yair, 2010, 845). Hertz-Lazarowitz and Shapira (2005), in a study of Muslim women who took up leadership roles in education in Israel, found that most of these women cited the encouragement of their families, particularly their fathers, to study, to advance professionally and to work for change within their schools. Shapira et al. (2011), studying the situation of women principals in the Arab school system, also acknowledge that higher education seems insufficient to ensure women's emergence into the public sphere given the diverse forms of pressure encountered by Arab women seeking management positions (see also

Abu-Rabia–Queder & Oplatka, 2008), from opponents inside the community as well as from members of their own family and tribe. The participants in the present study acknowledge the support and encouragement of their families and they also refer to opposition from within. However, the form of subjectivity expressed in the narratives is active: both Iman and Hiam are ready to challenge inequalities, to work for change, and to be creative in the use of their power in the situations where they find themselves.

Interactions of research and practice in life and career

With respect to their involvement in research and its interaction with educational practice, the participants are a diverse group. All of them have engaged in research, whether as part of their studies or in their academic positions, and all of them have found research compelling. Hiam, Iman and Fany express the drive to continue to develop as researchers, and Fany is currently engaged in doctoral research. Rachel, Devorah and Chava spoke directly about the relationships of research and practice; also, the women's circle of which four of the women were a part reflected on these issues and even gave a conference presentation on the topic.

At the time she told her story, Chava had recently completed her PhD and had just brought her 'baby' into the light of day, giving a presentation on her doctoral research to a group of teacher educators. She saw her research as clearly grounded in personal experience, in the example of her own father as a parent, in discussions she had with men engaged in teacher education, and in her reading of theory, particularly the work of Ricoeur. Chava was angry at the way the discourse of teaching ignored or silenced important issues: fatherhood in particular, parenting, gender, multiculturalism. She was determined to bring her research on the important insight regarding adult parental attitude to bear on teacher education, stating: "I want the students to be aware of themselves, where they came from, be empathic and not harm children"; the theme of parenting, and the possibility of bringing parental values into teaching, had become the central message in her work.

Rachel comments that "as a former teacher it was very important for me to continue my contact with future teachers, and over the years I also worked with teachers in the field. I didn't see this as being less important than being in the mainstream of psychology." This suggests a view of research in psychology as something separate from practice. But Rachel tells the story of a gradual rapprochement and blending of theory and practice. For example, in recent years she taught a seminar on social and cultural aspects of education, in which the students engaged in participatory research, studying the attitudes and interactions of Jewish and Arab students on the university campus (e.g., Zelniker et al., 2009) and exploring the 'hyphenated identities' of Arab and Jewish teachers who were graduate students at the university (Hertz-Lazarowitz, Farah & Yosef-Meitav, 2012). Still, she notes that this course was taught in the Education Department and not in the teacher education program, where, she implies, it might have had a more significant impact on practice. In her view, it is the institutional structure which enforces a certain distance between theory and practice. She is also somewhat critical of her own work on multiculturalism, feeling that it took her a long time to face the issues directly, to bring her personal perspective to bear in the classroom; and it seems to her that like-minded faculty members have not supported one another enough in working on the difficult issues of multiculturalism and Jewish-Arab relations.

Devorah finds a gap between what she as a teacher considers good teaching and what students remember, appreciate and think that they have learned from the teacher. She recalls acting out *Pygmalion* for her students, apparently with great flair: she still meets former students who remember her warmly for her performances in class. She taught the Shaw play (a staple of the English curriculum) this way because the students read English very badly, and she enjoyed doing dramatic reading for them, but she did not think it was "good teaching." Similarly, she found that both students and student teachers wanted to receive warmth, and while she certainly understood this, and had good relations with her students, she does not believe this correlates with learning. In a broader context, she obtained gratification from the program she taught in which Jewish and Arab student teachers worked together in pairs, a program which was highly successful. But after the program ended, "nothing was left," and this does not surprise her. As a sociologist Devorah believes that education is an outcome of the social order and cannot significantly change social arrangements. Only political change can make a difference, she argues. Understanding more about social life has made her more pessimistic about any possibility of changing existing structures although she insists it is still worthwhile to try. For both Devorah and Rachel, participation in research has provided meaning and purpose in their academic lives independently of the outcomes, and at the same time their contact with students at different levels has been a source of unfailing interest and gratification.

The members of the women's group also grappled with the issues of research and practice by formulating a question: Is the group's process of telling our stories and reflecting on them together an objective in its own right, or is it rather a means, a phenomenon to be investigated? They felt as yet unable to answer the question, because it seemed that the methodology of the group was being invented as the group went along. They wondered if the qualities that were developed over time in the group—qualities such as attention, respect, acceptance and resonance could be seen as 'outcomes' or rather, were aspects of the mode of inquiry adopted by the group. They also focused on the multiple and conflicting voices that came to expression in the circle (sometimes even in the same person), and in particular the diverse ideas held in the group about research. One voice expressed a reluctance to wear the hat of the "researcher" (at least as usually understood) which seemed to call for becoming more systematic and disciplined; the fear was that an engagement with the cold and dispassionate requirements of research would damage the living fabric of our circle—the sharing, interaction and sense of community that the group had created for itself. Another voice insisted that the group had something to contribute through studying its own processes and wanted to move forward, invest in analyzing the materials gathered (participants' stories, protocols of discussion) and work to develop a "product" and to formulate our insights clearly. A third voice thought it would be possible to do both: to preserve the "here and now" of the group's meetings and also to work towards research 'findings and insights as a result of the process.

The dilemmas that confronted the members of the women's circle with respect to the relative place of life versus research in the activities of the circle, and in their lives, are familiar (see Gemmell, Griffiths & Kibble, 2010; Knowles, Cole & Sumsion, 2000). Their deliberations call to mind the formulation of Oberg and Wilson (2002, 4): "the momentum that keeps the circle in motion does not come from a desire to produce a research topic, although a topic is eventually produced. Rather, the goal of the process is to keep the re-searching process going. In this process, the goal of writing is a living engagement."

History and place in the teachers' stories

Taken together, the teacher educators' stories provide a fascinating panoramic view of life and education in Israel over the years. Devorah, who arrived in the country in 1949, remembers the difficult economic privations of the early years. Recalling the urgency of political discussions in the kibbutz dining hall, she calls up an image of herself, dressed (somewhat inappropriately, it now seems) in a long flowered housecoat: "why was I in the dining room in this housecoat? ...I didn't know where I was, I still didn't know politically, why would I go and vote, and they were sure the country would go to the dogs because of Menachem Begin if I didn't vote." She recalls the lack of legitimacy for questioning of the country's leaders and the gratification she felt when the students she had taught to ask questions "went to the army and they came back in the course of the year to tell me I was right. I was so moved by that." Living in a 'development town,' she felt that while there was little genuine interest in or respect for the culture of new immigrants, there was also no prejudice about their ability to learn and adapt to the ways of the country. Rachel also grew up in an atmosphere of acceptance where it seemed that Arabs and Jews, immigrants from eastern and western backgrounds, religious and secular, rich and poor could all get along. But for all the participants more recent events show that social divisions are still prominent (in some cases perhaps even more so than in the past) and often very painful. It was interesting to note from Fany's story that as late as the 1970s a teacher still tried to change the name of a pupil because it was not an accepted Hebrew name. By the time Fany's family arrived in the country economic success was more central to one's social status, and a more privatized and materialistic view of life is something largely taken for granted by the younger participants, Hiam and Iman.

A disturbing account of how polarized relations have become among Israelis from the different communities is provided by Iman. When she participated in a prestigious educational program for young leaders from the periphery of Israeli society, Iman became close friends with another Arab participant, with a religious Jewish woman, and with a Jewish man originally from Ethiopia whose humor she appreciated greatly. However, although in the past Iman had met people from all sectors of Israeli society, she found the experience in this particular group very difficult. To her surprise, there were people in the group who had never before met an Arab, and while some were curious others would have preferred not to have this meeting at all. She recalled how painful it was to sit opposite someone with right-wing views who was "unable to say my name because if he did so, if he even said 'good morning' it would constitute an acknowledgement that I exist, which he did not want." The situation eventually erupted into open conflict despite the efforts of the program organizer (a supporter of critical pedagogy who had studied with Paulo Freire). Summing up this experience, Iman commented that "to think about it, in theory, it sounds very good, but to experience it, to experience the racism that exists in society, and in me as well, was a kind of 'reality shock'." The experience affected Iman physically: she often had headaches and other symptoms. Devorah also described an event in which Jewish students in her class expressed extreme racist views in a class discussion; after class Devorah apologized to the Arab students who were present and felt it as "a knife in my flesh" when the students dismissed the episode, telling her "we are used to it." Devorah, however, sees progress in the fact that nowadays the Arab community speaks out rather than remaining silent about such matters.

Discussion

The stories of six Israeli teacher educators portray a complex and shifting picture of the practices of teacher education over an extended period of time in Israeli education. The stories are themselves multi-voiced, and each one is reflective of inner diversity as well as being quite different from one another. However, a number of central ideas emerge from the teacher educators' stories: they speak to the inherent tensions and conflicts that characterize the work of educating teachers; to the necessity and the complexity of taking up an 'inquiry stance' in teacher education; and to the need for hope and some means of self-preservation when one engages in difficult work in a difficult time and place.

The tensions of teacher education have been addressed in the literature on self-study (Berry, 2007; Badali, 2004; Williams et al., 2012), and it is hardly surprising to find these same tensions arising in the present context. The stories reveal a 'duality of commitment' similar to that described by Weber (1990): the women educators clearly care about the future teachers with whom they work; they also derive personal satisfaction from engaging in research, and it is apparent that they manage somehow to navigate between the two poles of teaching and research. However, their duality of commitment seems more complicated and ambivalent than Weber suggested. First, the nature of the commitment seems to vary with the institutional setting, level of experience and background. For those working in universities the commitment to research is a given, but a certain ambivalence is built into the situation, because while the academic discourse clearly privileges research and the furthering of academic knowledge, the time that must be invested in teaching is significant, and the women are strongly committed to the learning and development of the future teachers with whom they work. Rachel speaks eloquently of her difficulty in changing her discourse openly, relating directly to student teachers' personal knowledge as part of her courses and making her concern for the actual diversity and multicultural nature of the student body central to her teaching. As Williams et al. (2012) indicate, "the debate around the perceived value of experiential teacher knowledge compared to academic knowledge" continues to preoccupy teacher educators. For those women who work in colleges in Israel, the importance of research involvement and output is increasing. Thus, bringing theory and practice, relationships and outcomes together remains an ongoing project in the lives of all the women.

Second, questioning and inquiry are central to all the stories. Each of the women has been and continues to be engaged in change processes of various kinds, personal, professional and intellectual, and their stories reveal that change is accompanied quite naturally by reflection as suggested by Asaf et al. (2008). The "inquiry stance" advocated by Cochran-Smith (2003) can be heard in the topics raised by the women, the implicit questions surfaced by their stories, and particularly in the emotional force of their language. The topics raised relate to dimensions of teacher education that are usually not given direct attention: the political, the personal and the institutional. The ongoing political conflict in Israel, and the intolerance and racism engendered by the conflict, are at the root of many of the women's implicit concerns. Thus Rachel speaks about the ongoing losses or "Nakbah" (catastrophe) of the Jewish as well as the Arab community in Israel; Devorah comments that her students' apparent acceptance of racist discourse was "a knife in her heart"; Iman mentions the physical suffering she experienced from being in the company of fellow students who refused to acknowledge her presence as a Palestinian. Fany is still outraged by the insensitive teacher who tried to change her name in elementary school because it was not a "proper" Hebrew name. The silencing of personal aspects of teacher education is evident in Chava's comment that daring to speak of sensitive topics like compassion and parental caring in teacher education is like "putting your hand in the fire." Similarly, Hiam refers to the painful backlash that she perceives coming from men in Druze society in the wake of women's growing empowerment. Direct confrontation with the institutional limitations of teacher education can be heard in Rachel's comments about how institutional structures limited her freedom as a teacher educator to actually meet students where they are. The embodied language of many of these comments highlights the intense, lived engagement of the women with their students and colleagues. As Latta and Buck (2007, 203) suggest, the "role and place of the mindful body within teacher education…(holds) implications for connected professional knowledge, empowering teachers and fostering the work of learning."

Third, the stories reflect many different facets of the complexity of life in Israel. But while they come from different backgrounds and have somewhat different preoccupations, the women seem to speak a common language: each of them would understand the concerns of the others, as was very evident in the work of the women's group. All the women have experienced intolerance, have sometimes felt excluded by the views of those around them, and all found this painful; sometimes, with hindsight there is compassion and understanding of how people looked at life then, while at other times even long-remembered experiences of injustice still sting. It also seems that while the women work for what they believe in, they also seem to protect themselves from the loss of hope by investing in their own development and by finding pleasure in the everyday interactions and small successes that are offered by their work (Bassett, 2012), in "the pleasure of simply meeting and having refreshments together, the ease of telling each other stories, the overall satisfaction of keeping the encounters going for two whole years despite suicide bombers and army raids" (Kalekin-Fishman, 2005, 21). Reflecting on a program of encounters of teachers from diverse communities (described in Elbaz-Luwisch & Kalekin-Fishman, 2004), Kalekin-Fishman found that the expectation of fragmentation of identity did not seem to hold for the participants in that program. The same seems to hold for the women whose stories are presented here: "as professional teachers, as women who care very much about family living, they demonstrate identities that are coherent and consistent —and at odds with the presumed crumbling of the person in light of the stress and strain of a society flooded with possibilities and saturated with information" (Kalekin-Fishman, 2005, 22).

Taken together, the teacher educators' stories lend significance to the comment made at the beginning: indeed teacher education is difficult work. It is complicated, puzzling, sometimes painful, and it does not get easier with time. Listening to their stories, the commitment to diversity, to inquiry and questioning of given pedagogical and institutional arrangements, and to caring for students, are evident. Their commitment to making room for diversity in teaching seems almost inevitable given the background stories the women told about their early lives. All of them were fortunate in having teachers or parents as models of caring in their lives. It may be that an inquiry stance grows almost inevitably out of the confrontation of these two elements—a valuing of diversity and caring for students—with schooling and teacher education as presently constructed. In any case, it seems clear that this particular combination of commitments is central in making possible lives of purpose and meaning for those who engage in educating teachers.

Note

1. The project was funded by the Israel Science Foundation, Grant No, 1038/04, 2005–2007.

CHAPTER 6

Auto/biography, Writing and Teacher Learning

It has already been noted that, paradoxically, the places where children go every day to learn are not inherently environments that encourage and stimulate learning for teachers (Sarason, 1982). Much has been done to address this situation through research on how teachers learn (Wilson & Berne, 1999), through the establishment of learning communities in schools (Cochran-Smith & Lytle, 1999), and professional development schools to promote shared learning of student teachers and experienced teachers (Lieberman & Pointer Mace, 2009; Vescio et al., 2008). In recent years there has been an increase in "systematic exploration that is conducted *by* teachers and *for* teachers through their own stories and language" (Johnson & Golombek, 2002, 6), through narrative research, teacher self-study (Kosnik et al., 2006; Loughran et al., 2004), teacher action research and teacher reflection (Oshrat, 2009).

This research presents a view of teaching as characterized by innovative developments such as reflection and collaborative inquiry, but there are also studies as well as statements in the public forum telling us that teaching has become a more and more difficult job over the years. The frequent use of terms such as "deskilling" (Apple, 1987), "intensification" (Ballet et al., 2006; Woods, 1999), and "marginalization" (Vongalis, 2004) reflect this. Research on teaching itself, particularly when conducted from instrumental perspectives, may tend to look at the negative side of the ledger rather than the positive, focusing on topics such as teacher stress and burnout (Byrne, 1994; Vandenberghe & Huberman, 1999; Wilhelm et al., 2000). Rapid changes in the work of teaching have left many teachers "grieving for a lost self" (Nias, 1993), struggling to make sense of the latest reform and wondering what—if anything—to invest of themselves in mandated new programs (Gitlin & Margonis, 1995). Casey's (1992) study of activist female teachers who leave the profession indicated that most of those committed and engaged women were ultimately defeated by the school system, by uncaring administrators or by school board regulations; rarely do teachers claim that they left their jobs because they stopped caring about their students.

Clandinin and Connelly (1996) formulated the idea of 'cover stories' to point to how teachers talk publicly about their work when their beliefs and actions are at odds with what seems to be expected of them in the school (see also Kainan, 1994, and Cole, 1997); likewise, Craig (2004) develops a provocative account of what happens when the atmosphere in the school makes teachers feel that communication is not safe. Webb (1996) talked about leaving teaching because of the realization that her knowledge of practice, developed over years of experience and reflection on her work, was not valued or taken seriously within the school.

These studies suggest that school is not always a place where one is able to speak out, to express one's views or to bring one's values and ideas to bear in interactions with colleagues. Many teachers come to graduate study hoping that the university environment will provide a safe place for speaking out and for elaborating their knowledge of the practice of teaching. Of course, teachers come to graduate study to do much more than simply speak their minds and formulate what they already know about teaching. Most of them expect to learn more about their subject, to acquire new pedagogies and understand the rationale behind new reform initiatives—all of this, labeled "knowledge for teaching" by Cochran-Smith and Lytle (1999), is clearly essential. But we know by now that it is not enough to simply present teachers with new knowledge. Drake et al. (2001) studied the literacy stories and stories about learning mathematics of a group of teachers who were engaging with new programs; their account suggests that how teachers story and restory their new understandings is critical for bringing this learning to bear on their work. As Cochran-Smith & Lytle (1999) argue, developing knowledge of practice in community appears to be essential for teacher development. Autobiography and personal writing are privileged means by which teachers can elaborate their new knowledge, so I turn now to look at autobiography and writing as forms of inquiry and teacher development.

Autobiography and personal writing as inquiry in teaching

Bringing personal experience into teaching and learning in academic contexts can make a significant contribution to the personal and professional development of adult learners and university faculty (Neumann, 1998; Schnee, 2009). In education, the benefits of telling and writing about one's own experience have been shown for diverse groups of teachers and learners in teacher education (Conle, 1996; Heikkinen, 1998) and in teacher development through self-study (Kosnik et al., 2006). Telling and writing one's own stories constitute powerful tools for fostering teachers' professional growth in both pre-service and in-service settings (Conle, 1996; Connelly & Clandinin, 1996; Diamond 1994; MacLeod & Cowieson, 2001; McNiff, 1990).

Thus writing about one's personal experience in an academic context has become almost ordinary; yet it can still be excruciatingly difficult (Elbaz-Luwisch, 2002; Richardson, 1994) and entails risks (Burman, 2003). Bleakely (2000) warns of writing that aims "to reveal a core or authentic self that is promised through 'growth' or 'development' techniques" (18), thereby turning autobiography into confession, exploiting pathos to solicit the reader's interest. This suggests that personal writing, particularly in an academic context, may unwittingly reproduce the values of bourgeois capitalism, positing the self as a form of property tied to particular class and gender positions. In writing about my mother, I worried about self-disclosure and about the justification for foregrounding this particular story, one which has more than its due measure of suffering on the one hand, and yet, on the other hand, is "less" painful than more familiar testimony of lives lived during the Holocaust (though the very idea that pain and suffering can be quantified or even compared does violence to survivors and to the memory of victims). Attended on every side by the risks of inauthenticity, pathos and having nothing new to say, personal writing begins to seem like an impossible task under postmodern views of the self (Bloom, 1996; Gannon, 2006).

Despite these risks, autobiographical writing is widely promoted as a practice which makes it possible for teachers to reflect on the sources that have influenced their current practice and to imagine the future (Heikkinen, 1998; Raymond et al., 1992). Yet one wonders, is this practice of telling, writing and retelling stories of teaching truly a practice with the potential to change teaching, to question and interrupt standard practice, or has it merely become one more feature of standard practice?

The answer to this question depends in part on the perspective adopted in relation to writing. Writing was traditionally viewed as a straightforward, even technical process whereby the writer formulates ideas in the mind and then puts them down on paper with the help of specific skills of composition and rhetoric. A postmodern conception of language, however, tells us that language is "not the result of one's individuality; rather, language constructs the individual's subjectivity in ways that are historically and locally specific" (Richardson, 1994). Thus writing is seen as a way to make meaning, a process whereby ideas are formulated in new ways through the writing process:

> The meaning of the world and of our existence is not given in advance, and the task of knowledge is not merely to discover this given. Rather, the perceived world imposes a task to be accomplished, which is to make out of what is given something meaningful. . .One of the ways language does this is to configure these givens into a narrative form in which desires and aspirations are used to transform the passing of life into an adventure of significance and drama. (Polkinghorne, 1988, 30–33)

But here postmodern thought raises a particular challenge: as Denzin (1995) argues, "the worlds we study are created through the texts that we write" (9). Experience is always already a text, and textuality helps to set the parameters of our experience. Perhaps it is partly in response to this dilemma of finding ourselves in the midst of what Denzin called "lived textuality" that autobiography has come into its own in recent years as an important social and educational practice (Griffiths, 1995b; Heilbrun, 1988; Swindells, 1995; Witherell & Noddings, 1991).

It is apparent that the writing process carries a special intensity (Schaafsma, 1996); this may contribute to the fact that the writing of educational autobiography is often conceived as an individual process of personal inquiry. Writers such as Cixous (1997), Mairs (1994), and Doll (1995) demonstrate some of the diverse ways that personal writing can also be critical. However, Clandinin and Connelly (1998b) point out that while personal inquiry can be difficult, and even putting a story down in writing sometimes seemed risky for them and their students, this is not enough: it is necessary to move from the simple telling of a story to retelling and reliving the story, "to engage in retellings that might lead to different social narratives lived out on the professional knowledge landscapes in schools and universities" (252). Many such retellings are collected in the volume edited by Mitchell et al. (2011). For example, Johnston (2011), who was born in post-war Germany and grew up under apartheid in South Africa, works to restore difficult personal and family memory through conversation and the reading of fiction, searching for personal meaning and for fictional accounts which can be brought to the teacher education classroom. Attarian (2011) explores her own history as an Armenian growing up in Lebanon, tracing her story back through the experiences of displacement and exile of her parents, grandparents and great-grandparents, weaving together documents, photographs and text to understand her own identity construction and to create a space where her students might do the same. And, as Hasebe-Ludt and Jordan (2010) suggest, life writing allows us to "write and live towards ontological and epistemological positions of being in the world truthfully, ethically, mindfully, and compassionately." By attending closely to the details of lived experience, such writing "constantly explores, contests, and negotiates the imaginative possibilities of knowing and being in the world" (1–2).

In the terms suggested by Bakhtin (1981), one might expect life writing to help the writer formulate his or her own "internally persuasive discourse," appropriating the various discourses that are available in society and using them to develop and express the writer's own ideas. By way of example, Ivanić (1998) followed non-traditional university students in different disciplines as they learned to give shape to their own thoughts while writing a research paper on their chosen subject. In a similar vein, in earlier work (Elbaz-Luwisch, 2002), I looked at the university as a site for personal writing and at the potential of the writing workshop as a transformative space where diverse voices can find expression and writers can experiment with the development of internally persuasive discourse.

Personal writing thus engages the writer as the subject of her own text. Smith and Watson (2001) identify five processes which construct the autobiographic subject: memory, experience, embodiment, identity and agency. Although their interest is with autobiography as a literary form, these five processes seem equally central to the construction of the teacher as subject. The narrative study of teaching, inspired by Dewey (1938), has emphasized giving an account of the teacher's experience, which remains central to personal writing. Memory—the retrieval of experience long past—is also evident when teachers write about their early experiences from childhood or as pupils; the reconstruction or re-imagination of those events can be key to retelling. Teaching identity and the development of agency have also been given attention in the literature on teaching and teachers' autobiographic writing; Heikkinen (1998), for example, saw such writing as helping student teachers become aware of "how I came to be myself." Embodiment, however, as already suggested in Chapter 3, has been given inadequate treatment in studies of teaching (see Estola & Elbaz-Luwisch, 2003) as well as in treatment of teachers' writing. I assumed that all these processes were likely to be important in varying degrees for teachers engaged in autobiographic writing. However, I wondered if embodiment in particular, which has been so marginalized in the literature on teaching, might provide a point of entry to a more critical perspective.

In the background, then, is a nested and overlapping set of purposes identified in the literature for autobiographic writing as serving in teacher development. First, writing to clarify one's personal story seems to be a basic purpose underlying all others (though it is not always the place where writers begin), enabling teachers to sort out issues of identity in and out of teaching, to hear their own voices and to become aware of their own purposes and motives. Second, teachers write to reflect: they describe and analyze various aspects of their work in order to consider and elaborate their pedagogy, to clarify its sources, and to work out their ideas about subject matter and their responses to reform. Third, teachers write to communicate, share their ideas with others, and contribute to the professional development of their peers—a purpose that has been salient in teacher self-study as well as in professional development projects for teachers of writing (see Lieberman and Pointer Mace, 2009). Finally and most generally, teachers write to create meaning, to make sense of puzzling or disturbing matters that come up in their lives and work, to question and critique, to gain new understandings. Given these purposes, I wonder if personal writing by teachers can serve to develop an internally persuasive discourse that is able to interrogate the authoritative discourse in teaching? Can such writing question given social arrangements and educational practices and call them to account? And what formats and practices can we call upon to encourage teachers to write this way?

Context and method

The context for the discussion of these issues is a graduate level course on autobiography and professional learning, the main purpose of which was to explore autobiographical writing as a tool of professional learning and development for teachers. There were 15 participants, thirteen women and two men, six teachers of English and four in special education, and one nurse. Several participants work as mentors of teachers in different contexts; about half were studying in a program for mentors. The students come from the diverse cultures and backgrounds that make up Israeli society: about half are Jewish, while the others belong to the Arab/Palestinian community and are also diverse in terms of religion (Christian, Moslem, Druse). The ways that Arab citizens of Israel are referred to, and refer to themselves, are not unproblematic matters. Here, unless I refer to a specific person in the way that he or she prefers, I use the term "Arab/Palestinian" as an approximation, knowing that many but not all of the students use the term Palestinian while some, in particular those belonging to the Druse community, refer to themselves as Druse and/or Arab.

The course is described in the syllabus as having a 'workshop' format to allow students to experience the process of personal writing in an open-ended way; discussion of the themes that came up in the writing would have a place alongside topics drawn from the research literature. The sharing of participants' writing in the large group was emphasized as a way to reach a more comprehensive and critical understanding of teacher development; the retelling and rewriting of participants' stories were also emphasized as a goal of the course.

Professional learning, the focal topic of the course, was explored in weekly reading assignments, in-class writing and discussions. Each week, in the first half of the class (90 minutes) we engaged in some kind of 'warm-up,' wrote for between fifteen minutes and half an hour and then shared the writing in pairs and in the whole group; the second half of the class was devoted to a discussion of the reading which usually had a strong connection to the writing just completed. In two written assignments, the students tried out various ways of bringing their autobiographic writing into relation with the research literature.

Autobiographical writing encompasses a very wide range of possibilities. As Smith and Watson (2001) point out, the forms of autobiographic writing include (among others): "apology, memoir, autoethnography, survival narrative, auto/biography, diary, confession, chronicle, genealogy, journal, life narrative, oral history, self-help narrative, testimonio. . ." I discussed this profusion of genres with my students at the beginning of the course, to un-

derline that there are no agreed-upon forms or "right way" of writing personally. We began the process of writing together with the exercise of "writing
for the garbage pail": we spent five minutes by the clock writing quickly,
putting down whatever came to mind, and then I passed around a large garbage can so that each student could consign his or her work to the trash with
due ceremony.

The exercises which began each class invited the students to write about
their experience and focused on the idea that writing is already an embodied
process (Anderson, 2001; Cixous, 1997; Gurevitch, 2000). I suggested that
working overtly with writing as embodied would help participants connect to
some aspect of their "tacit knowledge" (Polanyi, 1966) of teaching and to
elaborate on it. Some exercises focused specifically on bringing forward
memories from different periods in the lives of participants. Issues of agency
figured particularly when the teachers wrote about their lives in schools and
their purposes as teachers. Teacher identity was also addressed quite naturally in this writing, and issues of cultural and religious identity came up often, usually through discussion in our multicultural group. Thus all five of
the processes mentioned by Smith and Watson (2001) were given a place in
the course, sometimes implicitly and in some instances quite explicitly.

In developing the exercises I was informed and inspired by the process-
oriented psychology of Mindell (1981/2000), which assumes that the body—
physical sensations, symptoms, positions and movements—is an important
source of understanding that we rarely tap into; with very few exceptions this
'oversight' is also found in education (but see Hocking et al., 2001, for an interesting set of examples). Mindell refers to our awareness of "dreaming"
(which includes nighttime dreams but also daydreams, imagery and flickers
of awareness that come and go) as a realm of experience which is full of significance if only we pay attention, bringing us into connection with parts of
our identity that may simply be unfamiliar or perhaps actively marginalized.
This approach has generated a rich fund of ideas for developing awareness
and creativity (Mindell, 2005) and has been applied to the writing process
(Halprin, 2001) as well as in therapy with individuals and families, and in
work with organizations and large groups (Reiss, 2000). Based on my experience as a student of process-oriented psychology over the past 12 years, I

adapted, developed and brought to class a variety of exercises; some examples follow.

The scribble.[1] I invited students to think of a problem at work, something large or small that was of concern to them in the moment, and to make a note of it. Then, after relaxed breathing, they took a piece of paper and made a quick scribble or drawing. They were then asked to look at the drawing, pick out some bit of it that intrigued them and redraw it, enlarged on a new sheet of paper—drawn as if it were the whole world. Finally, in a third drawing they were to redraw the initial bit again, this time quite small within its particular surroundings. At this point they might have some new insight into the initial problem, or not; in any case, they began writing an account of the problematic situation, trying to be as concrete and descriptive as possible. Usually by the end of the writing period people had some understandings of their situation that had not been available to them when we began.

Who am I as a teacher? The participants were asked to relax and breathe deeply for a few moments, to close their eyes and pay attention to their bodily sensations, to find what seemed to be the deepest place in the body and attend to that until they could identify some quality associated in the moment with that spot. I then invited them to think of a place in the world that this sensation or quality called to mind and to go there in imagination, to experience being there and even becoming the place if possible, noting what it had to tell them. When they were ready to 'come back' from this journey, I asked them to write about the experience and to answer several questions: "Who are you as a teacher after returning from the place you visited? What new quality would you like to bring to your work, and how will you do that?"

The circle of meaningful learning.[2] The students were instructed to draw a circle and to mark on its circumference experiences of meaningful learning from various times in their life. They were also asked to note one small and concrete memory detail related to each experience. Then they picked at random one of the experiences, remembered and wrote about it in as much detail as possible. As they thought and wrote about the experience, they were invited to pay attention to some particular quality of meaningful learning that presented itself, to feel into that quality and to represent it with a small movement or gesture. When they shared their work in pairs, they were asked to help one another notice whether the identified quality was present in the other experiences around their circle. In this exercise one participant remembered the teacher who finally knew her name in her first year at a large high school; she used a hugging gesture to express the feeling of being held and confirmed as a learner.

Other activities that preceded our writing included working with clay to make a figure, followed by writing a letter that the figure would send to us; and choosing a picture of an animal and writing a dialogue with the animal. Several times the writing was preceded only by quiet relaxation or music: for example, writing a 'confession' about something we had done wrong in the past or writing about a time when we had wanted to speak out about something but had been unable to do so. I tried to vary the activities and prompts for writing as much as possible, finding that some participants preferred the more meditative 'inner work' before writing while others were more comfortable with an active start to the writing.

In addition to writing alongside students in class, I kept a journal during the course and read and reread their written work. Near the end of the course the students wrote personal summaries of what, for them, makes up professional learning, and we discussed this issue in the final class in January 2009. The present account of what we learned about professional learning, on the one hand, and about the contribution of autobiographic writing to the process on the other hand, is based on my interpretation of all these materials. Interpretation and writing went hand in hand as I found myself figuring out what had happened in the course as I wrote about it (see Colyar, 2009). It is important to note that I did not collect everything written by students during the course, believing that it was important to ensure that they retained maximum control over their personal writing. Thus I had access only to the in-class writing that students chose to share as well as to two written assignments submitted during the semester (in which they quoted and expanded on selected passages from their in-class writing). Thus I don't presume to give a comprehensive account of what took place for all the students in the course. Drawing on the writing and comments of the students where it was relevant to the matters discussed here, in dialogue with my own understandings, I do try to make sense of the experience of the course as a whole. I begin the account with a retelling (based on my journal) of an episode from the middle of the semester.

Not another reading assignment!

Since the beginning of the term we had been following a routine that seemed to be well established: each week the students read and responded to an article posted on the course website. The responses were due the day before class, so I had time each week to read them and take them into account in the class discussion. This ongoing assignment was worth 30% of the grade; students got full marks for submitting their responses on time, and I felt confident that this mechanism was contributing to a sense of orderly learning: we were doing many non-traditional exercises, yet still "covering the material." Then, halfway through the semester, there were exclamations of protest: the mid-term assignment was due the following week, holidays were coming up, and students insisted that the reading should be postponed. "What will we discuss if you haven't read the article?" I asked. I knew that most students worked full time and had families in addition to undertaking graduate studies. Still I stuck to my decision, and one of the students looked at me in surprise; "last year," she commented (referring to a course she had taken with me the previous year), "you were more flexible."

During the break, I sat in the teachers' room and wondered why, indeed, I felt so adamant about the reading assignment. I decided to try one of the exercises I had been facilitating all semester. I closed my eyes and relaxed, paying attention to my inner experience, following the tension I was feeling in my stomach. The tension made me aware of how much I wanted this course to be successful: I was trying something new, taking a risk, and it seemed to be working well. But I was still afraid the course might be reduced to an exercise in venting emotions and feeling good. The knot in my stomach reminded me of a fist, holding on to the requirements so that the course would be serious as well as fun. I took that fist and tried to imagine a place in nature that embodied its qualities; soon I saw myself hiking in the south of Israel near the small town of Mitzpe Ramon. The ground was rocky and I had to place every footstep carefully; if I let my attention wander I would trip or fall. I had walked in this area a few years earlier, during a silent meditation retreat: every day our group of some 30 people had spent three or four hours walking in single file, slowly and in silence, through the extraordinary landscape of the Negev desert. While sometimes we walked on clearly marked paths, often we were led across a rocky hill no different from other hills nearby, having to trust that we were going in the right direction. Each day's walk took a different path; the landscape was beautiful at every turn and sometimes spectacular.

In addition to keeping pace with those in front, we had been told to look back from time to time, to make sure that those coming after us were also keeping up. If the space behind us got too large, we were supposed to slow down; this way, the line of walkers would eventually learn to pace itself so that all the participants could stay together. This did not happen right away. In the beginning I found myself in a dilemma: if I slowed down to wait for those behind me, I would lose sight of the line ahead and might not know which way to go; yet if I waited, in effect, I would become the leader for all those coming after me and might be responsible for all of us losing our way. Worrying about this, I no doubt lost some beautiful moments; luckily after a day or two the group of walkers learned to keep pace. Remembering this experience I felt the knot in my stomach soften. I did want my students to keep pace with the program I had outlined for the course and to master the relevant literature on teachers' professional learning. But I also valued the journey and the experiences to be had along the way; I decided to trust that each of them would be engaged in his or her way. I returned to class with a lighter step, announced a compromise arrangement for the readings, and we continued with the topic of the day.

Aspects of professional learning

Many issues featured in discussions with the students about the important professional learning that they had experienced over the course of their careers. The main issues that I will take up here are: the expansion of their repertoire of professional knowledge and skills, the strengthening of reflective processes, inquiry into and clarification of their personal story and the development of 'narrative authority' (Olson, 1995), the building of a 'knowledge community' (Craig, 1995), and the integration of theory and practice. In this section I draw on quotes from the teachers' comments in class and in their writing to give an account of how they viewed professional learning and what it meant for them.

Expanding the teaching repertoire. Most of the students came to their studies with the simple expectation that they would learn more about teaching, or, in the words of one student, that they would "acquire knowledge, skills, strategies and a professional world view in relation to the subject matter that the teacher teaches." They saw this as an important stage in the teacher's professional development. It was equally important to them to be informed about pedagogical developments and reforms taking place in the school system. This expectation in relation to "knowledge for teaching" was almost taken for granted, and although many participants included it in their outline of professional learning, none felt the need to elaborate on it. It also seemed quite clear to them that our course was not meant to provide this type of knowledge.

Reflective processes. The students were particularly aware of the value of reflective processes in their studies overall. One student commented, "Autobiographic writing breaks down the old and fixed thought patterns we hold on to, and allows for a process of ongoing learning about the present, the past and the future. This is a process of professional learning." Another student emphasized the value of cognitive dissonance in promoting reflection: "In order to see the past in a new way, the teacher needs well developed skills of reflection, to see himself and think about his thinking and behavior, in order to make improvements and envision the future." One of the conditions for such processes of learning and change is the awareness of a problematic situation, an imbalance which awakens the need to reformulate one's professional knowledge, and following that, reflective thought is further enhanced. A third student commented that using "metacognitive processes of reflection, introspection and retrospection" helped to attain insights about practice and then to make changes in one's teaching in order to adapt to the particular needs of students. The language of 'cognitive dissonance' and 'metacognitive processes' was not introduced by me but was brought to the course by the students from their reading and knowledge in other contexts and was used by them to help them make sense of the material we were reading and discussing in our course.

Clarifying one's personal story. By the end of the course the students saw autobiographic writing as having made possible what one student referred to as a "journey to oneself," a personal exploration which, she felt, "made it possible to see the processes we are going through from a critical perspective, which leads to learning and development." Interpreting the present in terms of the past allows one to consider why he or she thinks or acts a certain way, and what influenced one's current perspective and identity. Another participant wrote about the writing exercise that began with a circle of meaningful learning experiences (described above), "I was excited when I found the connecting thread that allowed me to see all the experiences as related: This is my way!" A third student commented that getting to know one's own story, the influence of one's history and past experiences on the shaping of one's identity and worldview, would inevitably have an impact on one's teaching; she believed that her thinking had became more reflective and would make her a more aware and more effective teacher. A student who had written her own literacy story, from that perspective began paying more attention to watching her own child learn to read, as well as noticing how her students were learning to read English as a second language. The participants saw these experiences with autobiographical writing as contributing to their sense of "narrative authority" (Olson, 1995), which they perceived as something flexible, open to change and reconstruction.

Building a knowledge community. From the experience in our course but also in their studies overall, the students had become aware that professional knowledge communities in teaching were a powerful source of support that would generate important insights and contribute over time to the development of their teaching (Olson & Craig, 2001). They sharpened their understanding of this issue through an exercise which called for writing about difficult events in which they had been unable to speak out. One student recounted a painful event in which her principal had invited her to chair a meeting on a particular topic; after she opened the meeting by explaining her views and those of other teachers with whom she had consulted before the meeting, the principal simply ignored her statement, gave the teachers certain directives and ended the meeting without allowing for any discussion. The event was infuriating, but the real humiliation was in having been unable to speak out or do anything about it.

Bringing their understanding of different kinds of participation in communities to bear on our course, one of the participants pointed out, "What happens here in class is an example of a knowledge community." Indeed, as the students shared their writing in pairs, and in the whole group, little by little, they came to know one another, and this process went forward not just in class meetings but also in other courses and events on campus. It was clear that engaging in autobiographical writing in this way provided a catalyst for the development of friendships and a sense of community among the teachers. This sense of community is enormously valuable in itself, especially in the Israeli setting marked by painful divides, but does not necessarily indicate the presence of a 'knowledge community.' In order to assess the kind of community that took shape in the class, I will briefly examine the idea of "knowledge community" as it has been developed in some of the relevant literature.

The notion of a teacher 'knowledge community' draws from a variety of different sources. Craig's defining work (1995) refers to Dewey's understanding of inquiry and the development of knowledge in social context as well as to the important notion of an "interpretive community" as developed in literary studies. Pardales and Girod (2006) draw on the philosophy of Peirce for their understanding of a "community of inquiry" in education as "modeled after scientific communities of inquiry where the explorations of ideas and reasoning are publicly displayed and scrutinized. This display and scrutiny eventually lead to the creation/construction of knowledge about the self, and the world" (Pardales & Girod, 305). The common elements that come to the fore in these diverse sources confirm that it is indeed important for a knowledge community to be a safe and congenial space where teachers can "narrate the rawness of their experiences" (Craig, 1995, 670). However, Pardales and Girod suggest that "the term 'community' denotes a togetherness that may not be a necessary condition for the kind of inquiry we want in schools…'community' might be something to strive for yet, something that is not immediately attainable in a classroom setting." What they see as essential is rather that the community "works together, has mutual respect and concern, and a recognizable and agreed upon set of assumptions and procedures" (Pardales & Girod, 2006, 308).

Thus, in addition to being a safe space in which respectful talking and listening can and do take place, it is important for a knowledge community to have agreed-upon procedures for conducting discussion—shared interpretive strategies—even if these procedures may be informal and not spelled out, so that "individuals can tentatively articulate how they are making sense of situations, explain their own actions, and examine their stories in concert with others" (Olson & Craig, 2001, 670). Further, knowledge communities are not always places of harmony and consensual agreement where knowledge is validated but can also be places where competing stories are told and acknowledged (Craig, 1995), where "tensions are revealed and where insights are offered that enable situations to be revisited, reassessed, and re-storyed" (Olson & Craig, 2001, 671). Participation in such communities enables teachers to confront difficulties and to notice and act upon opportunities for change and growth. In doing so, teachers are not only constructing knowledge, individually and together, but making that knowledge public and visible to others in the community.

With these characteristics of teacher knowledge communities in mind, I want to revisit one particularly significant encounter that took place at the end of December 2008; I believe this event contributed significantly to the processes taking place in our class and helps to understand the nature of the knowledge community taking shape, even though the event took place in the department and not all the students in the course took part. Students in the mentoring program in our department (about half the participants in the course were in this program) organized a series of faculty-student meetings to foster dialogue between those two groups. As it turned out, the first such meeting took place just a few days after the beginning of the Israeli army's operation in Gaza. The Palestinian students who were part of the organizing group were in a dilemma, and one student chose to write about it in her mid-term paper for our course:

> I came to the meeting with a heavy heart, tense, with a lot of anger, sadness and pain. I felt conflicted...should I attend this meeting which we had been planning for a month, or should I join the strike?[3] Finally, I decided to attend. Since it was a mentoring meeting characterized by flexibility and sensitivity to the context we are part of, I saw that there was room to express my voice. After I spoke about the pain I was feeling, there were expressions of support and solidarity. When H., my professor whom I really appreciate, spoke, I felt the humanitarian aspect of his words. He said that specially in these difficult times, Arabs and Jews should meet, speak and make their voices heard.

While this discussion was indeed difficult, by the end of the meeting there was a feeling that something positive had been accomplished: strong emotions were voiced, grievances aired, differences of opinion given space, and those who spoke felt that their views had been respected and taken seriously. Although not all the participants in my course were present, it seemed that the provision of this space for dialogue within our department had a strong impact on other interactions in the department, including my course. The student quoted above was not alone in feeling relief that political issues were not excluded from discussion in our academic and professional context.

Shortly after the above event, two important articles featured on our reading list for the course (planned well in advance of the political events, needless to say). The first of these (Diab, 2002), written by a Palestinian-Israeli teacher educator, described her work with student teachers from the Arab community. She had found that many of her students were not well informed about the history of their families, and in particular they knew little about what their families had experienced before, during and after the war of 1948—Israel's War of Independence, referred to by Palestinians as the 'Nakbah' or 'Catastrophe.' Diab's course engaged the students in writing what she termed "the missing narrative" of their families, and her article described this process in some detail. This gave rise to lively reactions in class: the Palestinian students commented that it was the first time they had read a piece of academic writing that related directly to their own lives and experience as members of the Palestinian community in Israel. This in itself was an important revelation for them, and at first their reading of the piece was unqualifiedly positive. The responses of Jewish students to the article acknowledged the importance of the work described in the text but also pointed out that something was lacking: the author said nothing about her own experience as a member of that same community. They wondered if she too had grown up with a 'missing narrative,' and if so, how had she discovered her own family history and when?

This divergence in interpretation of the text at first caused some tension in the class. Some of the Palestinian students seemed to hear the criticism of the text as a challenge to their right to have the story of their community heard. However, the degree of friendship and shared professional interests in the class apparently served a purpose here. First, the Jewish students saw that they needed to explain further why they thought there might be more to learn from this case about the author's professional learning as a teacher educator and about how the historical and political story impacted her work. This in

turn made it easier for the Palestinian students to engage with the interpretation offered by the 'other side.' Ultimately, the class as a whole began to see
this position as a valid criticism of the text, and they came closer to a shared
interpretation.

The text which followed provided an example of an author who did make
the connection between her family history and her work in education: Neumann (1998) discusses the impact on her work as a researcher and university
professor of the life story of her father, a Holocaust survivor. This too was in
some ways a "missing narrative" in Neumann's early life, talked about in the
family but indirectly, in bits and pieces, in particular contexts and special
tones of voice, in Yiddish at first and only years later in English. Not until
her adult years did Neumann take deliberate steps to listen to and record her
father's full story. The article discusses the ways that Neumann's academic
work changed as listening to and dealing with her father's narrative began to
shape her understandings of herself and her work. Having kept her personal
and academic lives separate for many years, she eventually found herself
asking, "what is my intellectual life—what is my work in the world—without
my self?" (432) This question resonated for many of the students (not only
the Jewish students) and was quoted in a number of their written assignments. Later, one of the Palestinian students, in a meeting in my office, expressed his interest in my family story and wondered whether it was similar
to Neumann's, and this gave rise to an interesting conversation that was quite
moving for me.

These two readings, coming together near the end of a series of texts
dealing with the relatively matter-of-fact topics of professional learning and
autobiographical writing, and in the wake of the political events erupting
around us, evoked some strong responses. Finally, in one of our classes towards the end of the course, a heated political discussion was engaged, bringing out many of the conflicts with which we live. One Jewish student read
aloud a text she had written about her experience, a few years earlier, of
teaching young children in the south of the country in a place that had been
under regular rocket attack; this text was apparently written in response to
strong sentiment against the Gaza military operation, which could be seen as
denying Israel's right to defend the citizens of border communities such as
the one where the student had taught. Following this, a Palestinian student,

Raneen, told about an event from high school: she gave a speech at a school assembly, in which she quoted from a poem in Arabic whose author, unbeknownst to her, was apparently considered "too radical" by the authorities; her teacher was strongly censured by the school principal and passed the criticism on to her. Other students expressed their anger about the military operation which was still ongoing at the time. As might be expected, the discussion was heated, sometimes chaotic, and difficult; many students had strong personal reactions.

Eventually, as the time for a break approached, things began to wind down. At this point one of the Jewish students, Karen (who had spoken briefly earlier on) commented, "At the beginning of the discussion today, I told myself that I would not participate, but then I heard Raneen say how important it was just to talk, even if we disagreed. This threw me off balance, and then I changed my mind—I was wrong." It was interesting to me that Karen invoked terms that had been used during the semester to talk about learning; she saw that Raneen's remark had provided the cognitive dissonance which enabled her to reflect on her position and become aware of a possibility of changing her view. It seems that Karen came to the course not believing dialogue between Jewish and Arab/Palestinian Israelis was possible; however, knowing that someone from the 'other side' wanted both sides to be heard, i.e., wanted to hear her, was apparently a factor in facilitating her change of mind. This event, like the ones mentioned above, shows that the class had indeed developed into a knowledge community in the sense discussed earlier. First, the class was a safe enough place to talk to one another even when the discussion heated up and despite very wide disparities in their views. Second, they were able to hold the disagreements and keep talking with a view to understanding one another's stories even when it was not easy to listen. And finally, there was evidence that some of them were also enabled to restory their own experience and grow as educators. These events highlight the nature of community as a place where difference can be held, not necessarily a place where everyone thinks alike (Olson & Craig, 2001).

Integration of theory and practice. The teachers formulated their understandings of what is needed both for professional learning, on the one hand, and for educational development in the field, on the other, in a number of statements:

- "Mediating between theory and practice is one of the most important conditions, in my view, for professional development."

- "Professional learning is the bringing to bear of one's insights in praxis."

- "The connection between theory and practice is two-way...implementation of new programs and reforms in the school system is also a major factor in teachers' professional development."

These statements could be summaries of what the students had read in the literature, but the fact is that they came to these understandings at the end of a long process of writing and reflecting on their experiences in teaching and then using the theories we were reading to make sense of them. I will illustrate this integration with two brief examples, summarizing processes that were elaborated at some length in the teachers' writing.

The first example comes from Karen whose participation in the class discussion, above, demonstrated how she was able to restory her experience. At the beginning of the semester, Karen wrote about a humiliating experience in school, something that happened to her when she was only 8 and had just immigrated with her family to Israel; she wondered how it was that her teacher did not have the time to get to know her story, to realize she was not yet familiar with classroom procedures and rules, to sense her need for kind words and simple compassion. Her experience resonated with writing by Hankins (1998), Johnson (2007), and others, and drawing from her reading she formulated her own professional development as a journey "from confusion to compassion": the desire and intention to understand her students and empathize with them were central to her teaching, and she could trace this intention back to her early experience and forward through teacher education and graduate studies to her work in the present.

In the second example, in one class midway through the semester, the writing task of the day was to choose an image from a random pile of pictures of animals and write a dialogue; Nabil engaged in a dialogue with a rooster standing high on a rooftop, a picture which called up his experience as a pupil sent to a school where he felt alone and different from everyone around him. This childhood memory and the written dialogue brought to mind a much later time when he was a new teacher of math in a boarding school for youth at risk; he realized how much it had helped him at that time to draw on his own childhood experiences in working with his pupils. Thinking about the different kinds of awareness he had at different periods in his life, Nabil began to understand more clearly his interest in critical pedagogy (Freire, 1970) and could see how it was orienting his work in the present.

In both examples, the students wrote in a retrospective-prospective way, calling up significant memories from different times in their lives, exploring the qualities of the experiences that came to mind and often relating those experiences to concrete physical and bodily details. Through writing about the events, they were able to clarify different aspects of their identities, and at the same time to bring to bear the theoretical knowledge acquired in their studies to make sense of what was happening. They subsequently formulated professional insights about how their identities related to who they were as teachers, what their underlying purposes were as educators, what practices they espoused and how they enacted their identities in the classroom in the present. Both stories illustrate the integration of theory and practice in specific contexts as well as the authors' reflective awareness of that integration and the possibility of continuing to integrate theory and practice in other contexts in the future.

Does writing enable teachers to challenge the authoritative discourse?

As we have seen, in their writing the students related to what they considered central issues in professional development: they saw the role of story in enabling them to reflect on and make sense of their experience as teachers, and they emphasized the importance of monitoring their own learning and paying attention to cognitive dissonance. They stressed the contribution of developing of a knowledge community such as had taken shape in our class and were aware of how this facilitated the development of their own narrative authority and their ability to speak out about what mattered both in the university classroom and back at school. Their ideas were convergent with the literature on teacher development in general and on knowledge communities in particular but also show something of the ways that this particular university setting influenced their development. It is evident that their development was expressed in and through autobiographic writing, but it is important to try to tease out the specific contribution of writing, as we know, first, that teacher development does often take place in conversation and storytelling without benefit of writing; and second, that there can be learning and development which is engaging and meaningful for the learner yet fails to go beyond entrenched forms of discourse and does not challenge the authoritative discourse. Miller (2005) has warned that "telling one's story" may simply reinscribe already normalized identity categories, and similarly the discourse of reflection in education may lead to a routine form of practice in which "teachers learn about and then implement new pedagogical approaches and curriculum materials without a hitch (221)." Invoking terms like autobiography, reflection and communities of practice does not by itself provide a guarantee of change in the authoritative discourse of education.

I will address this question by consideration of a number of themes that emerge from the set of texts presented here and which point to the "added value" of autobiographic writing for teacher learning: *details, feelings, imagination, social concerns,* and *difference.* A few words about each of these points follow.

Details. I begin with the importance of paying attention to small details, generally thought to be one of the qualities that make for good writing (Goldberg, 1986). Typically the university classroom is concerned with theories, with large generalizations and with the abstract. In this context, attention to the concrete and to the small facts of everyday life goes against the grain, yet for teachers it seems to signal a respect for everyday life both in and out of the classroom. Detail is required for telling writing, but the opposite also holds: writing calls forth detail. In oral storytelling we are required to be more direct and concise, confining ourselves to what is essential for fear of losing our audience. But as we immerse ourselves in the writing of a meaningful story, the colors, sounds and textures present themselves and insist on being included. Paying attention to one's real life in this way is a practice which allows the writer "to pay attention to one's conduct" (Hasebe-Ludt & Jordan, 2010, 1) and perhaps also enables teachers to be fully present in the classroom, ready to teach and learn.

Feelings. Attending to feelings—whether happiness, pain, fear or the minor and less easily identified feelings that come and go—also challenges the taken-for-granted academic patterns, in this case that of divorcing thought from feeling (Miller, 2005; Zembylas, 2007). Noticing feelings helps teachers to figure out what is really important to them, including why they have come to the university and what they need from their studies. Of course feelings may also arise through conversation in a safe space, but writing allows more time and privacy to be present to one's feelings without risk of embarrassment.

One of the writing tasks focused on the topic of failure and invited the teachers to recall and set down an episode in which they made a mess of some professional situation; writing provides the chance to give form to the mess, to shape the event in a way that begins to reveal its meaning, even to suggest what may have been right about what the teacher did even in the midst of failure. The teacher who wrote about her frustrated attempt to lead a professional meeting, for example, began to see past her own humiliation to identify clearly what had been wrong in the principal's handling of the situation, and writing about this event became an empowering experience. Karen, who wrote about a childhood embarrassment, also clarified for herself through writing just how much this event contributed to who she became as a teacher.

Imagination and social concerns. Autobiographic writing made space for two further aspects of experience that are usually marginalized in graduate studies. Generally, imagination and social concerns are treated in separate disciplinary contexts, the humanities and social studies; social action is often relegated to an extra-curricular niche and not seen as an academic pursuit. For teachers who are immersed in the practical (and for their professors), this compartmentalization makes little sense. It seems clear that we need to draw on our imaginations to deal with important social issues such as gender, social justice, equality and power, not to mention the impasse of violent conflict. Allowing free rein to the imagination provided room to experiment with new thoughts and ideas, and it also introduced a light-hearted tone to balance the more difficult matters that were at the margins of our work. At the same time, the fact that the real and pressing issues of the day could be brought into the classroom was a relief, even though it made for some tense moments.

Difference. Finally, the recognition of cultural, social and religious differences in our classroom made the developing learning community an interesting and rich setting, despite its complications. All too often, diversity is thought of as a problem to be managed, but in our class it was apparent that multiculturalism is a factor that facilitates and empowers professional learning. The special contribution of writing was evident on a number of occasions, as it allowed the teachers to express themselves clearly and fully on matters of importance to them that might have seemed at first too controversial or provocative to be brought to the classroom conversation. Writing provided the space to release some of the tension of holding a difficult topic and then allowed the writer time to choose her words carefully. This was clear for the student who described her experience of teaching in a small community near the Gaza border, as for another student who wrote about a visualization of the terrors of the Gaza war and then imagined herself, her own body, as a place of refuge for all the children threatened by that war. In conversation alone, these experiences and images would likely have been expressed in the familiar terms of political debate that typically bring us to polarized views of right and wrong in the conflict, and rarely lead to new understanding (see Li, Conle & Elbaz-Luwisch, 2009). When these experiences were storied in writing, however, whether based on the writer's memory or a fantasized image of a lived, bodily experience, the sharing of these stories revealed our capacity to listen to one another even across boundaries of conflicting identities.

The themes of detail, feeling, imagination, social concerns and difference highlight the ways that autobiographical writing not only allowed the students to learn and develop beyond their own personal boundaries but also illuminate how such writing can challenge authoritative views of teaching and learning. Although I make no claims about the impact of the course for all the students, I was encouraged by how readily they took to the format of the course and by their willingness to experiment and learn in new ways; my impression is that almost all the students were afforded some important insights through their writing. It also seems evident that the various elements act synergistically: autobiographic writing was done not in isolation but in an academic milieu focused on the production of knowledge, in the context of reflection on teaching practice and its improvement, and in the setting of a developing community of practice. All these aspects work together to make the experience more significant for participants.

Students' assessments via the university-administered teaching survey indicated that there was also room for improvement. The connection between the two parts of the class—personal writing and conventional academic work—was unclear at times; some students needed this to be demonstrated more explicitly. Further, each student had preferred ways of easing into personal writing, but for some this continued to be difficult, and in future I would pay more attention to individual needs.

A final question is how experiences shared by the students could be taken further and brought into the real-life settings where they work. Unfortunately, I missed the opportunity to ask this question of the students themselves. Several students indicated at the beginning of the course that they already had the habit of keeping a journal and recording their teaching experiences, and I imagine that for them the course is likely to have enlarged their awareness of ways to make use of journaling. Others, however, will not find or make the time to write unless facilitated by some form of professional development activity. Laneve (2009) refers to the writing that is done by some teachers in 'in-between' moments during their working day as "stolen time writing," highlighting just how much of a challenge to the authoritative discourse teacher writing might be. Furthermore, many teachers associate writing with the carrying out of assigned academic tasks; for them a workshop that introduces writing not as a chore but a pleasure could be instrumental in making available the possibility of writing for one's own personal and professional development. Ideally, this should be done in a voluntary context where marks are not given! Probably the most important step would be to build time for writing into the schedule of activities of existing teacher communities where personal writing can support other development processes.

At the end of the course I invited the participants to write one of their conclusions about professional learning on a slip of paper and to exchange it with another class member. The slip of paper I received says "There can be no professional learning without challenging fixed ideas." In these times, under pressure from outcomes-oriented policies, there is a temptation for academics who work with in-service and pre-service teachers: as we try to bring ideas and activities that will contribute to teacher development and help them grow professionally, we may be limiting our suggestions to "what works." In my own case, I admit that for many years I held the fixed idea that Israeli teachers were too busy, overworked and tired to be interested in personal writing that did not promise ready solutions to problems of practice. It may be that graduate education will contribute more to the kind of teacher learning that is relevant for their everyday work if we are more courageous in challenging fixed ideas and asking hard questions. We might demonstrate our own willingness to take apart our knowledge and dwell in not knowing and uncertainty for a time. Autobiographical writing can also provide a safe space for those of us who work with teachers to be critical of existing arrangements even when we have no ideas (yet) for how to improve them.

Notes

1. The 'scribble' exercise was adapted from Salome Schwartz.

2. The 'circle' exercise was introduced by Arlene and Jean-Claude Audergon at the "Butterfly Intensive" in La Grange, Switzerland, in September 2006.

3. Public strikes and demonstrations were held in many of the towns in the Arab/Palestinian sector at this time.

CHAPTER 7

"Taking the Imagination Visiting" as Pedagogy: Journal Fragments

"To think with the enlarged mentality—that means you train your imagination to go visiting." *Hannah Arendt, 1978, 257*

One of the greatest privileges of university life is the opportunity to travel, and to get to know one's colleagues from different parts of the world. To be sure, there are many negative aspects to international travel in particular: it is wasteful of resources, expensive and often exhausting. Air travel involves much that seems like 'lost time': waiting in electronically controlled and artificially lit environments, being 'processed' from check-in through shopping areas to waiting rooms to crowded aircraft. On arrival one may confront language barriers, pressures of time and ever-present tourist inducements; whether on vacation or meeting with colleagues, there is rarely enough time to really get to know and understand the lives of local residents. And yet, it seems that the desire to learn about other people and other cultures, to be part of things, is almost inevitably awakened by finding oneself in an unfamiliar place; travel has been an important part of my learning over the years.

Devorah (interviewed in Chapter 5), spoke about the attitude with which she first came to Israel and which she still takes with her when she travels:

I was busy trying to be an Israeli, even when I thought I was going back, in that first year. It's more or less the way I think now, for example I was in India for a week, I wouldn't mind living in India for a year. I think I wouldn't mind so much, to get to know things. And even when I first came for a year, I thought, I want to be part of this.

Although it is all too easy to fall back into the defensive posture of the tourist, complaining about the food or bemoaning minor inconveniences, I note that many of the experiences I've had of seeing differently, connecting differently, understanding things in a fresh way, have happened away from home. Writing done in far-away places has a different quality: there is more 'wakefulness' (Elbaz-Luwisch, 2010a), 'beginner's mind' is evoked more easily, and I'm more likely to write poetry when in unfamiliar places.

In the present chapter I draw on Hannah Arendt's notion of 'taking the imagination visiting,' described by Zerilli as the "art of imaginatively occupying the standpoints of other people" (Zerilli, 2005, 176). Barr and Griffiths (2004) elaborate on the way that Arendt connected an understanding of storytelling and of using the imagination to understand the perspectives of others, with a concern for critical thinking:

> Being critical, for Arendt, does not call for disinterest, detachment or withdrawal from political commitment. Instead, it requires 'training the imagination to go visiting' and this is done by means of stories. By storytelling, she asks, 'How would you see the world if you saw it from my position?' (Barr & Griffiths, 2004, 7)

Putting this a little differently, Disch comments that "In order to tell yourself the story of an event from an unfamiliar standpoint, you have to position yourself there *as yourself*" (Disch, 1994,158). In Arendt's own words:

> I form an opinion by considering a given issue from different viewpoints, by making present to my mind the standpoints of those who are absent; that is, I represent them. This process of representation does not blindly adopt the actual views of those who stand somewhere else, and hence look upon the world from a different perspective; this is a question. . .of being and thinking in my own identity where actually I am not. (Arendt, 1993, 241)

Barr and Griffiths add that "By means of *taking the imagination visiting* I am both *distanced from* the familiar and *taken to* unfamiliar standpoints" (2004, 7). Visiting in this sense is not tourism—looking from the safe distance of a spectator, nor should it be reduced to empathy which involves putting oneself into the situation of the other. According to Disch (1994), "Visiting involves constructing stories of an event from each of the plurality of perspectives that might have an interest in telling it and imagining how I would respond as a character in a story very different from my own. It is a kind of representation that arrives at the general through the particular" (158).

Thus visiting, like narrative inquiry, involves immersing oneself in the details and particularities of a situation viewed from diverse points of view. Attention to detail and to the particular might seem to be focused on the 'surface' of the world, but the purpose of such visiting could not be more serious for Arendt. As both Disch and Zerilli explain, Arendt's driving concern is with judgment, with the search for ways to respond to totalitarianism and with the possibilities of freedom. The notion of visiting is elaborated in an ethical and epistemological context in relation to the work of Kant on judgment. The idea of 'visiting' has obvious educational implications, as it is intended to enlarge the understanding. In this, attention to detail is crucial: Arendt believed that "the essence of education is natality, the fact that human beings are born into the world" (Arendt, 1993); thus, children must be brought up and educated with great care, introducing them to the world as it is, in all its specificity, while also allowing them to become, to prepare for the task of bringing something new into the world.

An idea that is closely allied to Arendt's notion of 'visiting' is elaborated by Maria Lugones (1987) with the phrase "world"-travelling. Lugones speaks about the practice, imposed as a matter of course on people outside society's mainstream, and particularly women of color, of shifting flexibly "from the mainstream construction of life where she is constructed as an outsider to other constructions of life where she is more or less 'at home.' (3) Although such travelling is largely imposed and the world being travelled to is a hostile one for the outsider, Lugones points out that the practice of world-travelling can also be taken up voluntarily and that it can be seen as a "skillful, creative, rich, enriching and, given certain circumstances, as a loving way of being and living" (1987, 3). The potential of 'world'-travelling is found in the act of sharing, for some time and to some degree, the lives and perspective of the people whose world one is visiting—without this sharing, without interaction, there would be little potential for significant learning.

The terms 'taking the imagination visiting' and 'world'-travelling are both metaphors for coming to know other worlds, through travel that is intellectual, imaginative and emotional rather than geographical. However, I want to consider the potential of actual travel as a form of 'visiting' in the Arendtian sense. In travelling to unfamiliar places, I find that I am more open to construction and reconstruction of myself and my world(s), less concerned about being competent, not taking rules as sacred, and "finding ambiguity and double edges a source of wisdom and delight" (17). I'm also more likely to be "playful," as Lugones (1987) understands it: open to surprise and to "being a fool." All these qualities, in fact, are what for Lugones make 'world'-travelling possible and worthwhile.

This chapter consists of a series of fragments, some taken directly from travel journals written while visiting various places, some written later as retrospective accounts. Some of the fragments are narrative in form, some are poetic. I hope that in some cases I have been able to occupy the standpoints of others, to understand what it would be like to be where I am not, but often no doubt I have failed in this. I make no effort to analyze the fragments, to look for common threads, themes or insights. I do no more than put them in roughly chronological order and say a little about the context. The fragments are presented in a playful spirit: perhaps they are foolish and will not make sense, but perhaps the way this chapter is organized will convey something about 'taking the imagination visiting,' about seeing the world through different eyes, about being immersed in the particular, about connecting or failing to connect with others whose world is different.

It's time to set out on the journey—since I haven't provided any tickets, we'll have to jump over the turnstile when the guards aren't looking.

Zichron Yaacov, Israel, 1995

My journey begins at home, in my bed. In a dream: I am lying in bed and my mother appears standing next to me. She is quite pale, wearing a long white nightgown, eyes open but not really seeing me—in short, she looks like a stereotypical ghost. I'm a little taken aback to see her this way, a little scared. She takes hold of my hands and tries to pull me out of bed. Not speaking. I don't know where she wants to take me, but I know with absolute certainty that I cannot and must not take this trip with her. I also know that I'm dreaming and that I *must* wake up. *Wake up, wake up, wake up*, I tell myself, louder and louder. And I wake myself up: suddenly I'm awake, in the same room and in the same bed but awake and hearing what seems to be the faint echo of my voice actually saying it aloud "Wake up!"

I didn't know what the command to wake up meant exactly. I was already doing what I could to be present, in the moment. Having done yoga since my mid-twenties, I attended my first week-long meditation retreat at around this time. I went to different kinds of workshops that were focused on seeking awareness. I kept a journal. Obviously I needed to do more—my mother had always been so busy doing something or other; I never feel that I've done enough. Here, I think began the project of writing about my mother. It began as a vague idea, which I thought about in random moments; it was not yet a plan. I imagined it as a literary project, hence something I didn't really know how to do.

Jerusalem, August 1996

A trip to Jerusalem, with some official purpose I don't remember, but really, to visit my parents' graves on the 18th anniversary of my mother's death, to say a goodbye of sorts. On the way I listen to music in the car, the McGarrigle Sisters singing in French. The lilt of the accordion sent me to a dimly-lit kitchen, in Russia perhaps or in Montreal. People are laughing or worrying, but quietly, so as not to wake the children, the old people, the neighbors, the government, the spirits, or the desires in themselves.

I never saw you dance. Oh, except at my wedding. But there was dancing in your eyes. Even there, it was restrained, a modest little two-step, arms rising slightly with the sideways movement, then falling gently. But only with your eyes. Your body, which could have been soft, was held, not stiff but wary. Always alert for danger, ready to freeze, ready to run. Ready to sing, like Nina Simone? No, not sing.

The noise I thought was a mower is a trimmer. Soon the branches of shrubbery that shade Dad's stone will be cut. The worker sees me watching him. He's thorough, trims all the way down behind the stone. Now he's gathering up the branches that fell, placing them to one side. He looks at me and asks if it's okay. I'm touched that he cares if I think he's done a good job.

"Dans un endroit tranquille, tu trouves le repos," sang the McGarrigle sisters. It is very peaceful here, even with the buzzing of the trimmer which has moved on to another spot. There's a breeze, the air has a faintly spicy scent of pine. I'm sitting on the step in the shade of two tall pines, through which I see the wooded hill opposite. This, and the smell, remind me a bit of Greece. I always forget this piney smell of Jerusalem.

At the Museum I saw a Vietnamese figure—a "funeral post"—it was you, the evening you died—stick limbs, face hollowed, staring out at me, not seeing. Tall, simply carved in rough wood, geometric features. It spoke to me from centuries and continents away. It told me that many others have shared my experience of seeing someone they loved turn to wood, to a lifeless shell of what they lived. A nameless Vietnamese artist, perhaps not much farther from starvation than his dead friend, made this funeral post which allowed his friend not just to be remembered but to live two centuries and to travel and see the world. In his spot at the Israel Museum, s/he gets to see streams of tourists, people who fell asleep during the movie on the Chagall windows and now revive to find themselves facing a two-hundred-year-old wooden figure. Or the two-thousand year-old red clay Mourner from Bahia in the pre-Columbian exhibit. He too knows grief, sitting on the ground with arms resting on his bent knees; sad but present. "Here to be seen," in the words of an African greeting ritual.

Flashback: London, 1967

I land in London in June 1967, just days before the Six Day War. I've left Israel at the urging of my parents, worried about the impending dangers, and of the school principal, a religious man who for several weeks, during the tension and build-up to the war had been assuring me that as an only child my first duty was to my parents. In a letter I had received from home a few days earlier my father had written that he would contact his friends in Reading, Harry and Muriel Stevens, and that perhaps I could visit them. As I arrive in the terminal I see a man standing at the exit who looks rather like I imagine Harry Stevens would look—tall, with shaggy grey-blond hair and mustache and a tan tweed jacket, but I am too shy to approach him. I tell myself that surely all English gentlemen of a certain age look like this and proceed towards the exit. Before I leave it occurs to me to ask at the information desk if there is any message for me, and indeed I'm handed a letter from my father. I head toward the bus stop outside the terminal, planning to read the letter on my way to London, but then I think better of it and open the envelope. I turn my luggage cart around and head back to the terminal: my dad had phoned the Stevenses (with whom my father had not spoken in about 25 years; in fact he had probably *never* spoken to them on the telephone), and Harry said he would be at the airport to pick me up. I ask the woman at Information to page him and the man I had noticed comes forward. He tells me that he had noticed me too and thought I must be my father's daughter, but he also had been too shy, or too polite, to approach me.

I spend two magical days in Reading. It is no longer (and perhaps wasn't even then) the small village I had imagined from my father's stories, but the Stevens' home is a delight, full of comfortable old furniture, books, and pictures. Harry had been a teacher of draftsmanship at a local high school, and his woodcuts grace the walls; Muriel's hand is evident in the way things are arranged. She shows me to the same room my father stayed in when he was there and explains how to use the handmade leather latch to close the door. Harry shows me the spot at the bottom of the garden where my dad used to go to smoke his pipe now and again. (I'd never seen my father smoke, although his pipe and one that had belonged to *his* father were in a desk drawer at home.) For dinner Muriel makes a salad with tomatoes, watercress grown in her garden and raisins, an unfamiliar and delicious combination. She asks if I'd like chicken or "something harmless" like cheese with my meal, obviously remembering the Jewish dietary laws; I ask for "something harmless." They tell me stories about their sons, their daughters-in-law and the grandchildren. I tell them about my parents, and about the year I've just spent in Israel as a volunteer, teaching at a school not far from a small development town. When I'm about to leave Muriel asks me to sign their guest book, telling me that I am their first guest "from Palestine." I think there's a little hesitation, a hiccup, after she says this, realizing her mistake, perhaps wondering if she has offended. But I'd grown up around people who still referred to Israel as Palestine, out of habit, even those who were Zionists; and the Six Day War is still waiting to happen. I have no problems with her use of terms.

Oulu, Finland, February 2001

My connection with Finland began in 1998 when I was invited to participate in an international research project on change in teaching; the project didn't materialize but a lively and ongoing research collaboration began. I first visited Oulu in 1998, to take part in meetings of Leena Syrjala's research group. Leena had written beforehand that she and Eila Estola would meet me at the airport, and that I would recognize them easily enough: two middle-aged Finnish women. I responded that they would no doubt recognize me too: middle-aged and not Finnish-looking. And so it was. I felt at home in Finland, and with my hosts, very quickly. No doubt a shared academic language and interests have a lot to do with this, but there was more. Somehow, many of my experiences in Finland remind me of my mother: the reserved friendliness of Finnish people, the airy and clean lines of Finnish style which calls to mind my mother's kitchen, and the carefully prepared and delicately seasoned food.

On my first visit a young couple was part of the research group, and they brought along their infant son. When I asked the baby's name, I was surprised to learn that he did not have a name yet: it was autumn, and he would not be christened until the spring. This custom apparently dates back to the time before motorized transportation. Since it was difficult to travel with a baby during the winter, and in addition many infants did not survive their first year, it became customary to wait for warmer weather before christening babies. I wondered if the young parents had chosen their baby's name, and if they secretly called him by it, if only in their minds, but was too shy to ask; it was hard for me to imagine not giving one's baby a name for so long.

In 2000 Eila came to spend 6 months in Haifa to work on her doctoral dissertation, and over the years I've been lucky to visit Finland many times, at different seasons of the year: the long dark days of winter gently lit by the reflection of moon on snow, the coming of spring felt almost tangibly in the extra few minutes of light that poured into each passing day, and the spaciousness of summer nights in which families enjoyed visiting, hiking and playing, with no need to worry about children's bedtimes.

One concrete result of the cooperation with Finnish colleagues was a joint publication (Estola & Elbaz-Luwisch, 2003) at the end of which we reflected on the nature and quality of our work together:

> Our work together began when Eila came to Israel and noticed the voice of the body in the texts of a Finnish teacher, Helena. We agreed that this topic was worth exploring further. Once we had made this decision, bodies were suddenly everywhere, demanding attention—in our teaching, in the stories of teachers we had collected, but also in our everyday lives. We started writing in Israel in the sun and finished in Finland during midwinter. In breaks from writing we walked on the beach in Israel, went skiing in Finland, and had a Finnish sauna. We listened to music from the desert and Finnish tango music, and the different rhythms punctuated our thinking and writing. These bodily experiences of writing (Hocking et al., 2001) also taught us how deeply our identities are embodied, how many feelings and values we carry all the time in our bodies.

Based on our own experiences in two cultures and after visiting schools in both countries, we have the impression that there are many similarities in the embodied practice of teaching. On opening the door there is no doubt that you have come into a school: corridors, classrooms, blackboards, desks, teachers standing in front of the class or walking around. But as teachers' stories showed us, there are differences as well, in the amount of noise, in the rules of appropriate behavior, in patterns of relating and touching, in styles of movement. In a multicultural world it is becoming more and more important to understand the cultural ground of our bodies and the power different bodies have. (Estola and Elbaz-Luwisch, 2003, 715–716)

India, February 2003

India fascinated me for years, but the prospect of going there frightened me; I thought I would be overwhelmed by the poverty. But once I had made some Indian friends through involvement with process-oriented psychology, I decided to make the trip. I stayed with my friend Radhika in Mumbai, joining in the rhythms of everyday life: on my first days in Mumbai I went along to meetings of a group of women involved in a number of social action projects and in educating against racism; later I went to observe Radhika's music lesson (she was learning to play a traditional instrument, the rudra veena). I also participated in a two-day workshop for teachers given by my friends Marguerite and Taba and learned about some of the issues which concerned Indian teachers. I was grateful for the chance to visit in people's homes and hear about their lives. It was, however, challenging, to be in homes where there were servants as a matter of course; this was made more difficult because I could not speak with these people, and as a result they seemed to me almost transparent. Gradually, though, I became aware of the many small ways that my friends sensitively organized things to lighten the load of their workers; for example, after dinner they would suggest we move to another room for coffee, because the kitchen worker would be unable to clean up and finish his day's work as long as we were sitting at the table. I began to see the responsibilities that were entailed by having servants, a side of things I had not previously imagined.

Since reading Andre Malraux's writing on the art of India (see Malraux, 1965, 1968), I had dreamed of visiting Ellora and Banares (now Varanasi). Because of the weather, I had to postpone a visit to Varanasi but did go to Ellora, the site of more than 30 remarkable caves intricately carved into the rock, caves that had been places of worship for Hindu, Jain and Buddhist monks at various overlapping periods between the 5th and 10th centuries. The Buddhist caves served as monasteries and are decorated with figures of the Buddha and various saints, while the Hindu caves are decorated with carvings of the various deities. The caves are diverse in size, style and form of construction; one of them, carved downwards from the top floor, constitutes the largest free-standing sculpture in the world. These caves were seen by Malraux as the source of spiritual imagery of mothers, emerging from the depths of the earth. I experienced the caring of mothers when I was resting on a rock above one of the caves: a young girl came up to me, urged on by her mother sitting nearby, to tell me that there were too many mosquitoes in the spot I had chosen and that I should move to a seat lower down on the site. On my last evening at Ellora I sat outside looking at the caves in the near distance, reading and writing. Night had just begun to fall when there was a power shortage; a hotel employee brought me a candle, but when it had burned down I decided I had no choice but to go to bed as the entire complex was completely dark. I tried to sleep but it was too early and I was not tired. I checked the time on my cell phone and realized that the phone gave enough light to show me the way to the central building, where I could get more candles and perhaps some food. I returned to the terrace and continued reading by candlelight; sitting in that remote place with neither electricity nor phone connection, with no possibility of contacting my family, or even my friends in Mumbai, I was perfectly content.

Towards the end of my stay I went to Goa, which seemed a required destination for an Israeli tourist.

Goa, February 8, 2003.

The sun comes up a little before 7 to the sound of birds, loud and raucous crowing and calling. At 8 on the beach it is quiet but full of activity. Café workers are setting up, and lots of people have clustered around the boats and fishing nets. Eight or nine of them are getting a boat named "Jesus" into the water. The boats are blue, green, yellow, orange; a white one is trimmed in blue and called "Praise the Lord." On the beach a few kids and all the dogs are playing. Some of the dogs have collars, I see now, but all of them seem to be beach-dwellers. Some cluster in groups, and when one moves or gets up to stretch the others follow suit.

At 10 it's still breezy and cool on the shady side of the restaurant verandah. Pale tourists begin to walk the beach slowly. Across the river a truck is being unloaded, a porter carries tall boxes on his head to the Sun Set Restaurant. The curve of the beach is covered in brown and green fishing nets, yellow cords, bright blue plastic tarps. Two crows sit on the table next to mine, checking out the kitchen of the restaurant just inside. One flies away, the other follows a few moments later.

Two guys are squatting on the bottom of an upturned aqua boat named something Brothers. They are scraping away at the underside of the boat with files of some kind. Now a third fellow has joined them, he's wiping the other end of the boat. They are working steadily but slowly. Much of what's happening on this beach seems to be in slow motion. The porters are still going back and forth on the other bank. The one in the beige shirt is carrying a tower of four boxes on his head. He walks with the same springy gait going and coming back empty. Even the waves coming in on the beach are slow and deliberate. In my last hour in this place I begin to love it for this pace. Three buses have just arrived, parking right under the verandah next to the tree where five crows are perched. A whistle, horns, voices begin to intrude on the quiet.

Haifa, 2003–4

Overcraft: Obsession, decoration and biting beauty. All I have to do is cross the street. For the two-month period during which the Haifa University Art Gallery hosts the exhibition titled *Overcraft*, I feel as if I am at the center of the universe. At any time of the day, I can leave my office, go down two flights and out the front door of the Education building, cross the street to the Main Building, walk through the lobby and enter another world. The space, an ordinary white rectangle when other exhibits have been shown here, has been covered in paint and fabric in rich hues of red against which the works displayed all seem to glow and vibrate, drawing the visitor in.

Right at the entrance, however, something stuns me: it is a side of beef, dripping blood. No, it is a sculpture: Michal Shamir's *Untitled* (2003). It has been constructed of hundreds, perhaps thousands, of small jelly candies which glow under the lighting of the space. On the other side of the gallery, something else glows: it's a rendition of a news photo taken after a terror attack on Bus 32A in Jerusalem in June 2002. The work shows the burnt-out bus, with rescue workers in yellow and black vests standing in front of it (Merav Sudaey, "Line 32A," 2003). The photo has been reproduced in a large copy done entirely in sequins and embroidery; from close up the whole surface glitters almost obscenely, but viewed from farther away it seems to radiate an inner fire. Sheila Kobo takes as her subject children's pajamas, the kind worn on the kibbutz where she grew up in the 1950s; she has covered canvas with tiny beads to recreate the naïve patterns of fairy tale scenes, cars and flowers on a shimmering but hard beaded surface. As I move from one work to the next I am thrown repeatedly off balance: taken in and exhilarated by the exquisite color and energy of these works, then dropped to the depths when the harsh message hits me. The works speak about longing and loneliness, about grief, violence, exploitation, disappointment. And they are beautiful.

Kingston, Ontario, July 2005

Kingston is a city I have driven past countless times when making the trip between Montreal and Toronto; I visited there only once, when invited to give a colloquium presentation in the early 1980s. Now it is summer, twenty or more years later, and I am visiting the Thousand Islands area with a friend; a stop in Kingston seems like a good idea. At a gas station I look over at the car stopped at the next pump, and I see two large golden retrievers sitting in the front seat of the car, in poses of full entitlement. By the time I manage to scramble for my camera, only the driver is still in his seat; his mate, presumably, has gone to the bathroom.

At the gas station we are given a map which indicates various tourist sites, and we decide to go to the Union Gallery before lunch. We drive slowly down a well-marked main street, but the number at which the gallery is located doesn't seem to exist. We park and walk back, realizing that the gallery must be inside the huge, angular and ultra-modern building that looms uninvitingly over the street corner. It is the library of Queen's University and indeed, once inside we find the gallery immediately. Nothing, except perhaps the retrievers, could have prepared me for the experience of entering

Rebecca Soudant's installation, titled *Re-Cover*.[1] Soudant is a student of teacher education (and now a teacher and artist working in a wide range of media including fabric, metal and wood). Her installation is a classroom, and while it is instantly recognizable as a classroom, it is unlike any classroom I have seen before.

The classroom designed by Soudant was conceived to question the uniformity and homogenizing effect of conventional school settings. The space is recognizable as a classroom because it does contain desks, they are arranged in rows, and there is a book—apparently the same book—on each desk. From here on, any similarity to a real classroom, living or dead, ends. The desks were designed and built "to be as individualized as the students who might occupy them." (Soudant, 2005) They are of different sizes and shapes; most appear to be recycled and they are painted in bright shades of pink, yellow, turquoise, red and green. Most have chairs, while some are low and accompanied by cushions, and others are tall, podium-like and meant for standing only. One desk has a sort of steering wheel, one is enclosed by shutters for privacy; several desks would be impossible to write at: one is saddle-shaped; another is a round globe with a small cutout so one might place one's belongings inside. In a text accompanying the exhibit, Soudant states that this diversity of seating "acknowledges the natural differences in physical shapes and body types and promotes an acceptance of this truth of human difference as a norm, just as desirable as celebrating differences in spirit." The classroom flouts practicality but is joyous and inviting.

The books placed on all the desks (perched precariously in several cases) prove to be copies of *Oliver Twist,* all with the same red binding. However, the text inside has been altered with Photoshop in one of several different ways, allowing viewers to see the text as students might see them if they have one of a series of "exceptionalities: dyslexia, attention deficit, scotopic sensitivity syndrome, retinitis pigmentosa, racial slur sensitivity and for contrast, reading for enjoyment." I must confess that I did not read the artist's text carefully enough while visiting the exhibit. As a result, while I identified all of the texts intended to reflect what we might otherwise term disabilities, I entirely missed the text meant to reflect the student whose 'exceptionality' was an inclination to read for enjoyment.

A final thought-provoking feature of this classroom was the absence of a teacher's desk. Instead, at the front of the classroom was a life-sized *photograph* of a teacher's desk, red with a white top, with a ring binder and several books sitting on it and a calendar, with an illustration from St. Exupéry's *Little Prince*, hanging behind the desk. A magisterial red chair—empty—is placed behind the desk. A real teacher in this classroom would be unable to take refuge behind this two-dimensional desk and would have to be physically available to students, circulating among the desks.

I did not want to leave Rebecca Soudant's classroom; I wanted to try out all the desks and chairs, I wanted to bring some favorite books and a notebook to write in. I wondered what it would be like to be seated on a low cushion, with my fellow students around and above me at desks of various heights. I remembered the 7th grade, when the teacher seated the shorter students in front so that our view would not be blocked, and then she noticed that two of us were unable to reach the floor because the regulation desk and chair were too high. She announced to the entire class that this was bad for our posture and promptly had our desks and chairs replaced with the size used in a lower grade, without asking about our wishes in the matter. A few months into the year the other girl moved away, and I was left in the front in the only smaller-sized desk in the class.

Today most elementary school classrooms make some accommodations for the needs of children: many classrooms have a reading corner with cushions, mattresses or an easy chair. Round tables where children can work in groups are common, and of course there are computer stations. Physical discipline is also now conceived differently. Even in the prestigious primary school classroom I visited in Beijing in 2010, where children were very well disciplined, I noted that the fourth graders working in groups assumed a variety of postures—some were standing and moving around the table, others were lounging at their chairs while one tired lad was stretched out, almost asleep on the table, all the while taking part in the task of exploring electric circuitry. However, these phenomena reflect small accommodations to the prevailing view of schooling rather than major revisions. What has changed very little, and Soudant's installation brings this home sharply, is the underlying "ethic of sameness and assimilation" that undergirds the authoritative discourse of education as a transmission of knowledge from those who know to those who require instruction and guidance.

India, February 2006

This is my second visit to India, and the plan is to tour the southern state of Kerala.

After a few days relaxing on a Goan beach, we buy train tickets and wait at the local train station at 11 p.m. for a train that will take us south to Kochi, the capital of Kerala. The train station is dark and almost deserted, but a half-dozen other travelers are waiting for the same train, which we are told is going to be late. There's nothing to do but pace up and down the platform, sit on our suitcases, and pace some more. Finally we hear the train approaching; there's quite a lot of fuss on the platform, but finally we locate the correct car and board the train. It pulls away quickly and we find ourselves standing with our luggage in a narrow passageway, beside berths that all seem to be occupied by sleeping passengers. It is hot, the lights are off, there seems to be no chance of locating the correct berths and the air is thick with the smell of feet. I am expecting to spend the night standing up or perhaps sitting on the floor. Then suddenly the lights are on again, a conductor appears asking for our tickets, he finds our places and unceremoniously dispatches the passengers who had temporarily occupied our berths.

I doze on and off all night, am just falling into a deeper sleep when the train stops at a station and an army of vendors board the train shouting "Tea, tea." The light has just come up and although I try to sleep some more, soon we are at another stop and this time coffee vendors march through the car, followed at the next stop by people with various breakfast offerings. The process of starting the day as a train traveler seems to be carefully orchestrated and there is little hope of maintaining one's personal rhythm; most of the passengers wake up and start to fold down their berths. We sit up, still only half awake, trying to read as we watch the countryside go by: people are beginning the day, children on their way to school, men on motorbikes heading to work, women doing chores on balconies. We should have arrived in Kochi by now, but time goes by slowly, one small town looking much like the next, everything green and lush and lazy and beautiful. Finally the train approaches the city which on first sight looks run down and chaotic. In the station porters rush at us offering to take our bags but we keep walking to the exit of the station where we finally find a taxi which takes us through industrial areas and across a bridge to the old part of the city.

I am spellbound by the deep blue of the Indian Ocean and fantasize dreamily about long ago voyages in search of gold, jewels and spices. My companion, who has spent time in the North of India on a previous trip, complains about the dirty and neglected appearance of the city, but I am determined to hold on to the romantic images I have created. At the synagogue, built in 1658, it is easier. There is an exhibit of naïve paintings describing the long history of the community, beginning, it is claimed, with the arrival of King Solomon. The main hall of the synagogue has a floor of blue and white Delft tiles brought from Holland in 1762, 1100 tiles of which no two are alike. The ark containing the Torah scrolls is decked in red velvet and brocade. Outside, the spice market is nearby, as is the palace of the ruler of the city, clearly indicating the status of Kochi's Jewish community in times past. How people might have lived then is harder to imagine, and after a while I am exhausted by the effort of trying to recreate the past of this community in my mind. In the Kashi Art Café, a pleasant yuppie-style place where things like granola and banana bread are served and a photograph exhibit lines the walls, I write in my notebook and sip coffee, relaxing back into my more familiar identity. I recognize someone from the Kathakali performance we saw the previous evening and when he comes over to say hello I am pleased; I feel less anonymous now. His job had been to introduce the story and provide narration as well as take tickets beforehand. It had been fascinating to watch the actors being made up and putting on their elaborate costumes, but even the drastically shortened version we saw had been far too long, and it was quite impossible to follow the story even with the aid of a printed summary.

Meenakshi Amman Temple, Madurai, February 21, 2006

The Meenakshi Amman Temple towers over the city of Madurai. The exterior surface is entirely covered in carved figures, flowers and animals; it is ornate, cheerful and brightly colored in blues, reds and yellows. We leave our shoes at one of the gates and go inside. We enter a vast world of its own, dimly lit, full of people and activity, relatively quiet considering all that is going on. There is a museum displaying many weathered statues, and long panels with drawings of the Ramayana; the exhibits are labeled unhelpfully: "ivory objects," "old coins." There are many kiosks selling food, drink and trinkets of all kinds. There are shrines to different deities, some of them closed to non-Hindus. In one area there are a number of statues on a raised platform decorated with carvings of the moon and stars; people line up to walk around this shrine in a brisk march. At other spots people prostrate themselves on the floor, praying to be granted children, sons.

Everything is fascinating, and very little of it seems to fall under the category of "religious worship" that I brought with me into the temple. It seems we could wander for hours and not see the same thing twice. Then suddenly I am tired and overwhelmed. In order to retrieve our shoes we have to leave by the entrance we came in, but it seems we are lost. We trace our way back past the elephants, past the market, past a shrine I can identify when I see it again because of the name I gave it, the "macaroni and vinegar" shrine (it is something like Mukkuruni Vinayagar). We are going in circles. A woman comes up to us—we had seen her earlier, selling beaded necklaces and when I declined to buy one, she argued with me, telling me that all the Israelis like them. Now she reappears, luckily bearing us no grudge, and tells us exactly where to go to find our shoes. Outside, the guard hands us our shoes immediately, without waiting to see the ticket. It is dark and we meet several cows on the way back to our hotel. I wonder what it was that I experienced in those last moments, when I really wanted to leave: was it claustrophobia? Or the simple weight of human feeling in all its complexity and confusion?

Kumily, February 22, 2006

Listening to the birds at this 'homestay' on the edge of the Periyar Nature Preserve. Language is not adequate to the variety of sounds produced by all of them—there's a hoot with a kind of burp at the end of it, a long gurgle, now a hoot just preceded by a burp, a long warbley hoot, now suddenly it's quiet, broken by the engine of an arriving rickshaw. It's shady and there's just enough breeze. I could sit here and listen, and read, and write, for a long time.

Vienna, May 2006

In the course of an intensive genealogical search for information about my father's family, my daughter Maya turned up the whereabouts of my grandparents' graves in Vienna. We had not even imagined that my grandfather, who died in Buchenwald, would have a grave; but in the early years of the war Buchenwald was not a death camp, and when people died there their remains were sent back to their families for burial. We had planned to go to Vienna together, but I had a conference to attend, and Maya couldn't join me, and I was impatient; I didn't think too much about whether I wanted to do this on my own. I had the precise numbers of the graves and was given a detailed map of the cemetery, a huge place with many entrances and a tram line running alongside it. It was not difficult to find my grandfather's grave in the new Jewish cemetery. In the older section where my grandmother, who died in 1909, was buried, the territory did not much resemble the map. I decided to return the next day when the office would be open. Although I had no language to explain myself to the woman in the office who spoke no English, I showed her the papers I had and she pulled a box off a shelf and from inside the box retrieved a small notebook with the names of the deceased written in pen. I copied down the name of my grandmother's 'neighbors', and set off again. I was not optimistic as many of the gravestones had been so eroded by the weather that no inscription remained, while others had simply fallen over. But I managed to find some of the names I had written down, and finally I was standing in front of a gravestone completely covered in vines and shrubbery. I started to pull away at the vines, and I began to see the familiar letters, and then my grandmother's name.

Mother is very ill, so be a good boy.
Be quiet,
Play nicely with your brother.
Shh, don't tell the children,
Not yet.
This disease has no cure
in 1909.
Vienna, Central Friedhof.
All the dead are gathered here.
Along the road, marble pillars
Stand tall to honour death.
In Gate 1, Section 20, row 33,

I find my grandmother.
In her 29th year,
Sadly missed by her husband
and children.
I have to take the tram
To Gate 4,
To find my grandfather.
Section 22, row 19,
Dachau 1939, it says,
contradicting the official information—
He died in Buchenwald.
Did the stonemason know
he made a mistake?
I am here
Contradicting history with blue flowers.

Einsiedeln, Switzerland, September, 2009

After my paternal grandmother died in 1909, my grandfather took his two young sons to Zurich where his sister Dora lived; my father had good memories of going to school there. I do not know why they left Switzerland after a few years, moving first to Reinfelden just across the border in Germany, and later to Wiesbaden. At the time there could have been no way of knowing that it would have been worth making every effort to remain in Switzerland. During the war some thirty thousand Jews were given refuge in Switzerland (Seidler, 2000), while an equal number were turned away.

A hundred years later, attending a seminar on the work of Marion Woodman in Einsiedeln, a small town in Switzerland, I found myself gazing at softly flowing green hills and listening to the constant chiming of cowbells. One morning we visited the town's cathedral, famous for a statue of the Black Madonna. I spent some time looking at a wall covered with icons gifted to the cathedral by people who had been healed there or by their families. I listened for a while to the mass being conducted in the small open chapel in the center of the cathedral. I tried to feel into the spirit of the place. Finally, I had to acknowledge that I was unable to see this very small figure draped in elaborate silks and brocades as a symbol of feminine strength, of cultural transformation and the valuing of diversity (Woodman & Dickson, 1996). There are no rational grounds for the feeling of threat that came over me on this visit to Switzerland, but I was beset by sights and sounds of war.

I remembered one of the first films about the Holocaust that I saw on television as a child; it portrayed a small group of Jews being led through snowy forests to the Swiss border. Most of the group made it to safety, but two members of the group were slower than the others—an elderly man and his young granddaughter. Shots rang out and the grandfather was killed. I left the cathedral, sat outside and opened my notebook.

The fires that burned my cousins
The earth that buried the others alive
The gunpowder, the bombs
The attacks from air and sea
The rivers of blood, the burnt-out bus
The bits of skin and bone picked carefully off nearby buildings
The scars, the severed limbs, the blinded eyes
The pain, the pain, the pain, the pain
Repeat four times, or six
Lest it seem like a meaningful series of three
Repeat again
This is the litany of terror
This is the poetry of despair
The song of destruction
The rhyming nonsense of war
This happened before I was born
It happened last week
It is happening now in my brain,
in my stomach,
In my toes, arms, liver and spleen
We are waiting for this to happen again

Poland, August 2011

In the summer of 2011 I visited Poland for the first time, together with my son Shai and his partner Michal. Before the trip I found myself telling people repeatedly that I had no personal connection to Poland; after all, my mother's family was from Russia, my father's from Galicia—both areas now in Ukraine. After a while my disavowals began to seem too glib. I remembered that many family members had died in Auschwitz. I remembered that the landscape and ways of living of Jews in Poland were probably very similar to the places where my family lived before the war in both Russia and Austro-Hungary. I realized that my efforts to deny any identification with Poland were a kind of protective measure that was unlikely to work. I decided that, for the week of the trip at least, I would be of Polish origin.

It was an intense week, led by a remarkable guide, Naama Golan, head of pedagogical services at the Yad Vashem Memorial Museum in Jerusalem. Our days began early: we boarded buses right after breakfast and were on the go usually until 7 or 8 in the evening. At every stop we were given detailed explanations of the place we were visiting; we heard stories of the people who had lived, and died, there. At Auschwitz-Birkenau one of the stories was read to the group by Michal from the autobiography of a survivor—her grandfather, Dov Weiss. Afterwards we crawled under the fence enclosing the area where the barracks had stood and Shai took a photo of Michal standing on the site of Block B, holding aloft the text of her grandfather's testimony.

Our bus was equipped with video, and when the travel between stops was long, we were shown films: most of them, like *Schindler's List* and *Escape from Sobibor*, were well-known films I had seen before. Viewing these films against the backdrop of the Polish landscape rushing past the windows of the bus was a strange experience which made the films seem simultaneously more and less genuine. Each night after dinner I went straight to bed and fell into a deep, dreamless sleep. The notebook that I brought with me remained empty; I was unable to put words to paper. Once home I began dreaming, every night the same dream: I was still on that bus, revisiting all the sites we had seen during the week, over and over until, after a couple of weeks, the dreaming ran its course. Only when I had completed the 'dream tour' of Poland was I able to write down some of what I had experienced.

July 31, 2011

It is a sunny but cool day in the north-eastern part of Poland, the last day of our trip. The trip began in Krakow, a charming university town, and the site of the Plashow concentration camp outside the city; the next day we went to Auschwitz-Birkenau. In the towns of Tarnow, Zamosc, and Lublin we saw the sites of the vibrant Jewish life there before the war. Outside the famous Lublin Yeshiva built only a short time before the war, we were fortunate: standing on the steps of the impressive building (now being renovated), holding our packaged sandwiches, we had a chance meeting with Phillip Bialystock, one of the survivors of the Sobibor camp. A cheerful, young-looking man in his 80s, he spoke mainly about his children and grandchildren and said little about the experience of the camp itself.

At Maidanek, much has been preserved to show what a 'working' concentration camp was like: some of the original barracks, the small building housing a gas chamber, another with the ovens where bodies were cremated. I stand outside the glass doors that were installed on the building where the gas was administered, to allow people to look inside. Our guide tells us that she was here recently with a group of teachers, and they had been allowed to spend time inside the chamber; placing their hands on the walls, they could feel the marks and striations caused by the fingers and nails of victims trying to get a hold and climb higher to be able to breathe. It is a sunny and cool day, and suddenly I feel that I am under water: my legs sway beneath me and I am being pulled by unknown currents. I want to go with those currents, perhaps lie on the waving field of grass and see where the currents take me; but I continue to follow the group. Recently, the noted Buddhist teacher and writer Tich Nhat Hahn was interviewed in *The Guardian* on the subject of climate change, and in his words I found an answer to the question I was not even able to formulate in Maidanek:

> So take refuge in Mother Earth and surrender to her and ask her to heal us, to help us. And we have to accept that the worst can happen; that most of us will die as a species and many other species will die also and Mother Earth will be capable after maybe a few million years to bring us out again and this time wiser. (Confino, 2013)

Later in the day we will make our final visit, to the site of Treblinka. Now we have come by bus from Warsaw to Tykocin, a picturesque and well-preserved town dating back to the 11th century. In 1941 some 2000 Jews lived in the town; the synagogue built in 1642 is a simple but elegant white structure in Mannerist style, restored in the 1970s; now it houses an exhibit of photographs of Jewish life in Poland before the Second World War. Nearby is a small wooden building that was the home of the local teacher or 'melamed.' From Tykocin, we are driven to the Łopuchowo forest outside the town. In the strange altered state induced by this week in Poland, my first thought is a pleasant one: at last, a bit of time in nature. Then I remember why we are here: almost 70 years ago, in August 1941, the Jews of the town were assembled in the town square and taken by truck or forced to march to this forest.

At the entrance to the forest our guide Naama tells us what happened here in August 25th and 26th of 1941. Each of us is given a memorial candle with a name printed on it, the name of a family living in Tykocin, a family that was brought here in August 1941, taken to a pit dug in the soft earth of a clearing in the forest, and shot.

I hold my candle—it bears the name of a mother and son—and walk alongside Shai and Michal down the forest path. History, family stories, and fiction mingle in my mind; it is impossible to distinguish between the real sites where horrific events took place many years ago and the landscapes I imagine, between film sets and the scenes depicted in drawings by survivors. All week this disjunction, confusion, paradox has been repeated. The site of the Plashow Camp outside Warsaw is now a rolling green hill topped by a large concrete monument. Maidanek is located just outside Lublin, and the residents of the town cross a field to walk there with baby carriages. As I walk I think of many other walks in forests around the world, in Canada and in Israel, in Europe, in India and in China. Many of the trees are familiar, some are different; the soil is not quite the same and the smell is different, but the feel of walking in the forest is just that, quiet and peaceful. I imagine that on those days in August of 1941 there would have been shouting and pushing; people who could not keep up with the pace would have been struck; children would have been crying, and there would have been the smells of panic and fear in the air.

In this place I think of my aunts, my mother's sisters Maika and Elka, who lived in Odessa with their families. I don't know what happened to them when the Nazis entered Odessa in October of 1942, but from what I've been able to figure out it would have been close to this. Two women in their 40s, with their children; by then Maika's daughters, Nussia and Freema, would have been young women. I picture them walking together. I try to imagine myself walking there with my daughter and granddaughter; I cannot, I will not imagine any of it. My body is wooden and I feel fear in my throat, feel the impossibility of imagining any kind of future in such a moment, in such a place.

London, November 2011: Navigating in the Dark

By simple good luck I happen to walk by St. Pancras Church on Euston Road in London and notice an ad for an exhibit being held there. I'm on my way to a seminar, so will have to come back later, and when I do, I enter a dim space, the crypt in the basement of the church. Several old wooden boats have been placed in the space; one of them holds coiled black snakes made of steel, on another a number of metal crows are perched. The third boat has figures, carved and shaped out of steel. They are seated, crouched, holding themselves ready for a long voyage. The figures are almost abstract, lacking individuality, yet in their physical proximity, sharing the small space of a single boat, they seem to be caring for one another. In a corner, a white cloud of paper bees are hanging from the ceiling of the crypt, and in one small nook there are dried grasses. The varied objects created or collected for this installation speak about voyages, about migration, and about shape-shifting. The crows, and the bees, seem to be following the travelers, showing them the way; or perhaps they *were* the travelers in an earlier time? The exhibit is the work of Kalliopi Lemos, a Greek artist living in London, the third of three installations on the same theme, the first two parts of which were shown in Athens and in Crete (see www.kalliopilemos.com). My mind can make no sense of what I am seeing here, but the scenes are primordial and familiar. In my heart, they speak to me of home.

Israel, 2010: Green Formica—a poem about writing

I volunteered to facilitate a short workshop on writing for my fellow students of process-oriented psychology. We did some of the same exercises I had done with my students (as described in Chapter 6). Danny, Einat, Rachel, Anat, Irena, Rami and Liad were willing participants, and we had a good time writing together. As they were presenting what they had written for the final exercise, I copied down some favorite lines. Later, I played with the lines and put them together, translated them into English. They became my own.

> *Green Formica,*
> *I wrote a story*
> *Rare and successful.*
> *Granny liked to do crossword puzzles,*

Soft-boiled eggs the way I like them.
The difficulty I had with Gila Birnbaum,
A question about the world.
Dear Anati, this is poetry!
Everything she brings,
I wrote and wrote so much,
It was at night,
I loved every word.
It happened this way:
A dream that came true too quickly,
Seeds cast in all directions
Small trees and big trees.
It was so pleasant,
In a spiral notebook,
The wise little girl that I was.

Note

1. http://uniongallery.queensu.ca/archive/MainSpacePages/2005_MSArchive_Recover.html

9.   Harry and Muriel Stevens, Reading, England—taken on my visit
     there in June, 1967.

10. View of Rebecca Soudant's installation, *ReCover*—Union Gallery, Queen's University, Kingston, August 2005.

11. *Oliver Twist*, pages from the book as it would be seen by a dys-
     lectic student, from Soudant's installation.

12.   Kalliopi Lemos, "Wooden Boat with Seven People." From the installation, *Navigating in the Dark*, St. Pancras Church, London, November 2011.

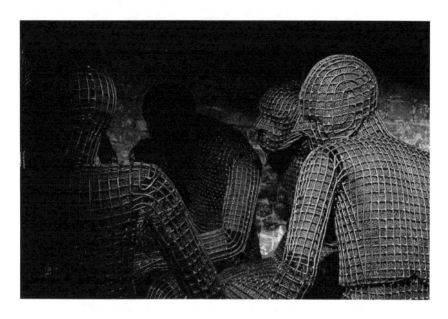

13. Kalliopi Lemos, another view of "Wooden Boat with Seven
     People."

CHAPTER 8

Auto/biography and Conflict in Teaching and Life

Introduction

Coming to the University of Haifa in 1986, I was troubled to see that, despite the diversity of the student body, the majority of students (particularly undergraduates and prospective teachers) chose to socialize and engage in discussion only with members of their own groups. At first I experimented with a variety of interventions, usually improvised on the spot with little success and some embarrassment. For a while I attempted to ignore the matter, consoling myself that in graduate courses the students, most of them teachers, shared their professional experience and concerns quite easily without any evident barriers of ethnic, linguistic, political or religious difference. But then I came across a significant book, *Sitting in the Fire* (Mindell, 1995), in which Mindell discusses his approach to working with conflict, claiming that "engaging in heated conflict instead of running away from it is one of the best ways to resolve the divisiveness that prevails on every level of society—in personal relationships, business and the world" (1995, 12). Reading this book and feeling the excitement of the possibilities I envisioned within Mindell's examples of his work, I began to understand that my efforts to bring students into dialogue were motivated by something beyond a preference for an active and engaged classroom. I took two actions as a result of reading the book: I arranged to study at the Processwork Institute in Portland, Oregon. And I volunteered to teach a course with the hopeful title, "Coexistence Workshop," a required course in the teacher education program in my faculty at that time (and about which my colleague Devorah Kalekin-Fishman spoke in Chapter 5).

A few years earlier, the Teaching Department had decided that all prospective teachers should learn something about the Arab-Israeli conflict and gain first-hand experience of meeting with members of the 'other' group. The "Coexistence Workshop" was taught by different teachers each of whom developed a syllabus according to his or her perspective and ideas about what such a course might accomplish. Based on my previous work with narrative I gave my section of the course the subtitle "Story as a tool for coming to know the Other" and planned a series of activities, mostly in small groups, which invited the students to tell stories about their lives. It was the fall of 1997; a peace process was ongoing and the public mood, at least in Israel (much less so in the Palestinian territories) seemed to be cautiously optimistic although with intermittent setbacks caused by terror attacks.

Thanks to a few friendly and sociable participants, a good atmosphere developed in class. Things were going well: students seemed to be interested in getting to know one another and willing to try the activities I suggested although I often had to invite the Arab students to join groups not of their choosing in order to create more heterogeneous small groups (at the time, Arab students made up about 25% of the class). About 5 weeks into the semester, on my way to class I noticed an exhibit of what seemed to be political caricatures, captioned in Arabic, being shown in the lobby of the building where our class was held. I thought it might be interesting to bring the students to view this exhibit together during the break. But once the class started I forgot about the exhibit, and when we stopped for a break I stayed in class for a while to speak to some of the students, and I was unprepared for the scene that greeted me when I finally went out to the lobby.

The exhibit was surrounded by a large group of students in heated and noisy argument, which was being stirred up even further by some members of the press who had arrived to cover the event. The exhibit, of work by Palestinian caricaturist Naji el Ali, included harsh depictions of the Israeli occupation, and the fact that the captions were in Arabic only seemed to have further inflamed the situation. I saw many of my students engaged in what looked like angry debate, and all I could think was that the work of the previous month had been completely undone. Our break was over and I went around reminding students to return to class, in some cases almost begging them to come back so we could discuss the issues quietly. When most students had returned, I suggested that rather than try to continue the debates and discussions that had taken place outside, people take turns saying what they were feeling. The students spoke soberly and clearly, many of them (on both sides) expressing the same feelings: disappointment that the "other side" did not seem willing to listen and hopelessness about the possibility of reaching mutual understanding, let alone peace. I commented about this sense of shared feelings despite obvious differences of opinion in the group, and the class ended. Outside I found a few of the students still in discussion around the exhibit. I saw one Palestinian student exchanging phone numbers with a Jewish student with whom she had been arguing only a short time before, and she came over to apologize for not returning to class: she had been caught up in the event, she told me, and it was too important to cut short.

I went home puzzled that day: the event had seemed a disaster while it was ongoing, but as I pondered what had happened I was no longer sure of its meaning. I had seen students looking shocked, and their shock had led them to share feelings in an honest way. I had seen argument wind down and turn into civility and perhaps the beginning of friendship. And the following week all the students were back, mostly smiling and ready to continue with the work of the course. My understanding of the role of conflict in education was beginning to change (see Elbaz-Luwisch, 2001, for a narrative account of the experience).

Before reading Mindell's work I would not have attributed any positive role to conflict in education. Living in the midst of conflict, I thought, one's thinking becomes solidified: not just "us" and "them," the most obvious and all-encompassing of distinctions, but "war" and "peace," "dialogue" and "argument" among others, come to be seen as clear and diametrically opposed concepts, polar opposites. It is also quite clear which are the positive and which the negative terms in each of these pairs. Polarized thinking seems to narrow the mind, giving rise to a lack of flexibility in thought and making criticism difficult. This seems to be an inevitable consequence of conflict situations, showing up in public debate and in media portrayals as well as in educational settings. At bottom, polarized thinking is grounded in early experience: it is in the family that we first learn where we belong, who "our people" are, who we consider to be others, and how we should relate to those others. In my case, growing up in a family that had experienced war and conflict at close quarters, I had been taught to avoid conflict at all costs: rather than expressing anger, I was taught (more by example than by precept) to try to understand and empathize with the other side, to accommodate, to forgive if possible and if not, to keep my distance.

It is hardly surprising that in the university classroom the Israeli-Arab conflict gives rise to a wide range of interactions, from polite distance to hot debates; polarized views can be identified in many of the interactions among students and faculty. However, it is not often noted that the tensions and pressures of globalization have fostered a sense of polarization in many parts of the world that would not be thought of as societies under conflict. According to Salomon (2004), education for peace in circumstances of conflict is thought to be categorically different from education for peace in other, more salubrious contexts; but my experience suggests otherwise, at least insofar as teacher education is concerned. Recently, together with two colleagues working in Canada and the United States (Li, Conle & Elbaz-Luwisch, 2009), we explored the phenomenon of polarization as it appears in the context of teacher education in Canada, the United States and Israel. We found many commonalities in our work in these three very different settings, though needless to say the issues around which polarization occurred were different in Israel, a society often described as 'deeply divided' (Al-Haj, 2002) and as living in the midst of an intractable conflict (Bar Tal, 2007), than the issues which came up for prospective teachers in Canada and the USA. Understanding that our practice as teacher educators was shaped by our own early experiences, my co-authors and I devoted one chapter of our book to an autobiographical account juxtaposing our three stories. In the next section I draw from that chapter to tell the story of what, for me, had led up to the class described above.

The roots of an approach to conflict

Born in Canada at the close of the Second World War, I was brought up to feel proud that I was a 'native' Canadian. For my parents, Canada was a refuge, a place of safety. For me, being Canadian meant supporting the Montreal Canadiens hockey team; it meant reading *Anne of Green Gables* (Montgomery, 1908), and *The Little Magic Fiddler* (Cook, 1951), the story of the childhood of Donna Grescoe, a Ukrainian-Canadian violinist. I loved both books, but the immigrant background of the latter, set in Winnipeg, was more familiar to me than the rural Prince Edward Island of the former; today both settings (places I have yet to visit) retain something magical and distant for me. Interestingly, I don't recall reading Richler's (1959) *The Apprenticeship of Duddy Kravitz*, set in Montreal largely in the pre-war period, until years later. rather than identifying with the characters in that novel—poor, uneducated immigrants—and the Yiddish-speaking setting of Jewish Montreal in the 1930s (when my mother immigrated to Montreal), I would have preferred to identify with a more cosmopolitan view of the city. Growing up in Montreal meant learning French at school and eating 'French' toast with real maple syrup, going skating in winter and building snow forts on the snow banks piled high at the edge of sidewalks. This sounds like a childhood thoroughly shaped by local culture and weather, but in later years I discovered just how different it was from a Québecois childhood lived out on the other side of the mountain.

At the same time that I grew up Canadian, I grew up Jewish. These two upbringings took place side by side and in many of the same spaces: I learned to be Canadian at home no less than in school, and I learned to be Jewish both at home and at school, attending a Jewish day school for the first three years of my schooling (regular subjects in the morning, Jewish studies after lunch) and after-school studies for several years later on. The two sides of my education did not often conflict, but they did not communicate much either—like the "two solitudes" of Montreal novelist Hugh Maclennan (1945). The Jewish part of my life was not reflected in any of the books I remember reading as a young child; only in my teens did I begin reading literature on the Holocaust, and popular novels like *Exodus* by Leon Uris (1958), which portrayed Jewish life in Europe and Israel, all very different from my own experience.

I don't know quite how I learned to keep the two parts of my identity separate, but separate them I did. In the 7th grade, we were asked in home economics to make up a menu according to rules of nutrition and meal-planning we had been taught. My menu (adapted from a women's magazine) featured roast lamb with mint jelly, accompanied by the requisite number of vegetables, an appetizer and dessert. This food was largely unfamiliar to me, but I adapted the menu to make sure it did not violate any of the Jewish dietary laws, which we observed at home. One of my classmates, also Jewish, volunteered to read out her menu in class: it consisted of chicken soup, roast chicken with potatoes…. I don't remember the rest, because she was stopped by the teacher before she finished: "No! You can't put chicken soup and roast chicken in the same meal—you should *never* use the same product more than once in a meal. You should have vegetable soup, or else serve roast beef instead of chicken." My classmate was confused. "But…but…that's what we eat!" she told the teacher, as many of the other girls (only girls took home economics in the 1950s) nodded and laughed. I remember looking down at my own menu with satisfaction, puzzled that my friend had so trustingly offered up for inspection the traditional Friday evening meal of Jews from Eastern Europe.

Was it because my parents were immigrants that they knew how to pass on to me without words the tacit rules which enabled me to do things like make up an appropriate menu—keeping family life private, adapting on the outside? Many years later I encountered a menu in a newspaper for a meal in which every course was made with zucchini: zucchini soup, pizza on a zucchini base, zucchini bread for dessert. The memory of the long-forgotten home economics teacher instantly came back to me as I imagined thrusting that menu in her face, telling her that, see, it IS permitted to use the same product more than once in a menu! This memory suggests that the 'two solitudes' (Maclennan, 1945) of my upbringing did not simply sit side by side in mute coexistence but were indeed polarized. Yet the clash between home and school cultures is significant for being so rare: if the two did not often conflict, how did I ever learn to keep them separate? I'm not sure, but perhaps the frequent movement between cultures and settings taught me how to constantly 'read' and appraise situations. Maybe growing up in a very traditional home which observed many of the religious laws of Judaism as well as customs and holidays contributed to my ability to move between the worlds, since I knew and appreciated both from an early age.

Although my parents had both experienced persecution as Jews, they'd been fortunate to have good relations with non-Jewish neighbors. Chapter 2 revealed how my mother's family had been taken in and hidden by their Christian neighbors during pogroms in post-revolutionary Russia, and how the Quaker family in England helped my father to escape from Vienna to England just before the outbreak of the Second World War. In Canada, my mother had worked and made friends with other immigrant women from many countries. On Christmas Eve my parents would go to visit our Christian neighbors and wish them well; as a child I went along and was always a little jealous of the colorful decorations and glowing lights on the tree. I assume that these patterns of coexistence had been laid down long before, under conditions that sometimes involved matters of life and death. My parents did tell me (and as a child I refused to believe) that anti-Semitism still existed in Canada and that one needed to be watchful; but their actions spoke much louder for me than their occasional words of warning and suspicion. Gradually I learned the dismal history of Canada's attitude toward Jewish refugees trying to enter Canada during the Nazi period (see Abella & Troper, 1983); it took even longer till a novel made me aware of the experiences of other groups in Canada during that same time (see Kogawa, 1981). Aoki's (1983) account of his experience as a Japanese Canadian educator was my first exposure to the educative potential of writing personally about this history.

After I finished my undergraduate studies I went to Israel, initially as a volunteer for a year; I met people from different backgrounds—native Israelis, Jewish immigrants from many countries, Holocaust survivors, Moslem and Christian Arabs from the Galilee, Bedouins still living a nomadic existence—and was moved and excited by what I perceived as the adventure of creating a new society in which all had a place. I stayed on to do graduate studies in education. I was astonished and angry to discover the existence of discrimination by Jewish Israelis of European origin towards Sephardic Jews of Middle-Eastern and North African origin. I encountered this discrimination on a personal level because my appearance was more Sephardic than European, but I spoke Hebrew with an English accent and my clothing and demeanor seemed to be western. In the very forthright Israeli culture, people rarely have difficulty asking direct questions of a stranger, so the fact that they squirmed and hesitated before asking the simple question, "Where are you from?" alerted me to the power of the stigma that could be attached to one's background.

Before going to Israel I had become interested in the philosophy of Martin Buber, and read what he had written (prior to the establishment of the state of Israel in 1948) about the idea of a bi-national, Jewish-Arab state in Palestine (see Buber, 1963). I was intrigued and told my parents about it; to my surprise they became upset and angry, telling me that questioning the Jewish state was tantamount to cutting myself off from my people. Later I came to understand that behind their anger was very deep pain: for them, in the aftermath of the Holocaust during which many members of their families had been murdered, the Jewish state represented an unassailable good. In 1938 when my father had been arrested on Kristallnacht and ordered to leave Austria, there had been no place to go; if not for the help of his Quaker friends, he would no doubt have been sent to Buchenwald as was his father. I thought I understood these historical facts well enough, but I only began to appreciate their emotional force when I went to Israel, and over the years, as new information has become available, and as the phenomenon of 'Holocaust denial' has appeared, despite the growing fund of knowledge of the events of the Second World War, I have continued to learn about this part of my family and national history.

As a result of all this, during those early years in Israel I did not question the official narratives of Israeli society. I met many Arab citizens and they were gracious and friendly; in 1967 the military rule over Arabs living in the Galilee and other areas ended, and their situation appeared to be improving. Whether I visited Arab Israelis in the north of the country or Palestinian residents of Jerusalem and the surrounding area, they invariably talked about the need to learn to live together. And I was grateful for the fact that they were more than willing to teach me about their culture.

Once I visited a student who lived in East Jerusalem but came originally from a village in the Galilee. He explained to me that in Jerusalem the custom was to serve coffee to guests as soon as they arrived, but in his home town a different custom prevailed: coffee would be served only at the end of the visit, and once one had emptied the cup it was time to leave. He assured me that he did not wish my visit to be over and asked if I wanted coffee, tea or a soft drink. I requested juice and we continued talking; a little later he again asked if I wanted coffee or tea, hinting he hoped I had time to stay a little longer. When finally he asked if I wanted to have coffee now, I understood that it was time to drink coffee and end the visit.

In the 1970s I returned to Canada to do doctoral studies at the University of Toronto, and when I came back to Israel in the 1980s I found many changes: the pace of life had increased, and although the term 'globalization' was not yet in use, the process itself was in full swing. The political situation, despite a peace agreement with Egypt, had become vastly more complicated as well as entailing greater risk: violence and suffering became commonplace both inside Israel and in the Palestinian territories (see Bassett, 2012; Masalha, 2003). It sometimes seems that every imaginable aspect of life in Israel has been polarized: the political spectrum is divided between right and left; the divide between religious and secular Jews has widened;

economic gaps have increased steadily. The population is even more diverse than before: while the distinction between Jews of Oriental (Sephardic) and European (Ashkenazi) origin has been blurred somewhat, new immigrants from the former Soviet Union are a prominent group that seeks to maintain its language and culture unlike previous immigrant groups which sought to adapt and fit in. There is a growing population of foreign workers who have few civil rights. And the Arab/Palestinian community continues to press for increasing autonomy and the fulfillment of the equality promised by Israel's declaration of independence. The only thing that seems to temporarily unite all these groups is suffering: during terror attacks and wars, it becomes clear that no group is untouched.

What emerges from my experience and has stayed with me until today is the sense of being a student of other peoples' lives and cultures. I have given up the naïve perspective with which I first came to Israel, and no longer assume that the way people arrange their lives is the way that they have freely chosen. I am aware of the many layers of discrimination and inequality in work possibilities for Arab citizens of Israel, in funding for education and public services, and many other problematic aspects of life in Israel for different groups; fewer Israelis than before enjoy the protection of trade unions, pensions and secure employment. A larger percentage and a wider range of the population (Jews and Arabs) now completes high school and attends university, but education no longer guarantees secure jobs and a higher standard of living. There is widespread dissatisfaction with the country's leaders. The hope of a peace agreement with Israel's neighbors seems to continually move out of reach, and debates in the media indicate that there is little consensus on anything except how bad things are.

Learning from conflict

Among teacher education students as in other sectors of society, the background conditions of conflict give rise to diverse opinions on political issues, economic and social issues, religion, and of course world views and educational ideologies; these opinions are accompanied by strong feelings arising from the difficult experiences undergone by many who have been affected directly or indirectly by the conflict. In addition, while some students are politically active on and off campus, most do not want these differences of opinion to interfere with the business of getting an education. When political views are expressed in class, there is a sense of a taboo being broken; for some students (and for me as their teacher) this can be energizing and bring a sense of relief, but for others it causes distress. My own experience of polarization has taught me not to assume that I know how other people live or understand what they think, particularly since so many aspects of life are changing rapidly and many people have hyphenated and multiple identities. Although it is difficult to remain detached and open-minded—I do have opinions and I care deeply about what happens—I hope that by retaining the sense of being a learner I can model for my students a way of being interested in and open to finding out about one another's lives and cultures.

My experience also leads me to think that there may be lessons to be learned from living with polarization and being in the midst of conflict that are relevant not just for those in the conflict situation itself but also for other contexts. This supposition is paradoxical. After all, by definition, a society that is beset by conflict does not know enough about its problems: if the group or groups involved did know enough, surely they would manage to end the conflict. One assumes that societies in conflict should be asking to learn from other countries that are not torn apart by war, or from societies have progressed to a post-conflict situation, and not the reverse. And yet Greenwood (2010) finds pedagogical work on the Israeli-Palestinian conflict highly relevant for his situation as an environmental educator in the United States in that it "brings forward the fact of war and the overtones of violence in my own culture and around the world" (352). So much for logic then or at least the binary logic of western thought.

Thinking on this further, it seems to me that war and peace are not really diametrically opposed, and that there are many situations that bear elements of war alongside elements of peace. The well-known story of German and French soldiers calling a spontaneous Christmas Day truce and coming out of the trenches to celebrate together with songs and football in the midst of the First World War comes to mind. Similarly, there are some life situations where a warlike attitude is needed to achieve a peaceful result: the war on poverty, on illiteracy, on racism, the battle of a patient diagnosed with cancer, and so on. Hillman (2004) suggests that the desire to end war is shared by many, but that the love of war is also shared and that indeed it is a basic human instinct. Lingis (2012) links violence and splendor, reflecting on the many instances in the history of art where war has inspired exalted aesthetic performance and monumental works of art. Clearly a simplistic polarization of war and peace is not adequate to capture the complexities of our relationship to the two terms.

The intricacies of the situation in the Middle East are highlighted by the work of Ben-Ze'ev (2011), who studied Palestine in 1948 by gathering a wide range of information, including the stories of rural Palestinians, women and men, stories told by fighters of the Palmach (the fighting force of the Haganah, set up by the Labor Party in 1920 to defend the Jewish "yishuv" or settlement) and of the women of the Palmach who served in a mainly noncombatant role. Her work seeks to "place the witness back in time" and avoid essentializing their stories. Her account demonstrates how the stories themselves were not static: "Palestinian refugees did not want to talk only of the village as it was in 1948, nor did they want simply to tell a story of suffering. Jewish men who fought in 1948 did not want to recreate themselves as flawless heroic figures, nor did they wish to venerate the war" (190; see also Spector-Mersel, 2011). At the same time, she finds that accounts of the war from opposing sides are not necessarily distinct:

> The villagers' oral accounts and the army documents often complement each other, and sometimes converge. Unlike Kurosawa's *Rashomon*, the testimonies of the witnesses do not tell a totally different story. . .(they) are characterized by an ability to inject life, volume and an internal logic to the story. In fact, the logic of certain chaotic episodes may continue to unfold long after their occurrence. (83)

Ben-Ze'ev adds that Palestinian women had had little opportunity to speak up about their memories, and when they did, their narratives "drew on everyday experiences, on their intimate knowledge of foodstuffs, plants, springs, or holy saints' shrines" (100); their narratives were fluid, "changed over time, were negotiated with other versions, and were manoeuvred according to the setting" (100). For the Arab-Palestinian population, "1948 was likened to a natural disaster" (84), whereas for the Jewish soldiers "war was a step towards building a state." Ben-Ze'ev's work makes concrete some of Rothberg's (2009) ideas about multidirectional memory discussed in Chapter 1, as do Menon and Bhasin (1998) who tell side by side the complex and sometimes unexpected stories of Hindu and Moslem women under India's partition.

The complexities highlighted by these 'multidirectional' accounts of the history of the conflict as well as stories of how the conflict plays out in the present, lead me to think that perhaps, instead of a crisp distinction between situations of conflict and situations devoid of conflict, there may be a continuum: different degrees of conflict and violence, diverse ways of dealing with conflict, mixing with diverse sorts of dialogue and processes of working through issues. If so, a group in the midst of conflict might still be getting some things right. It is clear that in local settings, in specific situations limited in time and space, we do occasionally manage things in decent, humane, democratic ways that take account of people's needs regardless of which side they are on. Taking a broader view, it may be that the ways we manage and work with specific small-scale conflicts, as they arise, may contain within them the seeds for dealing more productively with larger conflicts.

The approach formulated by Mindell (1995) suggests that conflict is actually the way a group or collective becomes aware of all its different parts. Thus conflict, when lived with awareness, serves to create community: within a society the polarization of divergent views and the division into opposing sides, can be ways of allowing all the voices to be heard, so that the society can grow and develop. Making room for the diversity of voices in society constitutes what Mindell terms "deep democracy." As he explains,

> If violence is admitted and addressed, it is less destructive than if it is repressed. Going consciously into battle is an intense experience, but one that revitalizes everyone. You are renewed in hope. You find not only solutions to issues, but something more precious. You find that a battle does not mean the end of the world, but the beginning of the river called community. (1995)

Mindell's approach is intercultural, influenced by Jungian psychology, theoretical physics, and the philosophy of Taoism, which sees seemingly opposed positions as being in constant dialectical interplay (see also Li, 2006). This perspective, and in particular its application in the Arab-Israeli conflict (Reiss, 2004), does not render conflict any less painful, nor can it guarantee a reduction in violence. However, it does suggest that there may be some purpose to conflict which we should not ignore and that working consciously with conflicts as they arise may not only be a way of preventing violence, but may even serve to enhance the development of community. This is the approach that lies behind my question, "What might we be doing right?" and in what follows I will draw on this approach to try to make sense of my own experience of working with prospective teachers.

Story and conflict in teacher education

As already mentioned, the student body at the University of Haifa represents the diversity of Israeli society. Studies at the university are in Hebrew (except in the departments of Arabic language and literature). Arabic-speaking students study in Arabic at the high-school level but also pass matriculation examinations in Hebrew language and literature, in Bible, and in history and civics similar to examinations passed by Hebrew-speaking students (see Al-Haj, 1995, for a comprehensive account of Arab education in Israel, and Al-Haj, 2002, for an updated view). Despite their high school studies, however, the Hebrew language often poses difficulties for Arabic-speaking students, and the spoken language, in particular, may constitute a barrier to communication between students from different groups. Language, of course, is only one layer of the existing diversity; religion, gender and politics also impact on students' complicated identities. Frequently, the campus serves as a stage on which many of the relationships and conflicts of the larger society are played out in small but vivid dramas (Hertz-Lazarowitz, 2003; Elbaz-Luwisch, 2001).

For the past fifteen years, beginning with the course described above, I taught a number of different courses with the terms "coexistence' and "multiculturalism" in their titles. Most recently I taught a course entitled "Curriculum development for multiculturalism," in which writing and working with personally meaningful stories served as the main focus of the course; some of the stories were retold above in Chapter 3. The course aimed to provide prospective teachers with a significant personal experience of encounter and dialogue with members of the diverse communities that make up Israeli society, something not all of them have had before, given the separation of the school system by language. At the same time the course aimed to help students develop a conceptual framework for thinking about the multicultural nature of Israeli society.

In addition to readings and discussion focused on curriculum development, multiculturalism and identity, the course invited students to write the life story of a person who had influenced them; the students were then organized into heterogeneous groups and spent a significant part of the semester working together to analyze and learn from the stories produced by their group members, leading up to a presentation in class and to a consideration of ways that life stories might be used in school curricula to teach pupils about the multicultural nature of Israeli society. The course was designed around personal stories with two main purposes in mind: facilitating the process of students getting to know one another and understanding one another's cultural backgrounds and life situations, and short-circuiting some of the conflict that is likely to arise in a course that deals head on with social and political issues related to the wider conflict. Life stories have the advantage of dealing honestly with the concrete situations being lived by people in Israel and in the region, yet framing issues in terms of a life lived usually makes it easier to read and relate to the experience of someone from a different group without immediately calling into play the preconceptions, stereotypes and grievances held by each side.

Narrative approaches have been shown to have a unique contribution to make in situations of multiculturalism (Elbaz-Luwisch, 2005; He, 2002; Phillion et al., 2005). My purpose in working with life stories in this course was not to avoid all conflict but rather to try to ensure that students would have an opportunity to make personal connections with fellow students from the 'other' group before putting to the test the very possibility of dialogue because of the eruption of a difficult issue. Life stories serve both purposes well, but of course conflicts still came up. Here, I want to ask a number of questions: What actually happens when conflict erupts? How do students respond? What may be learned from such instances of conflict? Are they just chilling reminders of the larger conflict outside, or do they serve a larger purpose? In what follows, I will present some examples to facilitate the exploration of these questions, first looking at ways in which conflict seems to be beneficial mainly because it promotes resolution and then considering what may be learned from conflicts in the classroom that cannot be resolved.

Conflict promotes engagement

Almost immediately, conflict brings people out of their shells; some of them, at least, become too angry or too engaged to remain on the sidelines. They are sometimes led to share personal information or do something active that allows them to make a genuine connection with people from the 'other' group. One example of this occurred a few years ago, when the class was involved in an open discussion around the political situation of the moment, and in the heat of an argument around Israeli military action in the territories, someone used the term "primitive," seemingly in reference to Arab culture. The comment immediately raised very strong feelings accompanied by many people talking at once, and it was not immediately apparent who had made the comment or why. After a few moments, the students became quiet and one Jewish student, Dana, acknowledged that she was the one responsible. She went on to tell the class that her parents had immigrated to Israel from Iraq, and that her father in particular held to the traditional culture in which he had been brought up. Her parents' roles in the family were clearly divided according to the traditional expectations for males and females: her mother took care of all household duties, served her husband and attended to his needs, while her father worked to provide for the family. When Dana wanted to study at university, her father insisted that higher education was unnecessary for a woman and refused to help pay for her studies. Dana saw her mother as deprived of any status in the home, and this, she insisted, was what she had had in mind when she used the term "primitive."

The class was quiet after this story; gender issues are still hotly contested in all sectors of Israeli society, but it is rare today that women are actively discouraged from obtaining higher education, and it could not have been easy for Dana to make this public confession. However, she then went on to say that during their childhood her father had been very warm and loving to her and her siblings and spent hours playing with them when he came home from work. When, towards the end of her studies, she encountered difficulties in paying her tuition fees, he had in fact given her money to help cover her expenses. It seems that the conflict which had erupted in class sparked Dana's motivation to contribute something of herself. Her story, spoken from the heart, was immediately effective in cutting through the polarized discussion and showing the diverse sides of the family culture in which Dana had grown up.

Conflict brings out the best in people

It usually seems that conflict brings out the worst in us, leading to the escalation of arguments, to extreme positions, intolerance, inability to compromise and, of course, to violence. This is unfortunately often the case, but sometimes it seems that conflict may help to connect people to their 'best' selves; people often express more compassion and concern for social justice during conflict situations. They reach out to one another. They search for common ground, and often they find it.

In a class some years ago, a few students proposed a group project which was enthusiastically accepted by about two-thirds of the class, but a small group of Jewish students seemed unwilling to participate; from a conversation with one student after class I learned that these students felt unable to express their right-wing views in the context of the class where most of the students appeared to belong to the left. Once the nature of this conflict became apparent, I suggested that the group look for several different projects rather than trying to agree on one project for everyone. Following this, a Moslem student became involved in a discussion with several of the Jewish students and invited them to visit her home; the Jewish students were curious and accepted the invitation, even filming their visit and showing the video to the class. Later, one of them wrote that she would never have had this experience outside of the setting of the course and that it had been very meaningful for her. Watching the video was a moving experience for many in the class; for me, the defining moment was seeing the Jewish visitors not only enjoying a meal with their hosts but feeling comfortable enough to get up and help to clear the table after lunch.

Conflict raises awareness

Dealing openly with conflict can help people become more aware of those areas that are not in conflict as well as those that are. One conflict that occurred repeatedly in the course is around the group assignment. Because instruction is in Hebrew, the Jewish students have an advantage when it comes to writing and submitting assignments. On one occasion, two Jewish students came to complain: Betty and Shira were in different groups, but both of them felt that they were doing more than their fair share of the work in preparing the group project: they were the ones to gather all the students' contributions, they were the ones writing the summaries and editing the overall product to ensure that it was written in correct Hebrew. Both said that they would have preferred to submit an individual assignment; they planned to go on to postgraduate study and high marks were important. However, when I suggested to Betty and Shira that they try to formulate some kind of differential marking of the group assignment, with each student stating how much he had contributed to the joint project, they rejected this idea immediately: "We have become good friends," they told me. They did not want to do anything that might jeopardize the friendships created during the course. They each acknowledged that the group work had been interesting and meaningful: they had learned from the group interaction, had not only developed friendships but become aware of interests and values shared with the members of their groups. And they could see that this would have been unlikely to happen if the group had simply met informally without the requirement of working together on a shared assignment.

Unsolvable conflict promotes learning

The conflict around language that came up in my class reappears frequently in different forms and reflects the basic inequality of the situation in which Jewish and Arab/Palestinian students find themselves; this conflict is difficult to resolve in the classroom just as it has not been resolved in wider society. But the example illustrates that it is not always necessary to resolve a conflict fully in order to reach a place of relationship and reconciliation. However, in the course of my teaching there have been a number of striking episodes when conflict erupted which could not be resolved and which have stayed in my memory clearly labeled as "failures." Recently, for example, a Jewish student dropped the course when he was assigned to a group with an Arab student who had expressed strongly anti-democratic views in class; he chose not to grapple with the difficulty, and I was unable to help because he did not respond to my mails.

On another occasion, a group of students seemed to be working well together, but at the end of the course it turned out that Dina, the only Jewish
student in the group, had done most of the work on their joint project; she
was so discouraged by her partners in the group that Dina—whose close
friend Carol was a Christian Arab—concluded that it was not possible for her
to relate to the Moslem students. Because the course had ended, there was
little to do but listen and empathize with her disappointment. These are
situations, which on the face of it had no apparent positive outcomes. Could I
have rectified these situations? What did I learn from them?

Personal limitations

The eruption of conflicts in the classroom has taught me a great deal about
my own personal limitations in situations of conflict. In one class, during a
highly controversial military operation in the West Bank, Shireen—a Druze
student whose father and brother serve in the Israeli army—told her group
that she believed the Israeli soldiers were committing murder in the territories. Shireen's inflammatory statement was unacceptable to the two Jewish
members of her group, Moti and Dita, who asked her to leave political matters aside, but Shireen insisted and repeatedly disrupted the group's work.
The group included three other students, Sahar, Anita, and Amal, who were
Moslem, Druze, and Christian, respectively; they did not get involved in the
discussion with Shireen but were not able to help resolve the issue. Shireen's
language seemed to be deliberately provocative, yet she obviously had strong
feelings; her words were clearly disturbing to Moti who we learned in the
course of the discussion had been injured by a rock thrown by a Palestinian
while serving in the army, and to Dita, whose aunt had been disabled in a
terrorist attack. In this situation it was hardly surprising that the group's
discussions sometimes degenerated into brief shouting matches (which
disturbed the rest of the class) followed by tense silence.

It seems that in this group, the personal stories were not powerful enough
to engage the students in a discussion that avoided the confrontational public
discourse; in fact, as it happened only two of the six participants had written
about close family members (Moti had written about his grandfather, a Zionist pioneer and Anita had written about her father), while the others had
chosen to write about public figures such as the Druze leader, Sheik Amin
Tarif, and Helen Keller. Although the students said that these figures had

and Helen Keller. Although the students said that these figures had been important influences on their lives, in retrospect it seems likely that because the writing had involved less personal disclosure, their involvement with the group work and with one another had remained more superficial.

During the group's discussions in class, I had tried to listen to Shireen and interact with her, but I could not be neutral in this conflict, and after a while she infuriated me too. However, as a result of this difficulty, I became much more aware of my own position; I realized what views I can listen to and engage with easily enough even when I don't agree and where my personal edges are. These edges—the points at which one's identity feels threatened by the views of the other—are of course different for every teacher, but we all have them, and there is a constant need to be reflective about our own limitations. This difficulty will come up differently for teachers in different situations, but it seems to be a constant as long as we are dealing with controversial and deeply felt issues. As long as we live and work in diverse, multicultural settings we will encounter difficulties in listening to one another, and we shall have to keep working on ourselves .

Over the years teaching in this area, I was forced to continually examine and re-evaluate my pedagogy and to realize that I have to listen to students all the time. In working with the life stories of people who influenced the students, I had developed a clever format that worked well much of the time, but I also had to be prepared for change. A few years ago, due largely to organizational changes, I found myself teaching the class to very small groups. It did not seem feasible to divide up into smaller groups, so I organized the students to work in pairs and to take on the task of telling the other person's story from a first-person perspective, trying to really "live into" the life of the person whose story it was (Min, 2001). This proved to be a valuable shift in the exercise, but I have to admit that it was difficult for me to let go of the group form which had worked so well and to risk doing things differently.

Maybe this is a message for the future? In education things are going to continue to change, and the same goes for the political arena: we may get a political agreement, but it is unlikely to solve everything for all time; we'll still have to pay attention, listen to one another, and be ready to adapt and work things out. Living with conflict, we want very much to believe that once it is resolved all will be beautiful; as we see from post-conflict situations in many countries, this is not always the case. But we should bear in mind that the skills we develop while trying to manage conflict situations are still there, and they remain useful.

Humility: Learning to accept that one can't always get it right

There is a sense in which, as the privileged side, Jewish Israelis are in a double bind. We can't always fix things. What has happened in history has happened. In the university, for example, those who speak Hebrew have an advantage and will probably continue to have an advantage. But we want to be "normal": that is, we do not want to acknowledge that we have an advantage. Having to acknowledge it, to accept and take responsibility for our privilege, can be difficult and painful. The need to do so sometimes makes us angry: it is, after all, not our fault that we have an advantage—or so we reason (see Reiss, 2004). And as a teacher, trying to help students engage with these difficult issues, I am not always going to be able to get it right. So, coming up against this sort of challenge helps me to understand the situation more deeply, to remember the need for humility.

To conclude, I want to return to the narrative of my experience in teaching issues related to multiculturalism in the teacher education setting in Israel. The narrative with which I began was one in which conflict disrupted my teaching, interfering with my efforts to facilitate dialogue among the student teachers in my classes. Thus my initial story was one in which conflict is an interruption to proper functioning; and indeed, while I may not believe this about conflict in general, I have to acknowledge that as a university teacher I am expected to teach without undue interruptions. In fact, on a few of the occasions when things went extremely well in my teaching, the classroom activity was accompanied by considerable noise, to a degree that it attracted the wrong kind of attention, bordering on complaint. However, over time I have come to see that conflict has value: on the one hand, it can further the goals of the course, increasing the sense of connection and community among students from diverse backgrounds; and on the other hand, even when it seems to serve no clear purpose in terms of the identified goals of the course, the encounter with conflict keeps me grounded in the immediate details of the concrete situation, makes me more attentive to students, to the pedagogy of the course, and to the moment.

It is of course only right that we aspire to end conflict: the Israeli-Arab conflict is one of the most painful being experienced around the world and continues to cause almost unbearable suffering on all sides. However, it seems that the usual definition of conflict as a disruption, as something to be eliminated and at least reduced to a minimum, is not always useful to our pedagogic efforts at fostering dialogue and understanding. I suggest that conflict in the classroom may be restoryed: perhaps we can begin to see conflict that erupts in the classroom as evidence of "things being stirred up," so that we can have interactions we have not had before and thereby come to new understandings .

Maybe we can regard conflict as evidence of things starting to cook, the pot coming to a boil, which is just the beginning of the cooking process. As mentioned above, in the Israeli university setting people from the different sides of the conflict are typically not in relationship at all. Communication can be difficult on many levels, because, as Barr and Griffiths remind us, "unequally empowered social groups develop unequally valued cultural styles, and the workings of political economy reinforces this imbalance by denying to them equal access to the material means of equal participation, including education" (Barr & Griffiths, 2004, 5). So perhaps we can view conflict in the classroom as evidence that people are finally "coming together" and beginning to relate to one another. I believe that if we continue to pay attention to the ways in which conflict plays out in the classroom, it will continue to teach us and accompany us on the path to mutual understanding.

CHAPTER 9

Presence and Dialogue, Auto/biography and Teaching

"A teaching life is only lived when it is pursued educationally…as a narrative of inquiry, a life filled with tensions and problematic situations and with the growth that ensues from moving successfully from one inquiry to another." Connelly, 1995, xv

An interest in narrative and story has been part of my life as long as I can remember, long before I understood that life is lived as a narrative, and this interest has motivated the work presented and discussed in this book. There are still many questions that can be asked about narrative as method, and many concerns have been raised by proponents as well as detractors (see, for example, Bullough, 2008). Now, however, I want to highlight several ideas that are made central by narrative inquiry as practice and as method, ideas which have been appearing and reappearing in previous chapters but that now ask to be looked at directly, in order to bring into focus the main themes that have been developing: the importance of presence and dialogue, body and imagination in teaching and in the study of teaching. All these themes are interrelated and it's difficult to look at them in sequence, but it seems important to give each one its due as they are all seriously undervalued in the current educational climate.

First, though, I want to address the notion of "wide-awakeness." Clandinin & Connelly (2000) highlight this notion on the landscape of narrative inquiry, saying that "it is wakefulness that in our view most needs to characterize the living out of our narrative inquiries" (185), and I agree (see Elbaz-Luwisch, 2010b). Bullough expands on the notion, citing the work of Maxine Greene to indicate how we might become more wide awake:

I've often thought about and been amazed by the emancipatory power of education, a generous liberal education, to open us so we can experience the world more fully and through others' eyes. Such power enables seeing things not as they are but as they might be, to become wide awake. (Bullough, 2008, 8)

It is wide-awakeness that allows us to be present with others as researchers listening to other people's narratives, and as teachers with our students. Being wide awake is a challenge, but luckily it seems that engaging in narrative inquiry is something that fosters awakening and facilitates being present; wide-awakeness is also essential in creating dialogue with others.

Presence

Although presence is a familiar concept and we generally feel that we understand its meaning, it is nonetheless a rather elusive notion that is difficult to define. "Presence" is not unlike the concept of identity which has two sides: identity as sameness, that which makes a person the same from one day to the next; and identity as uniqueness, that which makes a person just herself, in ways that may change in response to changing circumstances. Similarly the idea of presence evokes both sameness and difference. Presence clearly involves something stable and unchanging, as when we refer to an individual's unique presence, recognize a family member from a great distance, or feel an old sense of comfort with a friend we have not seen in many years. And presence also refers to a person's responsiveness, her way of being *for another*, available and ready to relate to others in dynamic ways given new situations. There are, however, many ways of speaking about presence, and rather than seeking a single definition of the term, I want to lay out some of the possibilities and consider how the concept may be useful in thinking about teaching. The definition of presence brought up earlier is worth repeating here:

> Presence is defined as a state of alert awareness, receptivity, and connectedness to the mental, emotional, and physical workings of both the individual and the group in the context of their learning environments, and the ability to respond with a considered and compassionate best next step. (Rodgers & Raider-Roth, 2009)

This definition refers to presence as responsiveness, calling for (at least) awareness of self, receptivity to others, and connectedness to what is going on in the situation at hand. Taking this a little further, consider Eisner's (1994) discussion of teaching as an art. He points out that "teachers, like painters, composers, actresses and dancers, make judgments based largely on qualities that unfold during the course of action." From this it follows that teaching presence cannot be merely a momentary thing but has to be sustained so that teachers can gain access to the qualities of the educational situation. He adds that teaching is "not dominated by prescriptions or routines but is influenced by qualities and contingencies that are unpredicted," meaning that the teacher's presence must be open minded, ready to observe what is new, both in students' behavior and in the unfolding situations.

Finally, Eisner holds that teaching deals with ends that are emergent, that is, "found in the course of interaction with students rather than preconceived and efficiently attained" (154–156), which, again, requires that the teacher be awake to possible ends in view that might be called forth in the moment and in the given circumstance. Eisner's conceptualization highlights the degree to which just talking about teaching presence as something to be fostered in schools largely runs counter to prevailing forces that aim at routinized, standards-based educational provision in which ends must be known ahead of time and clearly formulated. The intensification of teachers' work leaves little room or time for observing students and adapting to their developing needs and interests. Conceiving of presence as such a dynamic and responsive way of being, we can see that being present as a teacher even for a few moments at a time becomes a major achievement.

On the other hand, Mindell (2010) offers a definition of presence that tends to emphasize its unchanging aspect. He suggests that presence "is a *pre-sense*...something you can almost feel before you can describe it as a feeling...a kind of spirit that sends signals to others before you even know you've sent them!" (39) He distinguishes presence from the main part of identity with which we identify as well as from the 'secondary' part of identity, the 'dreaming process'; rather, he suggests that our presence is related to what he terms the 'essence' level, a deep and stable part of the self that is like an 'intentional field' (2010, 42) underlying and orienting who we are in the world. For Mindell, if we think of a teacher we loved, we may remember their words, but it is more likely that we remember their presence in just this sense of the term, as a particular person with particular intentions and a particular stance in the world.

Kelchtermans (2009) formulates an understanding of teaching with the statement that "Who I am in how I teach is the message," a way of speaking that begins to put together the two aspects of presence. He is concerned about the vulnerability of teachers, which inevitably makes it more difficult for teachers to be present. Kelchtermans highlights three elements that make up this vulnerability. First, teachers are not in full control of their working conditions, as "they work within particular legal frameworks and regulations, in a particular school, with a particular infrastructure, population of students, composition of the staff." This sort of vulnerability is political in nature; it may be intensified by such matters as the stereotypes and racist attitudes held by others in the situation (as exemplified by some of the stories told in earlier chapters) as well as by the stress on accountability which characterizes the current educational climate. A second aspect of teacher vulnerability stems from the fact that teachers cannot be in control of student outcomes, which are influenced by many personal, social and situational factors. In fact, he points out that

> Very often teachers are not allowed to witness when the seed of their efforts finds fertile ground to develop. That is why the quality control systems, being based only or primarily on students' test scores are felt by so many teachers as an unfair evaluation of their work, doing injustice to their specific working conditions. (Kelchtermans, 2009, 266)

Finally, the most fundamental meaning of the concept 'vulnerability' according to Kelchtermans lies in the fact that teachers are called on to make multiple decisions in the course of every day in order to promote learning, but they must do this without a clear ground for their decisions. Even if the teacher can bring justification for his actions and manages to take the time to do so even to himself, his decision can always be questioned on the basis of a different view or in light of conflicting research evidence. Teaching is what has been called an "essentially contested concept" (Gallie, 1956), and living with such uncertainty is never easy, especially since it is "this capacity to judge, to act and to take responsibility for one's actions which constitutes a key part of teachers' professionalism."

However, Kelchtermans is hopeful that critical reflection can help to sustain teachers in their vulnerability: it is by "examining and unmasking the moral and political agendas in the work context and their impact on one's self-understanding, one's thinking and actions" that critical reflection can "open up perspectives for empowerment," and allow for new conditions to be created under which teachers might "regain the authorship of their selves," and thereby, I would add, be more present in the classroom. Kelchtermans' way of speaking about "who the teacher is" thus brings together the stable and unchanging aspect of who the teacher is and the qualities she brings to teaching, with her efforts to understand the complexities of her work and the way that she interacts in the rapidly changing situations of teaching. Taken together, all these aspects make it possible for the teacher to author her own work and thereby to be more present both to herself and to students.

The chapters of this book have offered evidence of teachers' presence. In the autobiographical writing of teachers shared in Chapter 4, we saw teachers fully present in writing about their early memories, telling about central events in their personal and professional lives, and considering their future career prospects. In the teacher educators' stories of Chapter 5, again early memories captured the teachers fully engaged in trying to understand their lives, and in their descriptions of their work one could see them present and trying hard to make a difference to their students. The writing process discussed in Chapter 6 was one in which the teachers had the opportunity to meet themselves on the page and to be in touch with whatever was important for them in the moment. These chapters suggest that narrative inquiry, in its different forms, can indeed be a means of enhancing teacher presence.

In addition to writing, other arts-based forms of work can also contribute to fostering presence. Cole (2009) offers examples of art installations which brought the viewer or visitor into direct contact with issues that are not easy to talk about (such as Alzheimer's disease), and which are likely to have a powerful educative impact. In Chapter 7 I discussed several examples of art exhibits which gave me direct bodily contact with important issues such as how educational experience is structured for diverse children, how culture shapes representation, and how memory can be understood non-verbally. Another instance is found in the work of the British sculptor Antony Gormley. In his project, "Field,"[1] the artist worked in different communities to create a very large number of small, rough sculptures of the human figure, which were then displayed standing close together in various settings. Viewing this work no doubt has diverse effects on different people; I was touched by the sense of human frailty, the need for solidarity and a sense that just standing side by side with others might be a restorative experience, one which paradoxically affirms the presence of each individual even though all are small and seemingly insignificant in making up the whole.

Embodiment

In reading Kelchtermans' (2009) article quoted above, I was struck by his simple and emphatic statement that "a teacher is *somebody*." This recognition is important, indeed absolutely essential, and yet it needs to be unpacked: the teacher is not only *some*body, but also some *body*. There is still far too little understanding of the need to acknowledge the teacher as an embodied human being. Discussion of teacher emotion is now common in the research on teaching, and feelings have been understood to be not just another, separate topic to be studied but an integral part of any teacher's work and being in the classroom. The body, however, is still in partial exile at best within the research literature: although the body is now seen as an appealing and trendy topic, it is often considered separately, in its own enclave. In writing Chapter 3, I found it difficult to avoid making false distinctions: the chapter was divided into sections on motherhood, embodiment and teaching only after I had attempted many other forms of organization and found it impossible to produce a coherent text. I could only hope that by placing the section on embodiment in the center, with links back to the first section on mothering and forward to the final section on teaching, some of the artificiality might be avoided.

I recall my late colleague Lia Kremer (z"l)[2] telling us that when she studied to become a teacher, they were taught how to stand in the classroom, how to write on the board and, in short, how to manage one's physical presence in the class. Today attention to such details seems quaint, especially in the context of the digital classroom. But teachers still have awkward moments, and their physical presence still matters. And the way that culture structures and shapes what bodies are acceptable and how they are to be viewed still impacts on teaching.

In looking at my mother's story I did the difficult work of tracing the impact of a mother's body and experience in the life and body of her daughter. This is only a beginning to thinking about the body in a pedagogical way, taking full account of the influence of early memories, of experience in the family, of history and of culture on how we are in the classroom. These questions also obviously impinge on the consideration of presence in teaching as well. I did not read the teachers' and teacher educators' stories systematically to look for their ways of storying the body, but bodies are certainly present in their early anecdotes, as well as in stories of difficult experiences. When a teacher educator says that she had headaches and pain in her jaw in a particular setting, we need to pay attention.

Imagination

The theme of imagination came up in relation to embodiment, and of course in the processes of writing discussed in Chapter 6. Reflecting on the work done in the course described in Chapter 6, I can see my own bias: although the prompts for writing were diverse and seemed to make room for some creativity, I must admit to being generally rather concerned with outcomes, with making sure that the participating teachers would see the work of the course as useful and relevant for them in practice. I never asked them to write poetry, for example, nor did I encourage them to produce fictional accounts. I held back from facilitating such activities, which I personally would have enjoyed, because I was afraid of possible consequences: students might find such activities too difficult, or worse: the course would be seen as frivolous, not serious. In looking back I think I did my students a disservice, but I don't think I should take all the blame for this on myself as an individual teacher. The lines were drawn long before I got there: literature versus science, hard versus soft, practical versus theoretical and so on, the binaries are well known. Like embodiment, imagination too is relegated to its own corner. I tried to release my own bonds by writing a chapter that is "not serious" in the usual way (though quite serious indeed in other ways), by including poetic passages. But then, I placed this discussion safely behind a fence in a chapter of its own (Chapter 7) with a 'reasonable' beginning if not an end. Releasing the imagination has enormous potential for social and educational change, as Greene (1995) has both told us and shown us by her own example. It's time to take up this challenge.

Dialogue

"Tall and straight my mother taught me, this how we dance. Tall and straight my father taught me, this is how we dance, battling feet on the city street, in pools of light on street corners, the proud bright carnival of the poor."[3]

A brilliant example of an embodied dialogue is found in the sequence called "Trading Taps" from the show, *Riverdance*, in which two groups of dancers, Irish and Afro-American, come together on a New York street. At first there is a stand-off, as the two groups eye one another suspiciously; then each group attempts to show off and impress the other. Gradually things begin to change: first the Afro-American dancers perform a stiff-limbed caricature of the Irish dance, and the Irish dancers follow with a sloppy (for them) impression of the Black tap dance. Then, each group tries dancing in its own style to the music of the other. They begin to pick up elements of one another's style and incorporate them into their own: the Irish dancers begin to move rapidly across the floor rather than dancing stiffly in place, and the Afro-American dancers invest their own steps with greater precision and intensity. By the end of the segment, which lasts seven or eight minutes, the dancers are performing together in one line, and it is hard to tell them apart or to put a label on the style of the dance.

This example shows in a way that is simultaneously concrete and metaphorical how dialogue can bring about change in action as well as in understanding. In my course on narrative methods described in Chapter 4, there were instances of a similar process. For example, in the course of the dialogue in class, through listening to the stories of each participant and working together, something changed for Marie who decided to bring forward an important piece of her history that had been missing from the account she initially wrote and shared with the group. In the same course in another year, the class engaged in an extended process of interpretation of one another's stories, and we were able to observe how misreading came about and what happened when it was explored through dialogue. For example, one Palestinian woman participant worked with a Jewish student who had emigrated from Ethiopia and whose story told, among other things, about life in the small agricultural village where she had grown up. The Palestinian student read this account through the lens of gender, suggesting that Ethiopian women in the village and in the family had had few rights. However, the teller of the story corrected this impression: she had not been obliged to help with the farming, only did so when she wanted to, when it was fun; the fact that she and other women in her family were now studying in higher education with the full support of both her parents backed up this view of her family. All of us, lacking knowledge, had been inclined to misread this story; the Palestinian student told how she herself had wanted to study a subject not typically chosen by women, and her family had channeled her towards teaching. This dialogue led to a fuller understanding of both women's stories as well as a greater sense of sharing and presence in the group (see Elbaz-Luwisch, 2010c).

That narrative inquiry is grounded in dialogue seems self-evident, perhaps so obvious that we don't need to discuss it. When the research process goes well, or when participants in a group feel comfortable telling and retelling their stories, we can safely ignore questions about what makes for fruitful dialogue. In the women's circle referred to in Chapter 5, we saw that the participants were free to argue and disagree about what kind of research activity—if any—should be undertaken by the group; they were also able to engage in difficult political discussion without harming, and indeed enriching the fabric of the group's connectedness (see Elbaz-Luwisch et al., 2008). But this kind of atmosphere is created with care and can't be taken for granted. Interestingly, embodiment and presence are important cues to what is happening in a group, and paying attention to them supports dialogue as well.

Goodson and Gill (2011), drawing on the hermeneutics of Gadamer, define the narrative encounter as "a situation in which, when the narrator begins, the listener is prepared for the stories to tell her something...the condition necessary for understanding is a sensitivity and an awareness of one's own bias as a listener, without which the story cannot present itself in all its otherness" (76) and failing which, the likelihood of learning something new is reduced. Lewis (2011) also stresses the importance of holding on to a sense of 'not knowing': "I don't know what to do at every given moment in teaching and I must acknowledge it, embrace it, and act from that awareness so that I remain open. Because when I act only from my knowledge and experience, I close the door on the entrance of other possibilities. When that door is closed, I lose and my kids lose" (509).

Conclusion

The themes of presence, embodiment, imagination and dialogue are intertwined throughout the discussion in this book, and coming back to them serves as a reminder of what has been done. These themes also serve to point the way forward: they are topics to be attended to if we wish to further our own development and participate with others, teachers and students, children and adults, in their processes of learning and growth. These themes might be taken as notes for the elaboration of an internally persuasive discourse in teaching, and eventually for a reformed authoritative discourse, a discourse of possibility.

Bullough (2008), in writing about his own story as a researcher and teacher educator, insists that research must find ways of bringing "personal troubles and social issues" together. A similar caution is expressed by Goodson et al. (2010) who warn that the contemporary 'celebration of the personal' risks making it easier to avoid "asking more difficult questions about the processes through which personal issues can be transformed into public issues that have political rather than just personal significance." The work of Hannah Arendt was centrally (if not unproblematically) concerned with the idea of the public sphere, and with storytelling as a methodology which can "dig under the rubble of history in order to recover those 'pearls' of past experience, with their sedimented and hidden layers of meaning, such as to cull from them a story that can orient the mind in the future" (Benhabib, 1993, 111). Benhabib's rereading of Arendt in the light of feminist critiques highlights a much-needed understanding of the private sphere as that place we usually call 'home,' which provides the nurturing and protection that might enable the individual to go forth and participate in the public sphere.

It is in the home that we learn the importance of particulars; narrative inquiry and teaching are both practices that rely on paying attention to the small details of our lives. It is not surprising that Arendt wrote: "One can't say how life is, how chance or fate determine people's lives, except by telling the tale. In general one can't say more than—'yes, that is the way it goes'..." (Brightman, 1996). In the words of Wyslawa Szymborska, from her speech in acceptance of the Nobel Prize (1996):

> In the language of poetry, where every word is weighed, nothing is usual or normal. Not a single stone and not a single cloud above it. Not a single day and not a single night after it. And above all, not a single existence, not anyone's existence in this world.

Our stories, Szymborska implies, are needed in the world. Narrative inquiry is the work of bringing stories to the places where they can be most useful; it is work that is in equal measure practical, political, and informed by spirit. In telling and writing stories, listening and falling under their spell, responding and arguing and questioning them, auto/biography is central to the practices of pedagogy, of nurturing children, fostering both individuality and community, and developing the unique abilities, inclinations and desires of children and adults to go out, by ourselves and together with others, to be present and make a difference in the world.

Notes

1. http://www.antonygormley.com/sculpture/item-view/id/245#p4

2. In Jewish tradition it is customary to refer to the deceased with the honorific "of blessed memory," or in Hebrew "zichrono livracha," usually written in an abbreviated form rendered in English by the letters *z"l.*

3. http://www.youtube.com/watch?v=nBUzyW8FGLA

BIBLIOGRAPHY

Abbey, S. (1999). Researching motherhood as a feminist: Reflecting on my own experiences. *Journal of the Association for Research on Mothering 1*(1), 45–55.

Abdo, N. (2002) Dislocating self, relocating 'other': A Palestinian experience. In N. Abdo & R. Lentin (Eds.) *Women and the politics of military confrontation: Palestinian and Israeli gendered narratives of dislocation*. New York & Oxford: Berghahn.

Abdo, N. & Lentin, R. (Eds.), (2002) *Women and the politics of military confrontation: Palestinian and Israeli gendered narratives of dislocation*. New York & Oxford: Berghahn.

Abella, I. & Troper, H. (1983). *None is too many: Canada and the Jews of Europe, 1933–1948*. New York: Random House.

Abu-Rabia-Queder, S. and Oplatka, I. (2008). The power of femininity: Exploring the gender and ethnic experiences of Muslim women who accessed supervisory roles in a Bedouin society. *Journal of Educational Administration 16*(3): 396–415.

Acker, S. (1997). Becoming a teacher educator: Voices of women academics in Canadian faculties of education. *Teaching and Teacher Education, 13*(1), 65–74.

Alayan, S. & Yair, G. (2010): The cultural inertia of the habitus: Gendered narrations of agency amongst educated female Palestinians in Israel. *British Educational Research Journal*, *36*: 5, 831–850.

Al-Haj, M. (1995). *Education, empowerment and control: The case of the Arabs in Israel*. Albany: State University of New York Press.

———. (2002). Multiculturalism in deeply divided societies: The Israeli case. *International Journal of Intercultural Relations 26*, 169–183.

Anderson, R. (2001). Embodied writing and reflections on embodiment. *Journal of Transpersonal Psychology 33*(2), 83–98.

Andrews, M. (2002). Memories of mother: Counter-narratives of early maternal influence. *Narrative Inquiry 12*(1), 7–27.

Aoki, Ted T. (1983). Experiencing ethnicity as a Japanese Canadian teacher: Reflections on a personal curriculum. *Curriculum Inquiry 13*(3), 321–335.

Apple, M. (1987). The de-skilling of teaching. In F.S. Bolin, J.M. Falk, (Eds.) *Teacher renewal: Professional issues, personal choices* (pp. 59–75). New York & London: Teachers College Press.

Arendt, H. (1958). *The human condition*. Chicago: University of Chicago Press.

———. (1978). Appendix/judging: Excerpts from lectures on Kant's political philosophy, *The Life of the Mind* (pp. 255–72), Ed. Mary McCarthy. New York: Harcourt.

———. (1993). *Between past and future: Eight exercises in political thought* New York: Penguin (first published 1968).

Arieli, M. (1995). *Teaching and its discontents.* Tel-Aviv: Ramot, Tel-Aviv University. (Hebrew)

Asaf, M., Shachar, R., Tohar, V., & Kainan, A. (2008). From superteacher to a super teacher: The career development of teacher educators. *Forum Qualitative Sozialforschung/Forum: Qualitative Social Research,* 9(3), Art. 19, http://nbn-resolving.de/urn:nbn:de:0114-fqs0803192.

Attarian, H. (2011). Narrating displacement: The pedagogy of exile. In Mitchell, C., Strong-Wilson, T., Pithouse, K. and Allnutt, S. (Eds.), *Memory and pedagogy* (145–160). New York & Abingdon: Routledge.

Audergon, A. (2005). *The war hotel.* Chichester, UK: John Wiley & Sons.

Aviram, R. (2010). *Navigating through the storm: Reinventing education for postmodern democracies.* Rotterdam: Sense.

Badali, S. (2004). Exploring tensions in the lives of professors of teacher education: A Canadian context. *Journal of Teaching and Learning 3*(1), 1–16.

Badinter, E. (1981). *The myth of motherhood: An historical view of the maternal instinct.* London: Souvenir E & A.

Baier, A. (1976). Mixing memory and desire. *American Philosophical Quarterly, 13*(3), 213–220.

Bailey, A. (1994). Mothering, diversity and peace politics. *Hypatia* 9(2): 188–198.

Bakhtin, M. (1981). *The dialogical imagination: Four essays by M. M. Bakhtin,* Ed. M. Holquist. Austin: University of Texas Press.

———. (1986). *Speech genres and other late essays/M. M. Bakhtin.* Trans. V.W. McGee, Ed. C. Emerson & M. Holquist. Austin: University of Texas Press.

Ballet, K., Kelchtermans, G. and Loughran, J. (2006). Beyond intensification towards a scholarship of practice: Analysing changes in teachers' work lives. *Teachers and Teaching: Theory and Practice* 12, 209–229.

Bar Tal, D. (2007). Sociopsychological foundations of intractable conflicts. *American Behavioral Scientist, 50,* 1430–1453.

Barnacle, R. (2009). Gut instinct: The body and learning. *Educational Philosophy and Theory, 41*(1), 22–33.

Barone, T. (1989). Ways of being at risk: The case of Billy Charles Barnett. *Phi Delta Kappan, 71*(2), 147–151.

Barr, J. and Griffiths, M. (2004). *Training the imagination to go visiting.* In Nixon, J. and Walker, M. (Eds.), *Reclaiming universities from a runaway world* (pp. 85–99). Maidenhead; London: Maidenhead SRHE and Open University Press.

Bassett, D. (2012). I need these stories to remind me that there is hope: Poetic representations of living in Israel during the *Al Aqsa Intifada. Qualitative Inquiry 18*(5): 432–437.

Benhabib, S. (1993). Feminist theory and Hannah Arendt's concept of public space. *History of the Human Sciences 6*(2), 97–114.

Benjamin, J. (1995). Recognition and destruction: An outline of intersubjectivity. In *Like subjects, love objects: Essays on recognition and sexual difference.* New Haven: Yale University Press.

Benjamin, W. (1999). *Selected writings*, Vol. 2, 1927–1934, trans. R. Livingstone & others, Ed. M.W. Jennings, H. Eiland & G. Smith. Cambridge & London: Belknap.

Ben-Peretz, M. (1995a). Educational reform in Israel: An example of synergy in education. In David S.G.Carter & M.H. O'Neill (Eds.), *Case studies in educational change: An international perspective* (pp. 86–95). London & Washington: Falmer.

————— (1995b). *Memory and the teacher's account of teaching.* Albany, NY: SUNY Press.

Ben-Peretz, M., Kleeman, S., Reichenberg, R., & Shimoni, S., (Eds.), (2013). *Teacher educators as members of an evolving profession.* Lanham, MD: Rowman & Littlefield.

Ben-Ze'ev, E. (2011). *Remembering Palestine in 1948: Beyond national narratives.* Cambridge, UK: Cambridge University Press.

Berry, A. (2007). Reconceptualizing teacher educator knowledge as tensions: Exploring the tension between valuing and reconstructing experience. *Studying Teacher Education: A Journal of Self-study of Teacher Education Practices, 3*(2), 117–134.

Bettelheim, B. (1969). *The Children of the Dream.* London: Macmillan.

Bhatt, S. (2000). *My mother's way of wearing a sari.* New Delhi & London: Penguin.

Bickman, D. (1996). Podolia and her Jews, a brief history. JewishGen, Ukraine SIG, downloaded from http://www.jewishgen.org/ukraine/PTM_Article.asp?id=18 (March 30, 2013).

Bleakley, A. (2000). Writing with invisible ink: Narrative, confessionalism and reflective practice. *Reflective Practice 1*(1), 11–12.

Bloom, L. (1996). Stories of one's own: Nonunitary subjectivity in narrative representation. *Qualitative Inquiry 2*(2), 176–197.

Bourdieu, P. & Passeron, J.C. (1990). *Reproduction in education, society and culture.* Second edition (first published in English 1977, in French 1970). London, Thousand Oaks & New Delhi: Sage.

Bresler, L. (2004). (Ed.) *Knowing bodies, moving minds: Towards embodied teaching and learning.* Dordrecht: Kluwer.

Brightman, C., Ed. (1996). *Between friends: The correspondence of Hannah Arendt and Mary McCarthy, 1949–1975.* Boston, MA: Harvest.

Brooks, P. (1984). *Reading for the plot: Design and intention in narrative.* New York: Knopf.

Brown, L.M. & Gilligan, C. (1992). *Meeting at the crossroads: Women's psychology and girls' development.* Cambridge: Harvard University Press.

Brown, R. & Kulik, J. (1977). Flashbulb memories. *Cognition, 5*(1), 73–99.

Buber, M. (1963). *Pointing the way.* New York & Evanston: Harper & Row.

Bullough, R.V. (2008). The writing of teachers' lives—Where personal troubles and social issues meet. *Teacher Education Quarterly 35*(4), 7–26.

Bullough, R. V., Knowles, J. G., & Crow, N. A. (1992). *Emerging as a teacher.* New York: Routledge.

Burdell, P. & Swadener, B.B. (1999). Critical personal narrative and autoethnography in education: Reflections on a genre. *Educational Researcher 28*, 21–26.

Burkitt, I. (1999). *Bodies of thought: Embodiment, identity and modernity.* London: Sage.

Burman, E. (2003). Narratives of 'experience' and pedagogical practices. *Narrative Inquiry, 13*(2), 269–286.

Butler, J. (2004). Bracha's Eurydice. *Theory, Culture and Society, 21*(1): 95–100.

Byrne, B.M. (1994). Burnout: Testing for the validity, replication, and invariance of the causal structure across elementary, intermediate, and secondary teachers. *American Educational Research Journal 31*, 645–673.

Campbell, S. (2003). *Relational remembering: Rethinking the memory wars.* Lanham, Boulder, New York & Oxford: Rowman & Littlefield.

Caplan, N. (2009). *The Israel-Palestine conflict: Contested histories.* Chichester, UK: Wiley/Blackwell.

Casey, E. (1993). *Getting back into place: Toward a renewed understanding of the place-world.* Bloomington: Indiana University Press.

Casey, K. (1990). Teacher as mother: Curriculum theorizing in the life histories of contemporary women teachers. *Cambridge Journal of Education 20*(3), 301–320.

———. (1992). Why do progressive women activists leave teaching? Theory, methodology and politics in life-history research. In I.G. Goodson (Ed.), *Studying teachers' lives.* London: Routledge.

Chapin, D. & Weinstock, B. (2000). *The Road from Letichev: The history and culture of a forgotten Jewish community in Eastern Europe.* San Jose, New York, Lincoln, Shanghai: Writers' Showcase, presented by Writers' Digest, iUniverse.com.

Cho, G.M. (2005). Regression analysis: Mother, memory, data. *Cultural Studies <=> Critical Methodologies* 5(1), 45–51.

Cixous, H. (1976). *The Laugh of the Medusa* (trans. Keith Cohen and Paula Cohen), *Signs* 1(4), 875–93.

Cixous, H. (1997). *Rootprints: Memory and life writing.* London: Routledge.

Clandinin, D. J. (1995). Still learning to teach. In T. Russell & F. Korthagen (Eds.), *Teachers who teach teachers* (pp. 25–31). London/Washington: Falmer.

Clandinin, D.J. & Connelly, F.M. (1996). Teachers' professional knowledge landscapes: Teacher stories—stories of teachers—school stories—stories of school. *Educational Researcher 19*(5), 2–14.

———. (1998a). Stories to live by: Narrative understandings of school reform. *Curriculum Inquiry 28*(2), 149–164.

———. (1998b). Asking questions about telling stories. In C. Kridel, *Writing educational biography: Explorations in qualitative research* (pp. 245–253). New York & London: Garland.

———. (2000). *Narrative inquiry: Experience and story in qualitative research.* San Francisco: Jossey-Bass.

Clark/Keefe, K. (2006, December). Degrees of separation: An ourstory about working-class and poverty-class academic identity. *Qualitative Inquiry 12*(6), 1180–1197.

Cochran-Smith, M. (2003). Learning and unlearning: The education of teacher educators. *Teaching and Teacher Education 19*, 5–28.

Cochran-Smith, M. & Lytle, S. (1999). Relationships of knowledge and practice: Teacher learning in communities. *Review of Research in Education 24*, 249–305.

Cochran-Smith, M. and Zeichner, K. M. (2005). *Studying teacher education: The report of the AERA panel on research and teacher education.* American Educational Research Association. Lawrence Erlbaum.

Cohen, E. (2004). *Hear O Lo-rd.* Ra'anana, Israel: Even Hoshen. (Hebrew)

Cole, A. (1997). Impediments to reflective practice: Toward a new agenda for research on teaching. *Teachers and Teaching: Theory and Practice, 3*(1), 7–27.

———. (2009). Living in paradox: Metaphors of conflict and contradiction in the Academy. *Educational Insights,13*(4), available at http://www.ccfi.educ.ubc.ca/publication/insights /v13n04/articles/cole/index.html

Cole, A. & Knowles, G. (2000) *Researching teaching: Exploring teacher development.* Boston: Allyn & Bacon.

Colyar, J. (2009). Becoming writing, becoming writers. *Qualitative Inquiry 15*(2), 421–436.

Confino, J. (2013). Zen master Thich Nhat Hanh: Only love can save us from climate change. *The Guardian*, January 21, 2013. Downloaded (01/04/2013) from http://www.guardian. co.uk/sustainable-business/zen-master-thich-nhat-hanh-love-climate-change

Conle, C. (1996). Resonance in preservice teacher inquiry. *American Educational Research Journal 33*(2), 297–325.

———. (1999). Why narrative? Which narrative? Struggling with time and place in life and research. *Curriculum Inquiry 29*(1), 7–32.

Conle, C., Li, X. & Tan, J. (2002). Connecting vicarious experience to practice. *Curriculum Inquiry 32*(4), 429–452.

Connelly, F.M. (1995). Foreword, in Ben-Peretz, M. *Memory and the teacher's account of teaching* (xiii–xviii). Albany, NY: SUNY Press.

Connelly, F.M. & Clandinin, D.J. (1995). Narrative and education. *Teachers and Teaching, Theory and Practice 1*(1), 73–85.

Connerton, P. (1989). *How societies remember.* Cambridge: Cambridge University Press.

Cook, L. (1951). *The little magic fiddler.* Toronto: Macmillan.

Cooper, M., Ryan, M., Gay, J., & Perry, C. (1999). Responding creatively to challenges in teacher education: Four women teacher educators tell their stories. *Asia-Pacific Journal of Teacher Education 27*(2), 143–158.

Cornell, D. & Dean, J. (1998). Exploring the imaginary domain. *Philosophy & Social Criticism* (24), 173–197.

———. (1995). *The imaginary domain: A discourse on abortion, pornography and sexual harassment.* New York: Routledge, Chapman & Hall.

Cosslett, T. (2000). Matrilineal narratives revisited. In T. Cosslett, C. Lury & P. Summerfield (Eds.), *Feminism and autobiography: Texts, theories, methods* (pp. 141–153). London & New York: Routledge.

Craig, C. (2010). Change, changing, and being changed: A study of self in the throes of multiple accountability demands. *Studying Teacher Education: A Journal of Self-study of Teacher Education Practices, 6*(1), 63–73.

Craig, C. J. (1995). Knowledge communities: A way of making sense of how beginning teachers come to know. *Curriculum Inquiry, 25*(2), 151–175.

———. (2004). Shifting boundaries on the professional knowledge landscape: When teacher communications become less safe. *Curriculum Inquiry, 34*(4), 395–424.

Darling-Hammond, L. and Bransford, J. (Eds.) (2005). *Preparing teachers for a changing world: What teachers should learn and be able to do.* National Academy of Education, Committee on Teacher Education. San Francisco: Jossey-Bass.

Davies, B. & Gannon, S. (2006). *Doing collective biography.* Maidenhead & New York: Open University Press.

Davis, D.A. (1994). A theory for the 90s: Freud's seduction theory in historical context. *Psychoanalytic Review, 81,* 627–640.

Day, C. & Gu, X. (2009). Veteran teachers: Commitment, resilience and quality retention. *Teachers and Teaching, Theory and Practice, 15*(4), 441–457.

Deleuze, G., & Guattari, F. (1987). *A thousand plateaus: Capitalism and schizophrenia.* Minneapolis: University of Minnesota Press.

Denzin, N. (1995). The experiential text and the limits of visual understanding. *Educational Theory 45*(1), 7–18.

Derrida, J. (1976). *Of grammatology.* (First published 1967, in French; trans. G. Spivak.) Baltimore, MD: Johns Hopkins University Press.

Dewey, J. (1938). *Experience and education.* New York: Macmillan.

Diab, K. (2002). The missing narrative: Search for self. In A. Shai and Y. Bar-Shalom (Eds.), *Qualitative research in the study of education.* Jerusalem: David Yellin College of Education. (Hebrew)

Diamant, A. (1997). *The red tent.* New York: Picador & St. Martin's Press.

Diamond, C. (1994). Writing to reclaim the self: The use of narrative in teacher education. *Teaching and Teacher Education 9*(5/6), 511–517.

Dinur, Y. (1961). Testimony at the trial of Adolf Eichmann, Jerusalem, June 1961. http://www.nizkor.org/hweb/people/e/eichmann-adolf/transcripts/Sessions/Session-068-01.html

Disch, L.J. (1994). *Hannah Arendt and the limits of philosophy.* Ithaca & London: Cornell University Press.

Dixon, M. & Senior, K. (2011). Appearing pedagogy: From embodied learning and teaching to embodied pedagogy. *Pedagogy, Culture & Society 19*(3), 473–484.

Doll, M. A. (1995). *To the lighthouse and back: Writings on teaching and living.* New York: Peter Lang.

Drake, C., Spillane, J. & Hufferd-Ackles, K. (2001). Storied identities: Teacher learning and subject-matter context. *Journal of Curriculum Studies 33*(1), 1–24.

Draper, P. (1985). "Refugee!" The adjustment of Jewish refugees from Nazism to Canadian life. *Refuge, Canada's Periodical on Refugees 5*(2), 15–17. Downloaded (13/4/2013) from https://pi.library.yorku.ca/ojs/index.php/refuge/article/viewFile/21487/20162

Ducharme, E. R. (1993). *The lives of teacher educators*. New York: Teachers College Press.

Ducharme, M. & Ducharme, E. (1996). A study of teacher educators: Research from the United States of America. *Journal of Education for Teaching: International Research and Pedagogy, 22*(1), 57–70.

Ehrenburg, I. & Grossman, V. (Eds.) (1980). *The black book*. New York: Holocaust Library.

Eilam, B. (2002). "Passing through" a western-democratic teacher education: The case of Israeli Arab teachers. *Teachers College Record 104*(8), 1656–1701.

Eisenstadt, S. (1995). *The absorption of immigrants*. Glencoe, IL: Free Press.

Eisner, E. (1994). On the art of teaching (pp. 154–170). In *The educational imagination*. New York: Macmillan.

Elbaz-Luwisch F. (2001). Understanding what goes on in the heart and in the mind: Learning about diversity and co-existence through storytelling. *Teaching and Teacher Education, 17*, 133–146.

————. (2002). Writing as inquiry: Storying the teaching self in writing workshops. *Curriculum Inquiry, 32*(4), 403–428.

————. (2004a). How is education possible when there's a body in the middle of the room? *Curriculum Inquiry, 31*(1), 9–27.

————. (2004b). Immigrant teachers: Stories of self and place. *International Journal of Qualitative Studies in Education, 17*(3), 387–414.

————. (2005). *Teachers' voices: Storytelling and possibility*. Greenwich, CT: Information Age.

————. (2007). Studying teachers' lives and experience: Narrative inquiry in K-12 teaching. In D.J. Clandinin, Ed., *Handbook of narrative inquiry: Mapping a methodology* (pp. 357–382). Thousand Oaks, CA: Sage.

————. (2010a). Writing and professional learning: The uses of autobiography in graduate studies in education. *Teachers and Teaching, Theory and Practice 16*(3), 307–327.

————. (2010b). Narrative inquiry: Wakeful engagement with educational experience. *Curriculum Inquiry 40*(2), 263–279.

————. (2010c). Analysis, interpretation and restorying: The contribution of a group process in the interpretation of personal narratives. In: R. Tuval-Mashiach & G. Spector-Marzel (Eds.), *Narrative inquiry: Theory, creation and interpretation*. Jerusalem: Magnes (in Hebrew).

Elbaz-Luwisch, F. & Kalekin-Fishman, D. (2004). Professional development in community: Fostering multicultural dialogue among Israeli teachers. *British Journal of In-service Education, 30*(2), 245–264.

Elbaz-Luwisch, F., Klein, S., Nasseraldin, H., Avni, I., Awadiyeh, I., David, D., Ben Hefer, A., Morag, H., Shaul, T., Shimoni, F., & Simon, C., (2008). Life stories and the development of a multicultural community of women educators. In A. Short & J. Kentel (Eds.), *Totems and taboos: Risk and relevance in research on teachers and teaching.* Sense.

Elbaz-Luwisch, F. & Pritzker, D. (2002). Writing workshops in teacher education: Making a space for feeling and diversity. *Asia Pacific Journal of Teacher Education, 30*(3), 277–289.

Eliot, T.S. (1922). *The waste land.* New York: Horace Liveright.

Ellis, C. & Bochner, A. (2000). Autoethnography, personal narrative, reflexivity: Researcher as subject. In N.K. Denzin & Y.S. Lincoln (Eds.), *Handbook of qualitative research* (2nd ed., pp. 733–768). Thousand Oaks, CA: Sage.

Erdreich, L. (2006). Marriage talk: Palestinian women, intimacy, and the liberal nation-state. *Ethnography 7*(4), 493–523.

Erikson, E. (1959/1980). *Identity and the life cycle.* New York: Norton.

Erlich, S. (2009). The place of the father in motherhood, and the motherhood of male therapists. In E. Perroni, (Ed.) *Motherhood: Psychoanalysis and other disciplines* (pp. 44–53). Jerusalem & Tel Aviv: Van Leer Jerusalem Institute & Hakibbutz Hameuchad (In Hebrew).

Esgalhado, B.D. (2001). For then and now: Memory and writing. *Narrative Inquiry 11*(2), 235–256.

Estola, E. (2003). *In the language of the mother—re-storying the relational moral in teachers' stories.* Ph.D. dissertation, University of Oulu Press.

Estola, E. & Elbaz-Luwisch, F. (2003). Teaching bodies at work. *Journal of Curriculum Studies 35,* 1–23.

Estola, E., Erkkilä, R., & Syrjälä, L. (2003). A moral voice of vocation in teachers' narratives. *Teachers and Teaching: Theory and Practice, 9*(3), 239–256.

Faber, M.D. (1998). *Synchronicity: C.G. Jung, psychoanalysis, and religion.* Westport & London: Praeger.

Felman, S., & Laub, D. (1992). *Testimony.* New York: Routledge.

Fine, M. (2002). The mourning after. *Qualitative Inquiry 8,* 137–145.

Fogel-Bijaoui, S. (1999). Families in Israel: Between familism and post-modernism. In D. Yizraeli et al., *Sex, gender and politics: Women in Israel.* Tel Aviv: Hakibbutz Hameuchad (Hebrew).

Franke, D. (1995). Writing into unmapped territory: The practice of lateral citation. In L.W. Phelps & J. Emig (Eds.), *Feminine principles and women's experience in American composition and rhetoric* (pp. 375–384). Pittsburgh & London: University of Pittsburgh Press.

Freeman, M. (2002). Charting the narrative unconscious: Cultural memory and the challenge of autobiography. *Narrative Inquiry 12*, 193–211.

———. (2007). Autobiographical understanding and narrative inquiry. In D.J. Clandinin, Ed., *Handbook of narrative inquiry: Mapping a methodology.* Thousand Oaks, CA: Sage.

Freire, P. (1970). *Pedagogy of the oppressed.* New York: Continuum.

Freud, S. (1899). Screen memories. *Standard edition,* 3, pp. 301–322. London: Hogarth.

———. (1991). A note upon the mystic writing pad (1925), in *On metapsychology: The theory of psychoanalysis* (pp. 429–34), trans. J. Strachey. Harmondsworth: Penguin.

Fullan, M., Galluzzo, G., Morris, P., & Watson, N. (1998). *The rise and stall of teacher education reform.* Washington, DC: AACTE.

Galea, S. (2005). Teachers as mothers: Practices of subversion. *Journal of Maltese Education Research 3*(1), 14–27.

Gallie, W.B. (1956). Essentially contested concepts, *Proceedings of the Aristotelian Society,* 56, 167–198.

Gallop, J. (1995). (Ed.) *Pedagogy and the question of impersonation.* Bloomington and Indianapolis: University of Indiana Press.

Gannon, S. (2006). The (im)possibilities of writing the self-writing: French poststructural theory and autoethnography. *Cultural Studies ↔ Critical Methodologies,* 6(4), 474–495.

Garrison, J. (1997). *Dewey and eros: Wisdom and desire in the art of teaching.* New York: Teachers College Press.

Gemmell, T., Griffiths, M. & Kibble, B. (2010). What kind of research culture do teacher educators want, and how can we get it? *Studying Teacher Education: A Journal of Self-study of Teacher Education Practices,* 6,2, 161–174.

Giddens, A. (1991). *Modernity and self-identity: Self and society in the late modern age.* Cambridge: Polity.

Gilat, A. & Hertz-Lazarowitz, R. (2009). Women's experience of personal and gender empowerment through university studies: The case of Jewish and Arab religious and non-religious women (pp. 133–148). In Hertz-Lazarowitz, R. & Oplatka, I. (Eds.), *Gender and ethnicity in the Israeli academy.* Haifa: Pardes. (Hebrew)

Gitlin, A. & Margonis, F. (1995). The political aspect of reform: Teacher resistance as good sense. *American Journal of Education 103*(4), 377–405.

Goffman, E. (1959). *The presentation of self in everyday life.* Garden City, NY: Doubleday.

Goldberg, N. (1986). *Writing down the bones*. Boston & London: Shambhala.

Golden, D. (2001). Storytelling the future: Israelis, immigrants and the imagining of community. *Anthropological Quarterly 75* (1), 7–35.

———. (2004). Hugging the teacher: Reading bodily practice in an Israeli kindergarten. *Teachers and Teaching, Theory and Practice 10*(4), 395–407.

Goldstein, L. S. (2002). *Reclaiming caring in teaching and teacher education*. New York: Peter Lang.

Goodson, I.F. (1992). Sponsoring the teacher's voice: Teachers' lives and teacher development. In A. Hargreaves & M. Fullan (Eds.), *Understanding teacher development* (pp. 110–121). London: Cassell, and New York: Teachers College Press.

———. (1998). Preparing for postmodernity: The peril and promise. *Educational Practice and Theory 20*(1), 25–31.

Goodson, I.F., Biesta, G., Tedder, M. & Adair, N. (2010) *Narrative learning*. London & New York: Routledge.

Goodson, I.F. & Gill, S. (2011) *Narrative pedagogy: Life histories and learning*. New York: Peter Lang.

Gotfryd, B. (2000). *Anton the dove fancier, and other tales of the Holocaust*. Baltimore & London: Johns Hopkins University Press.

Gray, B. (1978). *Manya's story*. Minneapolis: Lerner.

Greene, M. (1995). *Releasing the imagination: Essays on education, the arts and social change*. San Francisco: Jossey-Bass.

———. (2000). Imagining futures: The public school and possibility. *Journal of Curriculum Studies 32*, 2, 267–280.

Greenwood, D.A (2010). Education in a culture of violence: A critical pedagogy of place in wartime. *Cultural Studies of Science Education 5*, 351–359.

Griffiths, M. (1995a). *Feminisms and the self: The web of identity*. London & New York: Routledge.

———. (1995b). Biography and epistemology. *Educational Review, 47*(1), 75–88.

———. (2006). The feminization of teaching and the practice of teaching: Threat or opportunity? *Educational Theory 56*(4), 387–405.

Griffiths, M., & Macleod, G. (2008). Personal narratives and policy: Never the twain? *Journal of Philosophy of Education, 42*(S1), 121–143.

Gross, Z. (2012). Muslim women in higher education: Reflections on literacy and modernization in Israel. In T. Lovat, (Ed.), *Women in Islam: Reflections on historical and contemporary research.* Dordrecht: Springer.

Gross, A.S., Hoffman, M.J., (2004). Memory, authority, and identity: Holocaust studies in light of the Wilkomirski debate. *Biography, 27*(1), 25–47.

Grosz, E. (1994). *Volatile bodies: Toward a corporeal feminism.* Bloomington, IN: Indiana University Press.

Grumet, M. (1988). *Bitter milk: Women and teaching.* Amherst, MA: University of Massachusetts Press.

———. (1995). Scholae personae: Masks for meaning. In J. Gallop (Ed.). *Pedagogy and the question of impersonation* (pp. 36–45). Bloomington and Indianapolis: University of Indiana Press.

Gurevitch, Z. (2000). The serious play of writing. *Qualitative Inquiry* 6, 3–8.

———. (2002). Writing through: The poetics of transfiguration. *Cultural Studies <=> Critical Methodologies 2*(3), 403–413.

Gur-Ze'ev, I. (2007). *Beyond the modern–postmodern struggle in education: Toward counter-education and enduring improvisation.* Rotterdam: Sense.

———. (2001). The production of the self and the destruction of the other's memory and identity: Israeli/Palestinian education on the Holocaust/Nakbah. *Studies in Philosophy and Education 20*(3), 255–266.

Gutfreund, A. (2002). "This grief." In *The shoreline mansions.* Ganei Aviv–Lod: Zmora-Bitan. (Hebrew)

Hager, T. (2011). Making sense of an untold story: A personal deconstruction of the myth of motherhood. *Qualitative Inquiry 7*(1), 35–44.

Hakker, H. (2004). Narrative and moral identity in the work of Paul Ricoeur, in Junker-Kenny, M. & Kenny, P. (Eds.), *Memory, narrativity, self and the challenge to think God* (pp. 134–152). Munster: Lit.

Halbwachs, M. (1992). *On collective memory*, Trans. and Ed. Lewis Coser. Chicago: University of Chicago Press.

Halprin, S. (2001). So much depends on a red hook: The essence of writing. *Journal of Process-Oriented Psychology, 8*(2), 10–17.

Hamilton, E. & Cairns, H. (1961). *The collected dialogues of Plato.* Bollingen Series LXXI. Princeton: Princeton University Press.

Hamilton, M.L., Smith, L., & Kristen Worthington, K. (2008). Fitting the methodology with the research: An exploration of narrative, self-study and auto-ethnography. *Studying Teacher Education: A Journal of Self-study of Teacher Education Practices, 4*(1), 17–28.

Hampl, P. (1999). *I could tell you stories: Sojourns in the land of memory.* New York: W. W. Norton.

Hankins, K. H. (1998). Cacophony to symphony: Memoirs in teacher research. *Harvard Educational Review 68*(1), 80–95.

Harris, P. (2010). Mediating relationships across research, policy, and practice in teacher education. *Studying Teacher Education: A Journal of Self-study of Teacher Education Practices, 6*(1), 75–93.

Hasebe-Ludt, E., & Jordan, N., Eds. (2010). "May we get us a heart of wisdom": Life writing across knowledge traditions. *Transnational Curriculum Inquiry, 7*(2), 1–4.

Haug, F., et al. (1987). *Female sexualization: A collective work of memory.* New York: Verso.

He, M. F. (2002). A narrative inquiry of cross-cultural lives: Lives in China. *Journal of Curriculum Studies, 34*, 301–321.

Heikkinen, H. (1998). Becoming yourself through narrative: Autobiographical approach in teacher education. In R. Erkkila, A. Willman & L. Syrjälä (Eds.), *Promoting teachers' personal and professional growth* (111–131). Oulu: Oulu University Press.

Heilbrun, C. (1988). *Writing a woman's life.* New York: Norton.

Hertz-Lazarowitz, R. (2003). Arab and Jewish youth in Israel: Voicing national injustice on campus. *Journal of Social Issues, 59*, 51–66.

Hertz-Lazarowitz, R., Azaiza, F., Peretz, H., Kupermintz, H., & Sharabany, R. (2007). National identity and perception of the university as a context of coexistence vs. a context of conflict (pp. 159–167). In Rahav, G., Wozner, Y,. Azaiza, F., Wander-Schwartz, M. (Eds.). *Youth in Israel 2005.* Tel-Aviv: Ramot Tel-Aviv University Publishers. (Hebrew)

Hertz-Lazarowitz, R., Farah, A. & Yosef-Meitav, M. (2012). Hyphenated identity development of Arab and Jewish teachers: Within the conflict-ridden multicultural setting of the University of Haifa. *Creative Education 3*, 1063–1069.

Hertz-Lazarowitz, R., Mor-Sommerfeld, A., Zelniker, T. & Azaiza, F. (2008). From ethnic segregation to bilingual education: What can bilingual education do for the future of the Israeli Society? *Journal for Critical Education Policy Studies, 6* (2).

Hertz-Lazarowitz, R. & Oplatka, Y. (2009). (Eds.) (2009). *Gender and ethnicity in the Israeli academy.* Haifa: Pardes Publishers. (Hebrew)

Hertz-Lazarowitz, R. & Shapira, T. (2005). Muslim women life stories: Building leadership. *Anthropology & Education Quarterly, 36*(2), 161–185.

Heuer, F. & Reisberg, D. (2007). The memory effects of emotion, stress and trauma. In Ross, D., Toglia, M., Lindsay, R. and Read, D. (Eds.), *Handbook of eyewitness psychology: Volume 1–Memory for events* (pp. 81–116). Mahwah, NJ: Erlbaum.

Hiebert, J., Gallimore, R., and Stigler, J.W. (2002). A knowledge base for the teaching profession: What would it look like and how can we get one? *Educational Researcher 31*: 3, 3–15.

Hillman, J. (2004). *A terrible love of war*. New York: Penguin.

Hirsch, M. (2001). Surviving images: Holocaust photographs and the work of postmemory. In B. Zelizer, Ed., *Visual culture and the Holocaust* (pp. 215–246). New Brunswick: Rutgers: The State University Press.

———. (2008). The generation of post-memory. *Poetics Today 29*(1), 104–128.

Hirsch, M. & Smith, V. (2002). (Eds.) Feminism and cultural memory: An introduction. Gender and cultural memory, Special Issue, *Signs 28*(1), 1–19.

Hirshfield, J. (1998). *Nine gates: Entering the mind of poetry*. New York: Harper Perennial.

Hocking, B., Haskell, J., & Linds, W., Eds. (2001). *Unfolding bodymind: Exploring possibility through education*. Brandon, VT: Foundation for Educational Renewal.

hooks, b. (1994). *Teaching to transgress: Education as the practice of freedom*. New York: Routledge.

Ivanić, R. (1998). *Writing and identity: The discoursal construction of identity in academic writing*. Amsterdam/Philadelphia: John Benjamins.

Johnson, K.E. (2007). Tracing teacher and student learning in teacher-authored narratives. *Teacher Development 11*(2), 175–188.

Johnson, K. E. & Golombek, P.R. (Eds.). (2002). *Narrative inquiry as professional development*. New York: Cambridge University Press.

Johnson, M. (1987) *The body in the mind: The bodily basis of meaning, imagination, and reason*. Chicago: The University of Chicago Press.

———. (1989). Embodied knowledge. *Curriculum Inquiry, 19*(4), 361–377.

Johnston, I. (2011). Re-memoring colonial spaces of apartheid and the Holocaust through imaginative fiction. In Mitchell, C., Strong-Wilson, T., Pithouse, K. and Allnutt, S. (Eds.), *Memory and pedagogy* (131–144). New York & Abingdon: Routledge.

Jung, C.G. (1989). *Memories, dreams, reflections*. New York: Vintage. (First published 1961.)

———. (1991). The archetypes and the collective unconscious. In *The Collected works of C.G. Jung*. London: Routledge.

Kainan, A. (1994). *The staffroom: Observing the professional culture of teachers.* Aldershot: Avebury.

Kalekin-Fishman, D. (2004). *Ideology, policy and practice: The education of immigrants and minorities in Israel today.* New York: Kluwer.

———. (2005). Trio: Three (auto)biographical voices and issues in curriculum. *Language, Culture & Curriculum 18*(1), 3–26.

Kelchtermans, G. (2009). Who I am in how I teach is the message. Self-understanding, vulnerability and reflection. *Teachers and teaching: Theory and Practice, 15* (2), 257–272.

Kemp, A., Newman, D., Ram, U., Yiftachel, O. (2004). *Israelis in conflict: Hegemonies, identities and challenges.* Eastbourne: Sussex Academic Press.

Kfir, D. & Ariav, T. (2008). *The crisis of teaching: Towards reform in teacher education.* Jerusalem & Tel Aviv: The Van Leer Foundation and Hakibbutz Hameuhad. (Hebrew)

Klier, J. (1992). *Pogroms: anti-Jewish violence in modern Jewish history.* Cambridge: Cambridge University Press.

Knowles, J. G., Cole, A. L., & Sumsion, J., Eds. (2000). "Publish or perish:" The role and meaning of "research" in teacher education institutions. *Teacher Education Quarterly, 27*(2), 33-48.

Kogawa, J. (1981). *Obasan.* Toronto: Lester & Orpen Dennys.

Kosnik, C. Beck, C., Freese, A. & Samaras, A. P., Eds. (2006). *Making a difference in teacher education through self-study: Studies of personal, professional and program renewal.* Dordrecht: Springer.

Kumar, A. (2000). *Passport photos.* Berkeley: University of California Press.

Laneve, C. (2009). Reading educational practice through the "stolen time writing." *The International Journal of Learning, 17*(12), 281–292.

Langer, L. (1995), *Admitting the Holocaust: Collected essays.* New York: Oxford University Press.

———. (1998). *Preempting the Holocaust.* New Haven & London: Yale University Press.

Lappin, E. (1999). "The man with two heads." *Granta,* 7–65.

Latta, M.M. & Buck, G. (2007): Professional development risks and opportunities embodied within self-study, *Studying Teacher Education: A Journal of Self-study of Teacher Education Practices, 3,*2, 189–205.

Lavee, Y., & Katz, R. (2003) The family in Israel: Between tradition and modernity. *Marriage & Family Review, 35* (1–2), 193–217.

Lederman, M. (2012). The friends Canada insisted were foes. *Globe and Mail*, July 13, 2012. Downloaded from http://www.theglobeandmail.com/news/the-friends-canada-insisted-were foes/article4416458/?page=all (13.04.2013)

Lentin, R. (2000). *Israel and the Daughters of the Shoah: Reoccupying the territories of silence*. New York & Oxford: Berghahn.

Lewis, P.J. (2011). Storytelling as research/research as storytelling. *Qualitative Inquiry 17*(6): 505–510.

Li, X. (2006). Becoming Taoist I and thou: Identity-making of opposite cultures. *Journal of Curriculum and Pedagogy, 3*, 193–216.

Li, X., Conle, C., Elbaz-Luwisch, F. (2009). *Shifting polarized positions: A narrative approach in teacher education*. New York: Peter Lang.

Lieberman, A. & Pointer Mace, D.H. (2009). The role of 'accomplished teachers' in professional learning communities: Uncovering practice and enabling leadership. *Teachers and Teaching: Theory and Practice, 15*(4), 459–470.

Lieblich, A. (1993). Looking at change: Natasha, 21, New immigrant from Russia to Israel. In R. Josselson & A. Lieblich (Eds.), *The narrative study of lives*, Vol. 1 (pp. 92–129). Newbury Park, CA: Sage.

Lingis, A. (2012). *Violence and splendor*. Evanston, IL: Northwestern University Press.

Litvak, O. (2006). *Conscription and the search for modern Russian Jewry*. Bloomington, IN: Indiana University Press.

Lortie, D. (1975). *Schoolteacher: A sociological study*. Chicago: University of Chicago Press.

Loughran, J. (2011). On becoming a teacher educator. *Journal of Education for Teaching: International Research and Pedagogy, 37,3*, 279–291.

Loughran, J. J., Hamilton, M. L., Laboskey, V. K., & Russell, T. (2004). *International handbook of self-study of teaching and teacher education practice*. Dordrecht: Kluwer.

Lugones, M. (1987). Playfulness, "world"-travelling, and loving perception. *Hypatia 2*(2), 3–19.

Lunenberg, M. & Hamilton, M.L. (2008). Threading a golden chain: An attempt to find our identities as teacher educators. *Teacher Education Quarterly 35,*1, 185-205

MacCurdy, M. M. (2007). *The mind's eye: Image and memory in writing about trauma*. Amherst: University of Massachusetts Press.

Maclennan, H. (1945). *Two solitudes*. New York: Duell, Sloan and Pearce.

Mairs, N. (1994). *Voice lessons: On becoming a (woman) writer*. Boston: Beacon Press.

Malraux, A. (1968). *Anti-memoirs*. New York: Holt, Rinehart and Winston.

———. (1965). *Museum without walls*. London: Secker & Warburg.

Margalit, A. (2002). *The ethics of memory.* Cambridge, MA & London: Harvard University Press.

Marsh, M.M. (2002). Examining the discourses that shape our teacher identities. *Curriculum Inquiry, 32*(4), 453–469.

Masalha, S. (2003). Children and violent conflict. *Palestine-Israel Journal* 10(1). Downloaded from http://www.pij.org/details.php?id=82, 24/10/12

McAdams, D. (1988). *Power, intimacy, and the life story: Personological inquiries into identity.* New York: Guilford.

McLeod, D. & Cowieson, A. (2001). Discovering credit where credit is due: Using autobiographical writing as a tool for voicing growth. *Teachers and Teaching: Theory and Practice 7*(3), 239–256.

McNiff, J. (1990). Writing and the creation of educational knowledge, in P. Lomax (Ed.) *Managing staff development in schools: An action research approach* (pp. 52–60). Clevedon: Multilingual Matters Ltd.

Menon, R. & Bhasin, K. (1998). *Borders and boundaries: Women in India's partition.* New Brunswick, NJ: Rutgers University Press.

Miller, A. (1980). *For your own good: Hidden cruelty in childrearing and the roots of violence.* New York: Farrar, Straus & Giroux.

Miller, J.L. (2005). *Sounds of silence breaking: Women, autobiography, curriculum.* New York: Peter Lang.

Min, E. (2001). Bakhtinian perspectives for the study of intercultural communication. *Journal of Intercultural Studies, 22*, 5–18.

Mindell, Amy (2005). *The dreaming source of creativity.* Portland, OR: Lao Tse Press.

Mindell, Arnold (1982, 1998). *Dreambody: The body's role in revealing the self.* Portland, OR: Sigo Press, 1981/Lao Tse Press, 2000.

———. (1984). *Working with the dreaming body.* Portland, OR: Lao Tse Press.

———. (1995). *Sitting in the fire: Large group transformation using conflict and diversity.* Portland, OR: Lao Tse Press.

———. (2010). *ProcessMind: A user's guide to connecting with the mind of God.* Wheaton, IL: Quest Books.

Mishol, A. (2006). *Look there: New and selected poems of Agi Mishol.* (Translated from Hebrew by Lisa Katz) St. Paul, MN: Graywolf Press.

Mitchell, C., Strong-Wilson, T., Pithouse, K., and Allnutt, S., Eds. (2011). *Memory and pedagogy.* New York & Abingdon: Routledge.

Montgomery, L.M. (1908). *Anne of Green Gables.* Boston: L.C. Page.

Morris, M. (2001). *Curriculum and the Holocaust: Competing sites of memory and representation*. Mahwah, NJ: Erlbaum.

Morrison, T. (1989). *Beloved*. New York: Knopf.

————. (1995). The site of memory, in W. Zinsser (Ed.), *Inventing the truth*. New York: Houghton Mifflin.

Munro, A. (2007). *The view from Castle Rock: Stories*. London: Vintage.

Murray, F.B., Ed. (1995). *The teacher educator's handbook: Building a knowledge base for the preparation of teachers*. San Francisco, CA: Jossey-Bass.

Nasseraldeen, H. (2006). Personal and professional development of successful Druze women educators. Unpublished MA thesis, University of Haifa. (Hebrew)

Neumann, A. (1998). On experience, memory and knowing: A post-Holocaust (auto)biography. *Curriculum Inquiry 28*, 4, 425–442.

Nias, J. (1993). Changing times, changing identities: Grieving for a lost self. In R.G. Burgess (Ed.), *Educational research and evaluation* (pp. 139–156). London: Falmer.

Noddings, N. (2005). *The challenge to care in schools: An alternative approach to education* (2nd ed.). New York: Teachers College Press.

Oberg, A. and Wilson, T. (2002). Side by side: Being in research autobiographically. *Educational Insights*, *7*(2). [Available: http://www.csci.educ.ubc.ca/publication/insights/ v07n02/contextualexplorations/wilson_oberg/]

Oliver, M. (1986). *Dream work*. Boston & New York: The Atlantic Monthly Press.

Olson, M. (1995). Conceptualizing narrative authority: Implications for teacher education. *Teaching and Teacher Education, 11*(2), 119–135.

Olson, M. R. & Craig, C.J. (2001). Opportunities and challenges in the development of teachers' knowledge: The development of narrative authority through knowledge communities. *Teaching and Teacher Education, 17*, 667–684.

Oshrat, Y. (2009). *The transition from pre-service to first year teacher: A study of reflective processes*. Unpublished doctoral dissertation, University of Haifa. (Hebrew)

Otte, G. (1995). In-voicing: beyond the voice debate. In J. Gallop (Ed.), *Pedagogy and the question of impersonation* (pp. 147–154). Bloomington and Indianapolis: University of Indiana Press.

Palgi-Hacker, A. (2009). The mother as subject: On the mother and motherhood in psychoanalytic theory. In E. Perroni, (Ed.) *Motherhood: Psychoanalysis and other disciplines* (pp. 71–90). Jerusalem & Tel Aviv: Van Leer Jerusalem Institute & Hakibbutz Hameuchad. (Hebrew)

Pardales, M. J. & Girod, M. (2006). Community of inquiry: Its past and present future. *Educational Philosophy and Theory, 38*, 299–309.

Pemberton, C. (2012). *Getting there: Women's journeys to and through educational attainment.* Rotterdam/Boston/Taipei: Sense.

Pennebaker, J. (1997). Writing about emotional experiences as a therapeutic process. *Psychological Science 8*(3), 162–166.

Peters, M. (2004). Education and the philosophy of the body: Bodies of knowledge and knowledges of the body, in: L. Bresler (Ed.) *Knowing bodies, moving minds: Towards embodied teaching and learning.* Boston: Kluwer.

Phelan, A.M. (2001). Power and place in teaching and teacher education. *Teaching and Teacher Education 17*(5), 583–597.

Phillion, J., He, M.F., & Connelly, F.M. (Eds.) (2005). *Multicultural education: Narrative and experiential approaches.* Thousand Oaks, CA: Sage.

Pillay, V. (2008). Academic mothers finding rhyme and reason. *Gender and Education*, 1–14.

Pinar, William F. (1994). *Autobiography, politics and sexuality: Essays in curriculum theory, 1972–1992.* New York, Bern: Peter Lang.

————.(2004). *What is curriculum theory?* Mahwah, NJ: Erlbaum.

Pinnegar, S., Lay, C., Bigham, S. & Dulude, C. (2005). Teaching as highlighted by mothering: A narrative inquiry. *Studying Teacher Education: A Journal of Self-study of Teacher Education Practices, 1*,1, 55–67.

Polanyi, M. (1966). *The tacit dimension.* Garden City, NJ: Doubleday.

Polkinghorne, D. (1988). *Narrative knowing and the human sciences.* Albany: SUNY Press.

Pollock, G. (2010). The Long Journey: Maternal Trauma, Tears and Kisses in a Work by Chantal Akerman. *Studies in the Maternal 2*(1), 1–32.

Pollock, G. (2008). The long journey home. *Jewish Quarterly*, No. 211, Autumn.

Price, J. & Shildrick, M., Eds. (1999). *Feminist theory and the body: A reader.* New York: Routledge.

Pryer, A. (2001). 'What spring does with the cherry trees': The eros of teaching and learning. *Teachers and Teaching, Theory and Practice, 7*, 75–88.

Rabinowitz, D. (1997). *Overlooking Nazareth—The ethnography of exclusion in Galilee.* Cambridge: Cambridge University Press.

Randall, W.L. & McKim, E.A. (2008). *Reading our lives: The poetics of growing old.* Oxford: Oxford University Press.

Raths, J. D., & McAninich, A. C. (Eds.). (1999). *Advances in teacher education: Vol. 5. What counts as knowledge in teacher education?* Stamford, CT: Ablex.

Raymond, D., Butt, R., & Townsend, D. (1992). Contexts for teacher development: Insights from teachers' stories. In A. Hargreaves & M. Fullan (Eds.), *Understanding teacher development* (pp. 143–161). London and New York: Cassell and Teachers College Press.

Reisberg, D. & Hertel, P., Eds. (2004). *Memory and emotion.* New York: Oxford University Press.

Reiss, G. (2000). *Changing ourselves, changing the world.* Tempe, AZ: New Falcon Press.

——— (2004). *Beyond war and peace in the Arab Israeli conflict.* Eugene, OR: Changing Worlds.

Ribbens, J. (1998). Hearing my feeling voice? An autobiographical discussion of motherhood. In J. Ribbens and R. Edwards (Eds.), *Feminist dilemmas in qualitative research: Public knowledge and private lives* (pp. 24–38). London: Sage.

Rich, A. (1997). *Of woman born: Motherhood as experience and institution.* London, UK: Virago. (Original work published 1976.)

Richards, J. (2007). "Introduction" to Section I, Classical and early modern ideas of memory, in M. Rossington & A. Whitehead (Eds.), *Theories of memory: A reader* (pp. 20–24). Baltimore: Johns Hopkins University Press.

Richardson, L. (1994). Writing: A method of inquiry. In N.K. Denzin & Y.S. Lincoln (Eds.), *Handbook of qualitative research* (pp. 345–371). Thousand Oaks/London/New Delhi: Sage.

Richler, M. (1959). *The apprenticeship of Duddy Kravitz.* New York: Andre Deutsch.

Ricoeur, P. (1969). On consolation. In A. MacIntyre and P. Ricoeur, *The religious significance of Atheism*, New York, N.Y.: Columbia University Press.

Ricoeur, P. (1984). *Time and narrative*, Vol. 1. (R. Czerny with K. McLaughlin & HJ. Costello, Trans.) Chicago: University of Chicago Press.

———. (2004). *Memory, history, forgetting* (Trans. Kathleen Blamey and David Pellauer). Chicago: University of Chicago Press.

Rodgers, C. R. & Raider-Roth, M. B. (2009). Presence in teaching, *Teachers and Teaching, 12*(3), 265–287.

Rogers, A. (1993). Voice, play, and a practice of ordinary courage in girls' and women's lives, *Harvard Educational Review 63*(3), 265–295.

Rogoff, I. (2000). *Terra infirma: Geography's visual culture.* London & New York: Routledge.

Rossington, M. & Whitehead, A., Eds. (2007). *Theories of memory: A reader.* Baltimore: Johns Hopkins University Press.

Rothberg, M. (2009). *Multidirectional memory: Remembering the Holocaust in the age of decolonization*. Stanford: Stanford University Press.

Rothschild, B. (2000). *The body remembers: The psychophysiology of trauma and trauma treatment*. New York: Norton.

Ruddick, S. (1980). Maternal thinking. *Feminist Studies 6*(2), 342–367.

———. (1989, 1995). *Maternal thinking: Towards a politics of peace*. Boston: Beacon.

Rudoren, J. (2012). Proudly bearing elders' scars, their skin says 'never forget.' *New York Times*, Sept 30. http://www.nytimes.com/2012/10/01/world/middleeast/with-tattoos-young-israelis-bear-holocaust-scars-of-relatives.html?pagewanted=all (downloaded 13.10.2012).

Salomon, G. (2004). A narrative-based view of coexistence education. *Journal of Social Issues, 60*, 273–287.

Sarason, S. (1999). *Teaching as a performing art*. New York: Teachers College Press.

Sarason, S.B. (1982). *The culture of the school and the problem of change*, 2nd ed. (First edition, 1971) Boston: Allyn & Bacon.

Sarbin, T. (2001). Embodiment and the narrative structure of emotional life. *Narrative Inquiry 11*(1), 217–225.

Schaafsma, D. (1996). Things we cannot say: 'Writing for your life' and stories in English education. *Theory into Practice, 35*(2), 110–116.

Schnee, E. (2009). Writing the personal as research. *Narrative Inquiry 19*(1), 35–51.

Scott, Sara & Scott, Sue (2000). Our mother's daughters: Autobiographical inheritance through stories of gender and class. In T. Cosslett, C. Lury & P. Summerfield (Eds.), *Feminism and autobiography: Texts, theories, methods* (pp. 128–140). London & New York: Routledge.

Seidler, V. J. (2000). *Shadows of the Shoah: Jewish identity and belonging*. Oxford & New York: Berg.

Sermijn, J., Dervieger, P., & Loots, G. (2008). The narrative construction of the self: Selfhood as a rhizomatic story. *Qualitative Inquiry, 14*(4), 632–650.

Shapira, T., Arar, K., and Azaiza, F. (2011). 'They didn't consider me and no-one even took me into account': Female school principals in the Arab education system in Israel. *Educational Management Administration & Leadership 39*(1), 25–43.

Sharkey, P. & Ewert, F. (2011). The legacy of disadvantage: Multigenerational neighborhood effects on cognitive ability. *American Journal of Sociology 116*(6), 1934–1981.

Shimoni, F. (2004). Pre-service early childhood teachers' acquisition of professional knowledge. Unpublished MA thesis, University of Haifa. (Hebrew)

Shteiman, Y., Gidron, A. & Eilon, B. (2013). Writing, knowledge and professional development of teacher educators. In M. Ben-Peretz et al. (eds), *Teacher educators as members of an evolving profession.* Lanham, MD: Rowman & Littlefield.

Shulman, L. (1987). Knowledge and teaching: Foundations of the new reform. *Harvard Educational Review 57*(1), 1–21.

Silberstein, L. (1999). *The postzionism debates: Knowledge and power in Israeli culture.* New York & London: Routledge.

Simon, C. (2005). Parenting and teaching: A narrative study of the personal and practical knowledge of teacher educators in Israeli teacher colleges. Unpublished Ph.D. dissertation, University of Haifa. (Hebrew)

Simon, C. & Elbaz-Luwisch, F. (2010). Reflections on "idle chitchat," or chitchat as discourse. *Reflective Practice 11*(2), 185–196.

Simon, R. (1995). Face to face with alterity: Postmodern Jewish identity and the eros of pedagogy. In J. Gallop (Ed.), *Pedagogy and the question of impersonation* (90–105). Bloomington and Indianapolis: University of Indiana Press.

———. (2005). *The touch of the past: Remembrance, learning and ethics.* New York & Basingstoke, UK: Palgrave Macmillan.

Smeyers, P. & Verhesschen P. (2001). Narrative analysis as philosophical research: bridging the gap between the empirical and the conceptual. *International Journal of Qualitative Studies in Education, 14* (1), 71–84.

Smith, D.G. (2000). The specific challenges of globalization for teaching and vice versa. *Alberta Journal of Educational Research 46*(1), 7–26.

Smith, S.A. (2002). *The Russian revolution.* Oxford: Oxford University Press.

Smith, S. & Watson, J. (2001). *Reading autobiography: A guide for interpreting life narratives.* Minneapolis: University of Minnesota Press.

Smith, T. (2009). Portrait of a class: A case study of one teacher educator's practice. *The teacher educators' journal 16*, 1–10. http://ateva.org/files/2009/05/the-teacher-educators-journal-spring-2009.pdf

Somerville, M. (2004). Tracing bodylines: The body in feminist poststructural research. *International Journal of Qualitative Studies in Education, 17*(1), 47–63.

Sotirin, P. (2010). Autoethnographic mother-writing: Advocating radical specificity. *Journal of Research Practice, 6*(1), Article M9. Retrieved [14/03/2013], from http://jrp.icaap.org/index.php/jrp/article/view/220/189

Spector-Mersel, G. (2011). Mechanisms of selection in claiming narrative identities: A model for interpreting narratives. *Qualitative Inquiry, 17*(2), 172–185.

Spence, D.P. (1982). *Narrative truth and historical truth*. New York: Norton.

Springgay, S. (2008). *Body knowledge and curriculum: Pedagogies of touch in youth and visual culture*. New York: Peter Lang.

————. (2007). Intimacy in the curriculum of Janine Antoni. In S. Springgay & D. Freedman (Eds.). *Curriculum and the cultural body* (pp. 191–202). New York: Peter Lang.

Springgay, S. & Freedman, D., Eds. (2007). *Curriculum and the cultural body*. New York: Peter Lang.

Squires, C. (2012). Narratives and the gift of the future. *Narrative Works: Issues, Investigations, & Interventions* 2(1), 67–82.

Steedman, C. (1986). *Landscape for a good woman: A story of two lives*. London: Virago.

————. (1992). *Past tenses: Essays on writing, autobiography and history*. London: Rivers Oram.

Stratton, J. (2005). Before Holocaust memory: Making sense of trauma between postmemory and cultural memory. *Australian Critical Race and Whiteness Studies Association Journal, 1*, 53–71.

Strong-Wilson, T. (2008). *Bringing memory forward: Storied remembrance in social justice education with teachers*. New York: Peter Lang.

Sturken, M. (1997). *Tangled memories: The Vietnam War, The AIDS epidemic, and the politics of remembering*. Berkeley & Los Angeles, CA: University of California Press.

Suleiman, S.R. (2000). Problems of memory and factuality in recent Holocaust memoirs: Wilkomirski/Wiesel. *Poetics Today, 21*(3), 543–559.

Swanson, D.M. (2007). Silent voices, silent bodies. In *Curriculum and the cultural body*, S. Springgay & D. Freedman (Eds.) (pp. 63–78). New York: Peter Lang.

Swindells, J. (Ed.) (1995). *The uses of autobiography*. London: Taylor & Francis.

Szymborska, W. (1996). Nobel Lecture: The Poet and the World. Downloaded 17 Mar 2013, from http://www.nobelprize.org/nobel_prizes/literature/laureates/1996/szymborska-lecture.html

Tillema, H. & Kremer-Hayon, L. (2005). Facing dilemmas: Teacher-educators' ways of constructing a pedagogy of teacher education. *Teaching in Higher Education 10*(2), 203–217.

Turley, S. (2005). Professional lives of teacher educators in an era of mandated reform. *Teacher Education Quarterly*, fall, 137–156.

Tym, C., McMillion, R., Barone, S., & Webster, J. (2004). *First-generation college students: A literature review*. TG Research & Analytic Services. Downloaded from http://www.tgslc.org/pdf/first_generation.pdf, 20.10.2012

Uitto, M. (2011). Storied relationships: Students recall their teachers. *Acta Universitatis Ouluensis* E 122. University of Oulu, Finland.

Uitto, M. & Syrjälä, L. (2008). Body, caring and power in teacher-pupil relationships: Encounters in former pupils' memories. *Scandinavian Journal of Educational Research 52*(4), 355–371.

Uris, L. (1958). *Exodus*. Garden City, NY: Doubleday.

Vagle, M.D. (2011): Critically-oriented pedagogical tact: Learning about and through our compulsions as teacher educators, *Teaching Education, 22*:4, 413–426.

Vandenberghe, R. & Huberman, A.M., Eds. (1999). *Understanding and preventing teacher burnout: A sourcebook of international research and practice.* New York: Cambridge University Press.

Vescio, V., Ross, D. & Adams, A. (2008). A review of research on the impact of professional learning communities on teaching practice and student learning. *Teaching and Teacher Education, 24*(1), 80–91.

Vongalis, A. (2004). Global education policy directives: Impact on teachers from the north and south. *International Education Journal, 5*(4), 488–501.

Walker, M. B. (1998). *Philosophy and the maternal body*. London & New York: Routledge.

Warnock, M. (1987). *Memory*. London and Boston: Faber.

Webb, K. (1996). I have left my classroom. Why? Systemic denial of teachers' knowledge. *Teachers and Teaching: Theory and Practice, 2*(2), 299–313.

Weber, S. (1990). The teacher educator's experience: Cultural generativity and duality of commitment, *Curriculum Inquiry, 20*(2), 141–159.

Weber, S., & Mitchell, M. (Eds.). (2004). *Not just any dress: Narratives of memory, body, and identity.* New York: Peter Lang.

Wideen, M., Mayer-Smith, J., & Moon, B. (1998). A critical analysis of the research on learning to teach: Making the case for an ecological perspective on inquiry. *Review of Educational Research 68*(2), 130–178.

Wilhelm, K., Dewhurst-Savellis, J. & Parker, G. (2000). Teacher stress? An analysis of why teachers leave and why they stay. *Teachers and Teaching, Theory and Practice 6*(3), 291–304.

Wilkomirski, B. (1996). *Fragments: Memories of a wartime childhood.* New York: Schocken.

Williams, J., Ritter, J. & Bullock, S.M. (2012). Understanding the complexity of becoming a teacher educator: Experience, belonging, and practice within a professional learning community. *Studying Teacher Education: A Journal of Self-study of Teacher Education Practices, 8*(3), 245–260.

Wilson, S. M., & Berne, J. (1999). Teacher learning and the acquisition of professional knowledge: An examination of research on contemporary professional development. In A. Iran-Nejad, & P. D. Pearson (Eds.), *Review of Research in Education, 24,* 173–209.

Witherell, C., & Noddings, N. (1991). *Stories lives tell: Narrative and dialogue in education.* New York: Teachers College Press.

Woodman, M. & Dickson, E. (1996). *Dancing in the flames: The dark goddess in the transformation of consciousness.* Toronto: Knopf Canada.

Woods, P. (1999). Intensification and stress in teaching. In R. Vandenberghe & A.M. Huberman (Eds.), *Understanding and preventing teacher burnout: A sourcebook of international research and practice* (pp. 115–138). New York: Cambridge University Press.

Yeats, W.B. (1961). *The collected poems of W.B. Yeats.* London: Macmillan.

Young, I.M. (1990). Pregnant embodiment: Subjectivity and alienation, in I. M. Young (Ed.), *Throwing like a girl and other essays in feminist philosophy and social theory* (pp. 160–174). Bloomington: Indiana University Press.

Zeichner, K. (2005). Becoming a teacher educator: A personal perspective. *Teaching and Teacher Education, 21,* 117–124.

Zelniker, T., Hertz-Lazarowitz, R., Peretz, H., Azaiza, F., & Sharabany, R. (2009). Arab and Jewish students participatory action research at the University of Haifa: A model for peace education. In C. McGlynn, M. Zembylas, Z. Bekerman, & T. Gallagher (Eds.). *Peace education in conflict and post-conflict societies: Comparative perspectives* (pp. 199–214). New York: Palgrave Macmillan.

Zembylas, M. (2007). Risks and pleasures: A Deleuzo-Guattarian pedagogy of desire in education. *British Educational Research Journal, 33,* 331–347.

Zerilli, L. M. (2005) "We feel our freedom": Imagination and judgment in the thought of Hannah Arendt. *Political Theory 33,* 158–188.

OMPLICATED

A BOOK SERIES OF CURRICULUM STUDIES

Reframing the curricular challenge educators face after a decade of school deform, the books published in Peter Lang's Complicated Conversation Series testify to the ethical demands of our time, our place, our profession. What does it mean for us to teach now, in an era structured by political polarization, economic destabilization, and the prospect of climate catastrophe? Each of the books in the Complicated Conversation Series provides provocative paths, theoretical and practical, to a very different future. In this resounding series of scholarly and pedagogical interventions into the nightmare that is the present, we hear once again the sound of silence breaking, supporting us to rearticulate our pedagogical convictions in this time of terrorism, reframing curriculum as committed to the complicated conversation that is intercultural communication, self-understanding, and global justice.

The series editor is

Dr. William F. Pinar
Department of Curriculum Studies
2125 Main Mall
Faculty of Education
University of British Columbia
Vancouver, British Columbia V6T 1Z4
CANADA

To order other books in this series, please contact our Customer Service Department:

(800) 770-LANG (within the U.S.)
(212) 647-7706 (outside the U.S.)
(212) 647-7707 FAX

Or browse online by series:

www.peterlang.com